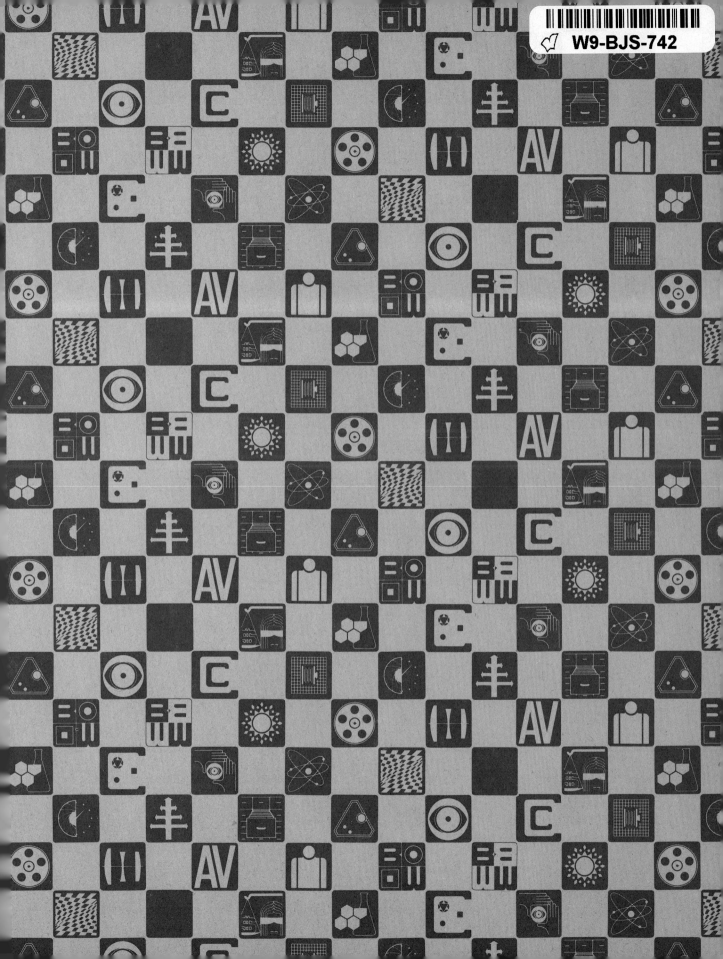

Encyclopedia
of Practical
Photography

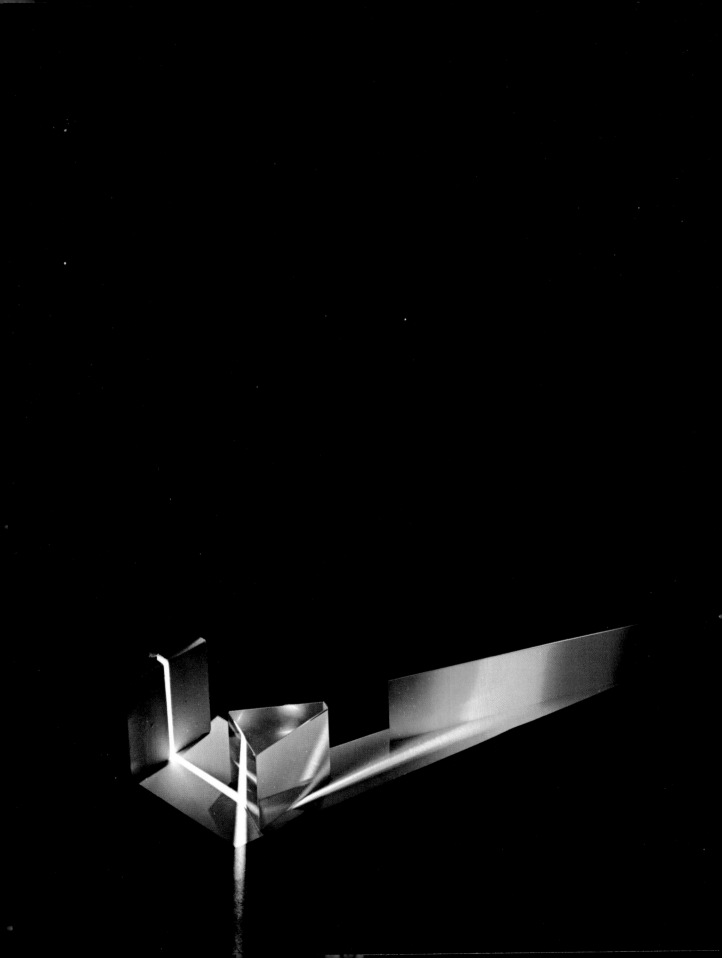

Encyclopedia of Practical Photography

Volume 1

A–Bab

Edited by and published for
EASTMAN KODAK COMPANY

AMPHOTO
American Photographic Book Publishing Company
Garden City, New York

Notes on Photography

The cover photos and the photos of letters that appear elsewhere in this encyclopedia were taken by Chris Maggio.

Frontispiece depicts white light entering a prism and being separated into its component colors. Page *vi* illustrates silver—the element essential to almost all photography—as found in its natural state. Page *x* illustrates light entering a camera lens.

Copyright © 1977 by Eastman Kodak Company and
American Photographic Book Publishing Company, Inc.

Library of Congress Cataloging in Publication Data

Amphoto, New York.
   Encyclopedia of practical photography.

   Includes bibliographical references and index.
   1.   Photography—Dictionaries.   I.   Eastman
Kodak Company.   II.   Title.
TR9.T34   770′.3   77-22562

ISBN 0–8174–3050–4 Trade Edition—Whole Set
ISBN 0–8174–3200–0 Library Edition—Whole Set
ISBN 0–8174–3051–2 Trade Edition—Volume 1
ISBN 0–8174–3201–9 Library Edition—Volume 1

Manufactured in the United States of America

Editorial Board

The *Encyclopedia of Practical Photography* was compiled and edited jointly by Eastman Kodak Company and American Photographic Book Publishing Co., Inc. (Amphoto). The comprehensive archives, vast resources, and technical staffs of both companies, as well as the published works of Kodak, were used as the basis for most of the information contained in this encyclopedia.

Photography and this Encyclopedia

A Form of Communication

Photography is at once an art, a science, a tool, and a toy. To some, photography is the simple recording of family events; to others, it is the recording of events important to the world. To some, it can be a way of earning a living; to others, it can be a way of exploring new frontiers. Some use photography to illustrate words; others can find no words for their photography. This most wonderful invention of man consists of so many diverse elements and means so many different things to different people, that pulling together all its varied aspects was an imposing task.

The Dimensions of Photography

There is though, one aspect of photography of interest to all photographers—that is the faithful reproduction of permanent images of scenes as they are perceived. All photographers are interested in the technical aspects of photography that will help them make the transition from the intangible to the tangible. In other words, they are interested in the practical aspects of photography. With this thought in mind, this encyclopedia was conceived and planned.

The Scope of the Encyclopedia

To be sure, you will find some photographic theory and chemistry on the pages that follow, as well as short biographies of important photographic innovators. Emphasis, though, is on the practical advice and instruction on using light, film, and chemicals to get the most use of your equipment. Here you will find the how-to information necessary for actual production of photographic images—the common ground for all photographers. The information in this encyclopedia will help you record exactly what you want, when you want, and the way you want.

THE PUBLISHERS

Symbol Identification

 Audiovisual

 Color Processing and Printing

 Picture-Making Techniques

 Biography

 Equipment and Facilities

 Scientific Photography

 Black-and-White Materials

 Exposure

 Special Effects and Techniques

 Black-and-White Processing and Printing

 History

 Special Interests

 Business and Legal Aspects

 Lighting

 Storage and Care

 Chemicals

 Motion Picture

 Theory of Photography

 Color Materials

 Optics

 Vision

Guide for the Reader

Use this encyclopedia as you would any good encyclopedia or dictionary. Look for the subject desired as it first occurs to you—most often you will locate it immediately. The shorter articles begin with a dictionary-style definition, and the longer articles begin with a short paragraph that summarizes the article that follows. Either of these should tell you if the information you need is in the article. The longer articles are then broken down by series of headings and sub-headings to aid further in locating specific information.

Cross References

If you do not find the specific information you are seeking in the article first consulted, use the cross references (within the article and at the end of it) to lead you to more information. The cross references can lead you from a general article to the more detailed articles into which the subject is divided. Cross references are printed in capital letters so that you can easily recognize them.
Example: *See also:* ZONE SYSTEM.

Index

If the initial article you turn to does not supply you with the information you seek, and the cross references do not lead you to it, use the index in the last volume. The index contains thousands of entries to help you identify and locate any subject you seek.

Symbols

To further aid you in locating information, the articles throughout have been organized into major photographic categories. Each category is represented by a symbol displayed on the opposite page. By using only the symbols, you can scan each volume and locate all the information under any of the general categories. Thus, if you wish to read all about lighting, simply locate the lighting symbols and read the articles under them.

Reading Lists

Most of the longer articles are followed by reading lists citing useful sources for further information. Should you require additional sources, check the cross-referenced articles for additional reading lists.

Metric Measurement

Both the U.S. Customary System of measurement and the International System (SI) are used throughout this encyclopedia. In most cases, the metric measurement is given first with the U.S. customary equivalent following in parenthesis. When equivalent measurements are given, they will be rounded off to the nearest whole unit or a tenth of a unit, unless precise measurement is important. When a measurement is considered a "standard," equivalents will not be given. For example: 35 mm film, 200 mm lens, 4″ × 5″ negative, and 8″ × 10″ prints will not be given with their customary or metric equivalents.

How Articles are Alphabetized

Article titles are alphabetized by letter sequence, with word breaks and hyphens not considered. Example:

> Archer, Frederick Scott
> Architectural Photography
> Archival Processing
> Arc Lamps

Abbreviations are alphabetized according to the letters of the abbreviations, not by the words the letters stand for. Example:

> Artificial Light
> ASA Speed

Contents
Volume 1

A A and B Roll Editing — 1

Abbe, Ernst — 4

Aberration — 4

Abney, Sir William de Wiveleslie — 7

Acetic Acid — 8

Acetone — 8

Achromatic — 8

Acid — 8

Actinic — 9

Action Photography — 9

Acutance — 15

Adams, Ansel — 15

Additive Color Synthesis — 17

Adurol — 17

Advertising Agencies — 17

Advertising Photography — 18

Aerial Fog — 30

Aerial Perspective — 30

Aerial Photography — 30

Aftertreatment — 41

Ag — 41

Agencies, Picture — 41

Agitation — 51

Airbrush — 52

Albada, Liewe Evert Willem van — 54

Albumen — 54

Alcohol, Denatured — 56

Alcohol, Ethyl — 56

Alcohol, Isopropyl — 56

Alcohol, Methyl — 56

Alkali — 57

Alkaline Salts — 57

Alum, Chrome — 57

Alum, Potassium — 57

Ambrotype — 58

Amidol — 58

Ammonium Chloride — 58

Ammonium Persulfate — 59

Ammonium Thiocyanate — 59

Ammonium Thiosulfate — 59

Anaglyph — 59

Anamorphic Systems — 60

Anastigmat — 60

Andresen, Momme — 60

Animal and Pet Photography — 60

Animation — 73

Anschütz, Ottomar — 94

ANSI — 94

Antifoggant — 94

Aperture — 95

Apochromatic — 96

Archer, Frederick Scott — 96

Architectural Photography — 97

Archival Processing (B & W) — 111

Arc Lamps — 120

Armat, Thomas — 120

Art, Photography of — 121

Artificial Light — 138

ASA, ASAP Speeds — 139

Aspheric — 140

Astrophotography — 140

Atmospheric Haze — 158

Audiovisual Planning — 159

Automatic Exposure Systems — 165

Available-Light Photography — 166

B Baby and Child Photography — 183

A and B Roll Editing

A and B roll editing is a system of "checkerboard" editing used in the preparation of 16 mm motion-picture film copies, and sometimes of super 8 films as well. The system came into use because of two problems with 16 mm films. The first was that there existed no means of adding optical effects, such as fades and dissolves, during the editing of a film. The other was that there is too little space between frames of 16 mm film for splices, hence all splices encroached on the picture area and were visible on the screen.

By preparing the original material in two rolls of equal length, in which successive scenes appear on alternate rolls and the corresponding space in the other roll is filled with an equal length of opaque black film, it is possible to produce a final copy with no visible splices. By printing the two rolls in succession on the same length of duplicating film, it is also possible to produce dissolves, fades, and double exposures during the printing operation. The latter effects can only be done on printing machines having automatic fading shutters, but prints having only "invisible splices" can be made on any kind of printing machine.

A process similar to A and B roll editing is used to mass produce film strips and slide sets. This technique is useful because a variety of original material is often necessary for the making of film strips and slide sets.

Both invisible splices and effects can be, and usually are, included in the same set of A and B rolls. Furthermore, it is possible in special cases to prepare a third roll (C roll) containing scenes that are either too short to allow normal operation of the fading shutter in the printer or, more often, are carrying titles to be superimposed over certain scenes in the picture. The C roll must then be added to the process of combining the A and B rolls.

It is important to use the correct type of splicer for A and B roll assembly. The ordinary "positive" splicer, which makes a splice that is symmetrical around the frame line, will not do; the splices will always be visible. The correct type of splicer is the so-called "negative" splicer, which makes a splice beginning at the frame line; the width of the splice for this technique is immaterial.

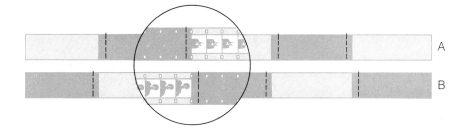

A   B

In the preparation of original A and B rolls, the checkerboard technique for making invisible splices is used. Scrape the picture emulsion only; never scrape the black leader film.

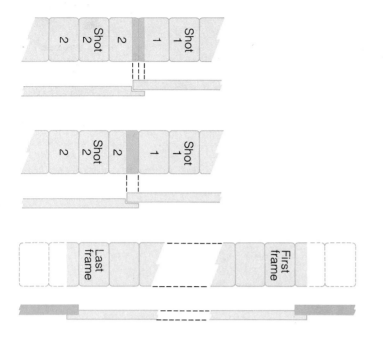

The positive-cut splice bridges the frame line. Cut film edges are visible in two frames. (Note: In this and the next figure, film edges with sprocket holes are not shown for simplicity.)

The negative-cut splice extends from the frame line into a frame. The cut film line is visible in only one frame.

In A and B rolls, cut and splice must fall in the frame preceding the first frame of a shot and in the frame following the last frame of a shot.

Scrape the emulsion only from the picture to make the splice. Do not scrape the emulsion from the black leader film or the splice will print through.

Equipment Required

The following equipment is necessary for A and B roll assembly:

Splicer producing the correct negative overlap.

Rewinds with long shafts to handle two or more reels at the same time.

"Synchronizer"—a measuring machine with two or more sprockets to keep the two films in synchronization, frame for frame, through the assembly process.

NOTE: If the master is being edited to match an edited workprint, then the rewinds and synchronizer will have to be able to handle three films: the workprint and the A and B rolls of the original master material.

How To Do It

Probably the best procedure in making a pair of A and B rolls is first to gather all the original scenes and assemble them in order on a single reel; they need not be spliced nor trimmed to length.

First, place the reel containing the edited workprint to be matched on the left arm of the rewind. Then, place the reel of original material on the same spindle. Finally, place a reel containing black opaque leader film on that same spindle.

Punch a "start mark" in the leader of the workprint, if one is not already there. Now, take two strips of white leader film, mark them "A" and "B," and about four feet from the beginning, punch a start mark in each. Thread these two strips of leader into the synchronizer so that the punched start marks are aligned and attach the heads of the three strips to the three empty reels on the right rewind.

Next, wind slowly until the first frame of the first scene on the workprint is on the synchronizer. Mark the leader strips at this point. Locate the first frame of the first scene of original material and splice it to the white leader on roll A. In exact alignment to this splice, splice the black opaque film to the white leader of roll B. Now, slowly wind the three films ahead until you reach the first splice in the workprint.

At this point, mark the end of the original picture film on roll A. Now, locate the beginning of the second scene of original film and mark the beginning frame. Cut the end of the original picture on roll A and splice it to the black leader film. Splice the beginning of the second scene to the end of the black leader film on roll B. Be sure that these splices are correctly made; always scrape the end of the picture film, never the end of the black film. This will necessitate looping the films so that picture film is always on the left jaw of the splicer.

With these carefully aligned splices made, you will now be winding black film onto roll A and picture onto roll B. At the next splice the procedure is repeated, but transpose the picture and opaque film rolls so that the third scene is spliced to roll A and the black leader to roll B. This procedure is continued through the entire roll. When finished, roll A will contain scenes 1, 3, 5, 7, and so on, while roll B will contain scenes 2, 4, 6, 8, and so on.

Effects

Dissolves, fades, and superimposures are simple effects that can be edited into a film with A and B roll editing.

Dissolves. If a point in the workprint is reached where a dissolve is indicated, a slightly different splicing arrangement is followed. It is essential that there be at least 24 frames of action film on the first scene—beyond the cut point on the workprint. Likewise, there must be at least 24 frames of material on the incoming scene—ahead of the splice point. A minimum of 48 frames is needed to provide the necessary overlap for a dissolve. If the editor of the workprint has not allowed this much material, then a dissolve cannot be made.

When you reach the splice on the workprint that has been marked for a dissolve, mark this point on the edge of the outgoing scene, continue 24 frames, and splice it to the black leader. Now, locate the starting frame of the action on the incoming scene and mark it in the edge. Go back 24 frames and splice it to the black film on the opposite roll. When you wind forward again, you should find the edge marks on the two original films aligned with the splice on the workprint.

Note that the shutter of the printer requires a certain definite time to recycle; if there are two dissolves in succession, there cannot be less than 12 frames between the end of one dissolve and the beginning of the next. This is shown in the accompanying diagram.

Note that the 24-frame overlap does not add to the length of either roll; it is merely deducted from the amount of black opaque film between scenes. The final length of each roll must be exactly the same as that of the workprint. This is essential in the case of sound films, since the final print must match the sound track, recorded in synchronism with the workprint, frame for frame.

Fades and Superimposures. Fades are produced during printing by progressively closing or opening an adjustable shutter. Superimposures, or "double-exposure" effects, result when part of roll A overlaps

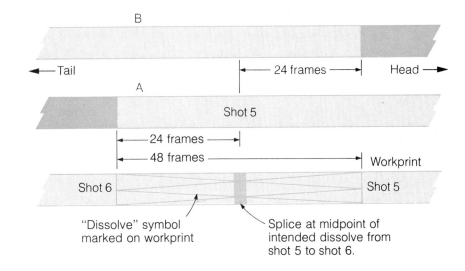

The shot that ends in a dissolve must extend at least 24 frames beyond the midpoint of the dissolve. The shot that begins in the dissolve must begin an equal number of frames before the midpoint. In a print made from these A and B rolls, shot 5 will dissolve into shot 6.

B

←— Tail |←——— 24 frames ———→| Head —→

A

Shot 5

|←——— 24 frames ———→|
|←——————— 48 frames ———————→| Workprint

Shot 6   Shot 5

"Dissolve" symbol marked on workprint

Splice at midpoint of intended dissolve from shot 5 to shot 6.

part of roll B so that a portion of the print is exposed to both segments.

Final Step. When finished, splice about eight feet of white leader into the A and B rolls and again punch start marks directly in line with each other. These will serve as a check on the matching of the two rolls. The punch marks can also be used to print the picture roll backwards, to avoid having to rewind the raw film to print the sound track.

• *See also:* EDITING MOVIES; SPLICING FILM.

Further Reading: Brodbeck, Emil E. *Handbook of Basic Motion Picture Techniques.* Garden City, NY: Amphoto, 1974; Burder, John. *16mm Film Cutting.* New York, NY: Hastings House, 1975; Callaghan, Barry. *Van Nostrand Reinhold Manual of Film-Making.* New York, NY: Van Nostrand Reinhold, 1973; Churchill, Hugh B. *Film Editing Handbook: Techniques of 16mm Film Cutting.* Belmont, CA: Wadsworth Publishing Co., 1972; Happé, L. Bernard. *Basic Motion Picture Technology,* rev. 2nd ed. London, England: Focal Press Ltd., 1975; Provisor, Henry. *8mm 16mm Movie-Making.* Garden City, NY: Amphoto, 1970.

Abbe, Ernst

(1840–1905)
German scientist and optician

Ernst Abbe's long connection with the firm of Carl Zeiss at Jena began in 1866. He realized that it was impossible to make lenses of the degree of correction he desired with the crown and flint glasses then known. In collaboration with Schott in 1880, he began work on new types of optical glass, which led to the introduction of the boro-silicate crown glasses, barium crowns, barium flints, borate flints, and others. These glasses made possible lenses with superior color correction and the first *anastigmats*—lenses with a high degree of correction of all aberrations. Abbe also designed the microscope condensers still known by his name and the first *apochromatic* (three-color-corrected) microscope objectives. He established the first basic theory of perfect optical systems, which was later expanded by Conrady. The *Abbe number* of a glass indicates how much it disperses, or spreads apart, the various colors of light passing through.

Aberration

A characteristic of a lens or mirror that prevents the formation of a perfect image. There are seven inherent aberrations that affect the quality of photographic images; their visible effects include degraded sharpness, lowered contrast, distorted shape, and color fringing. *Geometric aberrations* prevent the light rays from a common origin in the subject from coming to a common point or plane of focus in the image because light rays passing through various portions or zones of the lens are not refracted (bent) in equal degrees. The geometric aberrations are: spherical aberration, coma, astigmatism, field curva-

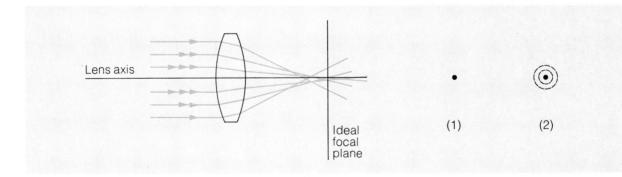

Spherical aberration. Light rays parallel to the lens axis that pass through the outer portions of a lens are brought to focus at a point nearer the lens than those passing through the central portions. Visually, the image of a point is surrounded by a halo of increasing sharpness.
(1) Ideal image of subject point at focal plane.
(2) Actual image at focal plane with spherical aberration.

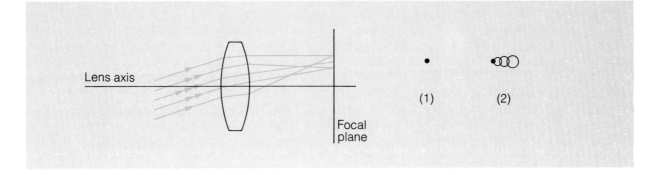

Coma. Light rays not parallel to the lens axis become a series of overlapping but displaced circles of diminishing size, depending on the portion of the lens they pass through. The result is a spot with a cometlike tail.
(1) Ideal image of subject point at focal plane.
(2) Actual image at focal plane with coma.

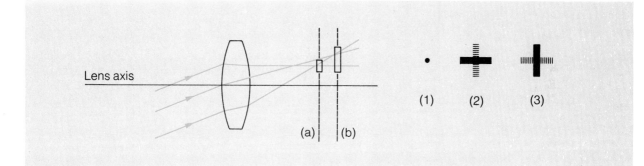

Astigmatism. Light rays from a single subject point are refracted as two short lines at right angles to one another at different focal distances. Radial astigmatism creates a blurred image of the line at right angles to the lens axis; tangential astigmatism creates a blurred image of the line pointing toward the lens axis.
(1) Ideal image of subject point.
(2) Image with radial astigmatism; focal plane at (a).
(3) Image with tangential astigmatism; focal plane at (b).

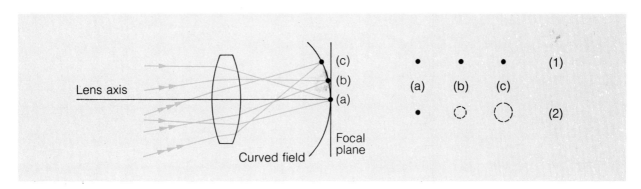

Field curvature. Light rays from subject points progressively farther from the lens axis are brought to focus at points progressively closer to the lens, forming a curved-field image sharply focused on a spherical plane rather than on a flat plane such as normally presented by a film or plate. The common appearance is decreasing sharpness outward from the center of the image.
(1) Ideal images of separate points at (a), (b), and (c).
(2) Actual images with field curvature.

ture, and distortion. *Chromatic or color aberrations* disperse or spread the wavelengths of a light ray passing through a given zone of the lens so that various colors come to different positions of focus, according to wavelengths. The two color aberrations are: longitudinal chromatic aberration and lateral chromatic aberration.

Aberrations are inherent characteristics of lenses, usually relatively severe in simple lenses. The effects of some of the aberrations can be reduced by closing down the lens aperture or by using selective filtration. However, modern compound lenses are well corrected in design and manufacture. Geometric aberrations are corrected by controlling the shapes of the various lens elements and by combin-

ing elements made from glasses, or other materials, with differing refractive characteristics. Well-corrected lenses may have from 3 to nearly 20 lens elements to provide corrections for aberrations. Chromatic aberrations are corrected by combining elements made of materials with differing dispersive characteristics, while the other aberrations are corrected by choice of glass, curve shape, element thickness, and air space. Even the most highly corrected lenses have traces of all the aberrations; their effects combine for a total influence on image quality. However, the appearance of individual aberrations can be observed by testing a lens on an optical bench or under similar controlled conditions.

• *See also:* ANASTIGMAT; LENSES; OPTICS.

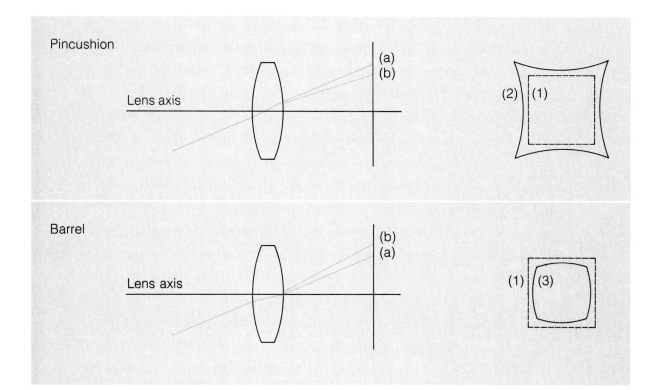

Distortion. Although sharply focused, the successive points that make up a straight line in the subject are refracted progressively closer to or farther from the lens axis than their ideal positions. The result is that imaged lines bend inward like the edges of a pincushion or outward like the sides of a barrel.

(a) Actual point position in image.
(b) Ideal point position in image.
(1) Ideal image of rectangle.
(2) Image with pincushion distortion.
(3) Image with barrel distortion.

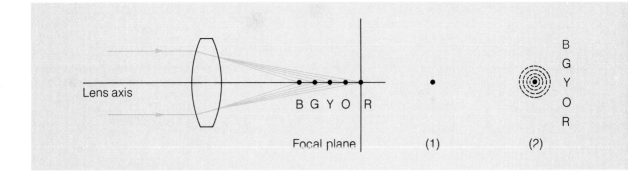

Lateral chromatic aberration. In rays not parallel to the lens axis, wavelengths are focused different distances outward from the lens axis, forming progressively larger images as wavelength decreases.

(1) Ideal image of subject form at focal plane.
(2) Actual image with lateral chromatic aberration.

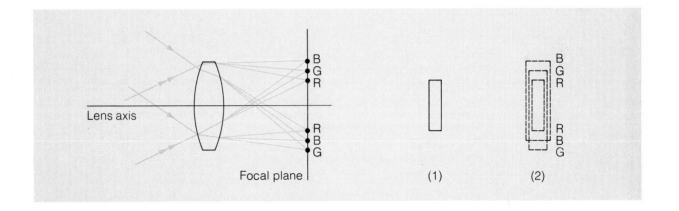

Longitudinal chromatic aberration. In rays parallel to the lens axis, longer wavelengths are focused closer to the axis than shorter wavelengths.

(1) Ideal image of point at focal plane.
(2) Actual image of point with longitudinal chromatic aberration.

Abney, Sir William de Wiveleslie

(1843–1920)
English chemist

Abney invented many photographic procedures and materials, including the first gelatino-chloride printing-out paper in 1882. He introduced hydroquinone as a developing agent and invented the copper bromide-silver nitrate method of negative intensification. He also discovered the Abney, or intermit-tency, effect in which a large number of very short exposures produces less of an accumulated effect in an emulsion than that produced by a single exposure equal to the total time of the intermittent exposures. Abney wrote numerous books and articles on various aspects of photography, photographic chemistry, sensitometry, densitometry, solarization, photometry, and spectral analysis. He was President of the Royal Photographic Society in London for five years and twice received the Progress Medal of the Society. He was also advisor in science to the Board of Education.

Acetic Acid

Methanecarboxylic acid, ethanoic acid, vinegar acid

Used in acid rinse stop baths to halt development and as the principal acid in fixing baths.
Formula: $CH_3 \cdot COOH$
Molecular Weight: 60.05

Clear colorless liquid with a very strong acrid odor; weaker solutions smell strongly of vinegar. Normally supplied in 99 percent strength (called glacial acetic acid because it freezes at a relatively high temperature—about 15.5 C [60 F]) and 28 percent dilution.
NOTE: Acetic acid is very corrosive in the glacial strength; the vapor of this concentration is flammable. It dissolves in water, alcohol, and other solvents. It dissolves gelatin, oils, and resins, and also certain cellulose plastics, and hence is sometimes used as an ingredient in film cements. The dilution used in stop and fixing baths does not materially affect the emulsion gelatin.
• *See also:* FIXERS AND FIXING; STOP BATH.

Acetone

Dimethyl ketone, propanone

Solvent for cellulose plastics and similar materials. Formerly used as an alkali in pyro developers and also as a solvent for the color couplers in some chromogenic (color-forming) developers.
Formula: $CH_3 \cdot CO \cdot CH_3$
Molecular Weight: 58.08

Colorless liquid, very volatile and inflammable. Dissolves in water and alcohol.

Achromatic

Literally, achromatic means "without color." As applied to lenses, the term refers to a type of lens in which two colors are brought to the same focus. The choice of the colors depends upon the use to which the lens will be put. With lenses to be used for visual observation, such as those in telescopes, the colors chosen are usually red and blue. In photographic lenses, the achromatization is for yellow and violet: yellow, because focusing is usually done with the brightest light (in the vicinity of yellow on the spectrum); violet, because most photographic emulsions are strongly sensitive to violet light. Bringing two colors to a common focus does not result in all other colors also being in focus. If this were the case, there would be no need for different types of achromatism. The residual color error in an achromatic lens is called "secondary spectrum."
• *See also:* ABERRATION; APOCHROMATIC; LENSES; OPTICS.

Acid

A photographic acid is a hydrogen compound that, in a chemical reaction, gives up hydrogen ions and accepts metal ions from another compound. The result is called a salt and, if the other compound is a base, water. (A few acids in the Lewis group do not contain hydrogen; they are not used in photography.) Acids are liquids at room temperature; they may be acidic gases dissolved in water. Acids generally exchange hydrogen ions for other cations.

In concentrated form, acids are generally highly corrosive. When mixing them into solutions, always pour the *acid into the water solution* while stirring slowly. Water poured into an acid solution may boil at the surface and spatter acid and hot water.

Acid strength depends on the chemical characteristics of the compound and its concentration. One measure of strength is expressed in pH, increasing from pH 7 (neutral) to pH 1 (extremely acidic).

Acids have two major uses in photography. In acid stop baths, they neutralize alkaline developing solutions to halt development quickly and to protect fixing solutions from being neutralized by developer carry-over. In acid hardening fixing baths, they provide the chemical conditions required for potassium alum to have a toughening or "hardening" effect on gelatin, make the hypo act more readily, and give the fixer a longer life.
• *See also:* ALKALI; pH; STOP BATH; and entries by specific acid names.

Actinic

Actinic is the property of radiant energy that changes the nature of materials exposed to it. Photographically, light, ultraviolet radiation, and infrared radiation (as well as x-rays, gamma rays, cosmic rays) have actinic properties. The spectral sensitivity of a photographic emulsion determines which wavelengths of radiant energy are actinic for the emulsion. For panchromatic film, ultraviolet radiation and most wavelengths of light are actinic, but infrared radiation is not.

• *See also:* BLACK-AND-WHITE FILMS; LIGHT.

Action Photography

Speed has always been one of photography's most appealing aspects. A century ago, people marveled that a portrait could be made in a matter of minutes or seconds, for they still thought in terms of portrait painters and the weeks and months a painting involved. When snapshots with shutter speeds of about 1/40 sec. came along, the age of speed was truly here.

Today, of course, the much greater speeds of modern shutters coupled to "faster" lenses and films are taken for granted. Even the cheapest, simplest camera works at something like 1/60 sec., and better cameras operate at shutter speeds of 1/250 sec. up to 1/2000 sec. When electronic flashes of light are used instead of relatively cumbersome shutters (as in stroboscopic work), speeds become astronomical.

But speed is relative. Even in picturing action, the top speed of which a camera's shutter is capable often may not be needed.

It is in the photography of straight-line action—a moving car, a train, a race—that relative motion becomes most important. When you stand beside a highway watching the cars, you will observe a phenomenon. While the cars are still a hundred yards

Use of smooth, perfectly timed panning and a fast shutter speed provided a clear shot of this racing car, with the blurred background giving an extra sense of speed. Kodak Ektachrome-X film, 1/500 sec. at f/4. Photo by John Paul Murphy.

or so away, they give no strong impression of speed; they merely grow larger. As they come nearer, they grow larger faster. And as they whiz past, you have to swivel your head quickly to see them at all. As they recede from you, the process goes into reverse; they grow smaller, quickly at first and then more slowly.

With a camera in hand, this phenomenon means merely that it takes a much higher shutter speed to "stop" action as it crosses in front of you than when it is either coming or going.

Back to the highway again. This time, stand back about a hundred feet from the nearest lane. Now the angle between you and the oncoming cars is less acute; their speed, at a distance, is a little more apparent but, oddly enough, not at the instant of passing in front of you. You can almost pick out details. You don't have to swivel your head quite as

violently to follow the action. Thus, for such a situation you may need a little more shutter speed for the approach and not quite as much for the pass-by.

Blur vs. Sharpness

There are two different and opposite schools of thought about the best way to picture speed. One demands the *stop-it-cold* technique and the other favors the *let-it-blur* technique.

The best possible illustration of the stop-it-cold concept is the classic picture of a speeding bullet. Made by the light of an electronic flash, automatically triggered, the bullet is pictured sitting serenely in space, going nowhere in particular and threatening no one. It is *so* "stopped" that there is no more sense of speed in it than in a still-life portrait of a banana.

The momentary poise of the skater is counterpointed by the feeling of movement created by panning a camera set at 1/30 sec.

The panning technique has created a sharp central image, while the blurred background and foreground emphasize not only speed but also the bright colors of the main figure.

Action Photography

The opposite of this is a shot that is so "*un-stopped*" that it is nothing but a fuzzy blur. It is speed, but it is speed without meaning.

Obviously, the photographic answer—a picture that both identifies the subject and gives a sense of speed—must lie between *stop-it-cold* and *let-it-blur*.

Shots of unstopped action, particularly in color, interpret movement. They give a "feel" of the action, but little or no information. Just enough significant shape or outline is shown to hint at the subject. They are interesting and sometimes effective, but their very novelty forces photographers to seek more revealing answers.

There are at least two answers. One is an oblique or nearly head-on shot of action in which there is enough contributory evidence of action—flying dust, straining muscles, feet off the ground—to convince the picture viewer that things are happening, fast. The subject of the picture may be truly "stopped," but the circumstances spell speed and action.

The other answer is to pan with the action so that the camera, as it swings, gets a good look at the subject but registers everything else as a blur of horizontal streaks. Actually, a good pan shot recreates your optical experience as a car goes by; your eye follows the car and disregards all else.

Motion-Stopping Shutter Speeds

Knowing what shutter speed to use to almost stop subject motion often permits the photographer to select the shutter speed and *f*-number for a given exposure that will give adequate subject detail and maximum depth of field for the conditions. The degree of blur used as the basis for the following table and formulas is .37 to .50 mm (.015" to .020") on an 8" × 10" print enlarged from the entire negative. The table is based on the use of a normal-focal-length lens. The type of motion column gives an idea of the types of activity that generally result in the speeds given in the first column.

The table can also be used to find shutter speeds that will show a predictable amount of blur in moving subjects. If you use the next slower shutter speed, the amount of blur will double (about 1 mm or .040") in an 8" × 10" print. If the speed called for

MOTION-STOPPING SHUTTER SPEEDS
(FOR LENSES OF NORMAL FOCAL LENGTH)

Speed		Type of Motion	Distance		Direction of Motion		
Mi/Hr	Km/Hr		Ft	M	◀ OR ▶	↖ OR ↘	↕ OR
5	8	Slow walk, hand work, sitting or standing people	12	4	1/500	1/250	1/125
			25	8	1/250	1/125	1/60
			50	16	1/125	1/60	1/30
			100	33	1/60	1/30	1/15
10	16	Fast walk, children and pets playing, horses walking, slow-moving vehicles	12	4	1/1000	1/500	1/250
			25	8	1/500	1/250	1/125
			50	16	1/250	1/125	1/60
			100	33	1/125	1/60	1/30
25	40	Running, sports, very active play, horses running, vehicles moving at a moderate speed	12	4	1/2000	1/1000	1/500
			25	8	1/1000	1/500	1/250
			50	16	1/500	1/250	1/125
			100	33	1/250	1/125	1/60
50	80	Fast-moving vehicles, birds flying, race horses running	25	8	1/2000	1/1000	1/500
			50	16	1/1000	1/500	1/250
			100	33	1/500	1/250	1/125
			200	66	1/250	1/125	1/60
100	160	Very fast-moving vehicles	25	8	—	1/2000	1/1000
			50	16	1/2000	1/1000	1/500
			100	33	1/1000	1/500	1/250
			200	66	1/500	1/250	1/125

Estimate between table values.

Action Photography

The fast action of a football game was stopped by a particularly high-speed shutter that was specially developed by the photographers for the 17-inch lens of a Colorama camera. Photo by Wes Wooden and Pete Culross.

in the table is 1/1000 sec. and you give 1/30 sec., the amount of blur will be about 12 mm or .5″. If you pan the camera to follow the subject, the background will be blurred by this amount, provided direction of action is across the camera field.

If the lens to be used is a wide-angle lens of about half the normal focal length, the next slower shutter speed than that given in the table should be used. If the lens is a telephoto of about twice the normal focal length, use the next faster shutter speed to get the same amount of blur.

Photographing Sporadic Motion

The previous discussion has been about continuous, more or less straight-line action. But much of the action, in ball sports particularly, is anything but continuous or uniform. Part of baseball's charm, for example, is the way exciting action erupts, often without warning.

Good sports shots are based as much on the photographer's knowledge of the sport and his intuition as on his mastery of his equipment. He knows that there are moments of seemingly suspended animation in sports and that those moments are, fortunately, just as pictorial as any others. Sometimes, they're better. Consider a baseball pitcher; in the middle of his delivery, he appears to have a broken arm and is awkward to boot. But when he rears back, ready to uncoil, he looks great; similarly, he is 100 percent pictorial when, fully extended, he releases the ball. And at both of those points you can stop the action with ease.

Much depends on your reaction time. It doesn't matter whether it is fast or slow; the important thing is that you need to be aware of it so that your action pictures can be tailored accordingly. Look for a big clock with a sweep second hand. Try a series of shots from about five feet, catching the second hand *exactly* as it points to ten-second mark intervals. After a few such experiments, you'll know fairly well what your reaction time is; obviously, it can be improved with practice, but don't assume it is very good until you have proved it.

Veteran sports photographers know their sports and also know their reaction times. In boxing, for example, they shoot for the impact of a blow.

The panning technique was combined with a slow shutter speed to convey the vivid sense of speed and strain in the movement of this racing athlete. Kodak Ektachrome-X film, 1/15 sec. at f/22. Photo by John Paul Murphy.

Poise vs. Pose

Simulated or imitation action looks silly. Usually, it is evident at a glance, and it is silly because it is not necessary. With high shutter speeds, with fast flash, and, most of all, with an understanding of what's going on, no pretension is needed.

A possible exception might be the standard head-on shots of football players in the signal-calling crouch. That's classic. Moreover, it's a matter of poise and not pose. Poise makes sense; pose doesn't.

Panning with Action

The pan technique for capturing passing action is simple, but it justifies experiment and practice.

First, set your focus for the distance at which the car will pass directly in front of you. Then with

shutter cocked, pick up the car in your viewfinder as it approaches. Keep your eye glued to it, pivoting your head and shoulders as the car comes nearer. Swing with it. Make the exposure when the car is squarely in front of you, but don't stop there. Follow through, as in golf. The smoother your swing, the straighter the blurred lines in your picture will be, and the better those blurs will suggest speed.

Try it at several shutter speeds, beginning at about 1/25 sec. The higher the shutter speed, the less blur. Then you can decide which of the effects you like best and try it on other subjects.

Focal-Plane Phenomena

Many sports cameras as well as a majority of the SLRs now in use have focal-plane shutters—shutters that travel across the face of the film. At, say, 1/500 sec., all parts of the film get their allotted 1/500 sec. of exposure, but they do not all get it at exactly the same time. The slit in the shutter has to travel across the film, and that takes a little time. So the first exposed parts of the film record their parts of the image just a fraction of a second before the last exposed parts.

If the shutter travels in the same direction as a fast-passing subject, there will be some pictorial elongation; if the direction of shutter travel is opposed to that of the subject, you can get a compressed effect. Therefore, the effect depends on the shutter's direction of travel.

Speed

To get a good record of fast action is fine and well worth doing. But, once you have mastered the basics of speed shooting, check over your work. Have you gained speed and lost pictures?

Pictures, good pictures, are the ends of photography. So, do not succumb to the temptation to accept any reasonably successful action shot as good enough.

• *See also:* SPORTS PHOTOGRAPHY.

Further Reading: Callahan, Sean. *Photographing Sports.* New York, NY: T. Y. Crowell Co., 1975; Self, Charles. *How to Take Action Photographs: The Right Way to Photograph Animals, Children, Nature and Sports.* Garden City, NY: Doubleday & Co., 1975; Turner, Richard. *Focus on Sports: Photographing Action.* Garden City, NY: Amphoto, 1975.

Acutance

Acutance is one measure of the sharpness of a film image. It is primarily a measure of the sharpness of a boundary between a light and a dark area and is not the same as resolution, which merely specifies the minimum separation between two lines or details. In fact, some materials of high resolution produce images that have less acutance than other materials of lower resolving power.

Acutance in a photographic image can be improved by the use of thin-emulsion negative films, because the thin emulsion spreads the image less than a thicker emulsion. The *appearance* of sharpness can often be enhanced by the use of a developer that releases bromide during the process; the ac-

cumulation of bromides at the edges of large highlights causes them to be surrounded by a thin line (*See:* MACKIE LINE.), which emphasizes the contrast at the edge.

Overexposure and overdevelopment both cause a loss in acutance; so do halation and irradiation in the emulsion coat. An out-of-focus or poorly corrected lens produces a similar apparent loss in acutance.

• *See also:* MACKIE LINE; RESOLVING POWER.

Adams, Ansel

(Born 1902)
American photographer

At age 28, Adams turned away from a career as a concert pianist to greater loves: photography and nature. He became one of the greatest masters of realistic black-and-white photography in the 20th century. His masterpieces are views of U.S. national parks and monumental landscapes in the American West, exquisitely printed from large-format negatives. He was one of the founders of the *f*/64 school of photography in 1932. This was a group of photographers who rebelled against the fuzzy pictorial school in vogue at the time. They used large camera formats and very small lens apertures to obtain pictures that have the qualities of great depth and clarity of image.

A superb technician, as well as a sensitive visual artist, Adams formulated the *zone system* to provide practical procedures for testing and evaluating negative and print materials, and processing methods, without the need for scientific conditions or instruments. The zone system attempts to put controlled photographic procedures at the service of artistic expression by relating negative exposure and development to the final tones desired in a black-and-white (or color) image. It is most fully explained in his series of technical books (N.Y. Graphic Society, Boston, MA). *The Eloquent Light,* by Nancy Newhall (Sierra Club, San Francisco, CA), is a biography of Adams up to 1938. The major published collections of his photographs are *Ansel Adams: Images, 1923–1974* and *Photographs of the Southwest* (both N.Y. Graphic Society, Boston, MA).

• *See also:* ZONE SYSTEM.

Ansel Adams: Monolith, The Face of Half Dome, Yosemite National Park, California; c. 1927.
From the photographer's collection.

16

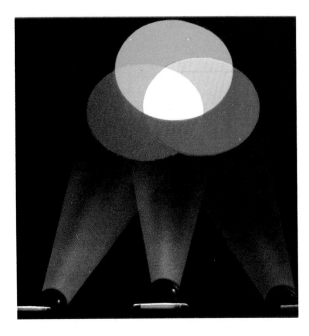

plates used starch grains dyed in the primary additive hues to achieve color separation in the taking stage and color synthesis in the viewing stage. Finlay color and Dufay color used ruled filter screens to achieve the same purposes. Color television is the only current usage of this principle.
• *See also:* Color Theory; Subtractive Color Synthesis.

Adurol

Trademark of Hauff, Ltd. for the developing agent chlorhydroquinone

NOTE: The name *Adurol* was also applied by Schering to bromhydroquinone; this latter had no particular advantage over the chlor- form and is no longer manufactured.
• *See also:* Chlorhydroquinone.

Additive color mixture. Projectors with red, green, and blue filters cast overlapping circles, creating pairs of cyan, magenta, and yellow. Where all three overlap is white.

Advertising Agencies

Although companies of all sizes may have internal advertising departments that buy or commission pictures, most advertising photography is purchased by or through specialized advertising agencies. It is agency-generated assignments that involve the largest fees for this kind of work.

The function of an agency is to create advertising ideas for a client, execute the ads, and arrange for their appearance in various media, such as magazines and newspapers, brochures, reports, catalogs, television, and outdoor boards. An agency may be a small organization of less than ten people or a concern with hundreds of employees. Some are located in cities of moderate size and operate successfully on a strictly local or regional basis; others are national or international corporations. All are sources of a great deal of photographic work.

For a photographer, the most important individual in an advertising agency is the art director. This person is responsible for the visual design of the advertising for one or more clients. The art director and staff create visual ideas, which are assigned to the photographers who can best execute them. While the largest agencies may have a few staff pho-

Additive Color Synthesis

Additive color synthesis is the creation of color by presenting to the eye various proportions of one, two, or three narrow bands of wavelengths—commonly those corresponding to pure red, green, and blue spectral hues. The stimuli may be colored lights projected on a white surface or dots of color placed side by side, as in Impressionist and Pointillist paintings and color television images.

The additive process depends on the use of the additive, primary hues to cause the eye to build up, or synthesize, a composite multiple-wavelength color impression. Its opposite, the subtractive process, depends on using filters or dyes—nearly always cyan, magenta, and yellow—to remove unwanted wavelengths from white light, leaving only those that make up the intended color sensation.

The first camera color films or plates were based on additive color synthesis. The Lumière color

tographers, most work is contracted with outside studios and independent photographers.

Although an individual campaign may have a particular style and theme, an agency usually has dozens or hundreds of campaigns, in as many styles, in progress at any given moment. Therefore, it must be able to draw on the talents of many different kinds of photographers for the required visual material. It is essential that a photographer show his or her work to as many art directors as possible, at as many different agencies as possible, in order to secure the assignments that best fit his or her talents.

In reviewing a photographer's portfolio or slide presentation, an art director looks for evidence of taste, style, and technical excellence. The last is an assumed basic quality; without it little else counts. Seldom does an art director look at a photographer's work to find a particular picture—for that a researcher is sent to a picture agency. Rather, an art director looks for evidence of professional competence and the kind of talent that can produce the sort of pictures needed for a specific ad or campaign. Essentially, the art director is looking for specialists who have mastered various styles or kinds of subjects. A portfolio that goes in too many directions will not leave a lasting impression.

When an art director sees the kind of work he or she can use, the photographer will be given an outline of a visual idea—often with a sketch or rough script—and a trial assignment. The photographer's job is to make sure the assignment is clearly understood, to clarify the business details, and to deliver the picture that actually was ordered. Alternate versions, other treatments, and creative approaches may also be turned in to demonstrate the photographer's talent, but the agency's primary demand and expectation is to receive the picture it wants delivered on time. A photographer who meets these criteria will receive repeated assignments. As the photographer's capabilities become familiar to the agency art directors, the scope of assignments will broaden. The rewards can be great. An agency will pay the top price within the available budget to obtain the best results, because that is what they in turn must produce. If the advertising they create does not do its job, they lose their client.

• *See also:* ADVERTISING PHOTOGRAPHY; AGENCIES, PICTURE.

Further Reading: Keppler, Victor. *Man + Camera.* Garden City, NY: Amphoto, 1970; Miller, Gary E. *Freelance Photography.* Los Angeles, CA: Petersen Publishing Co., 1975; Perry, Robin. *Photography for the Professionals.* Waterford, CT: Livingston Press, 1976; Stern, Bert. *The Photo Illustration.* New York, NY: T. Y. Crowell Co., 1974.

Advertising Photography

Advertising photography is illustrative photography; it is the production of pictures that embody or express a predetermined idea. Other kinds of photography do not always have the primary aim of making ideas visible. Record photographs (photojournalism, documentary or scientific photography) present the physical reality of what was in front of the lens. Expressive, artistically intended photographs communicate an experience or aesthetic reaction caused by the subject or—in the case of an abstract image—by the photograph itself.

The Function of Advertising Photography

An illustration may contain something of these approaches, but its primary function is to find a visual way to tell a story or make a promotional statement. In accomplishing this, almost any style or technique of photography may be used. Typical kinds of advertising illustrations and the intended message or idea include the following:

A picture of the product—this is a handsome, well-made thing.

A glamorous picture of a girl in a gown—this dress will make you beautiful.

An impressive, towering modern building—this is a large, substantial corporation.

A smiling, informal, or candid portrait—we are a friendly, helpful organization.

A scientific photograph—the work we do is complex, technical, important.

Children in a hospital ward—we need your help to help people like these.

A slum neighborhood—this ought to be corrected.

The list could be extended almost indefinitely. In every case, the ultimate function of the advertising

Deep, rich colors project the image—a fine and elegant wine. Photo by Jerry Sarapochiello.

Advertising Photography

This experimental photograph ties together the ideas—Americanism and business/typing/correspondence. It might be used as a poster for the Secretary of the Year competition; obviously, there are a number of other possibilities. Photo by Henry Ries.

photography is to *sell* its subject, either literally by making the viewer want to purchase the product or service shown, or indirectly by creating a positive attitude toward the organization or the activities presented.

These kinds of illustrations are used in many more ways than just newspaper and magazine advertisements. They are the major part of catalogs, brochures, and promotional literature; of posters, billboards, and car cards; of in-store and point-of-purchase displays. They are used in instruction manuals, annual reports, mailing pieces, product packages, and wrappings. In technique and application, advertising illustration is probably the most

all-encompassing area in the field of photography.

The equipment, materials, and techniques used are determined by the nature of the desired picture; there is no limit to what may be required. The way in which they are used is determined by the underlying idea.

Content and Message

An advertising illustration may or may not have a product as a portion of its content, but it must always have an idea as its starting point and some sort of story as its end. The story may be as simple as a message of beauty, goodness, taste, or size. Or it may be so complex that its effect is to conjure up a totally imaginary experience in the viewer's mind —an experience suggested, but not shown, in the illustration.

Whatever its message, a successful advertising photograph must do three things:

> *Stop the eye*—Without visual impact, nobody stops and nothing happens. The photograph must create awareness.
>
> *Set the mood*—Visual pleasure invites the viewer to stay a while and participate in a way the advertiser desires. A need must be defined.
>
> *Start the sale*—The whole point of an ad-

vertising illustration is to sell, to encourage the action to buy. The ability to persuade often depends on the degree of promise and the way in which the product is presented.

Illustration Content. There are advertisements that are catalog pages. Here's the product; here's what it looks like; read what it does. There are advertisements that suggest a result. Use our product, get your man—or girl. Or, use our product, don't lose your man—or girl. Still others suggest benefits, some tangible, some not. The marketing ideas are different among them; illustration ideas, therefore,

This photograph is a simple exercise in technique and design. Photo by Jerry Sarapochiello.

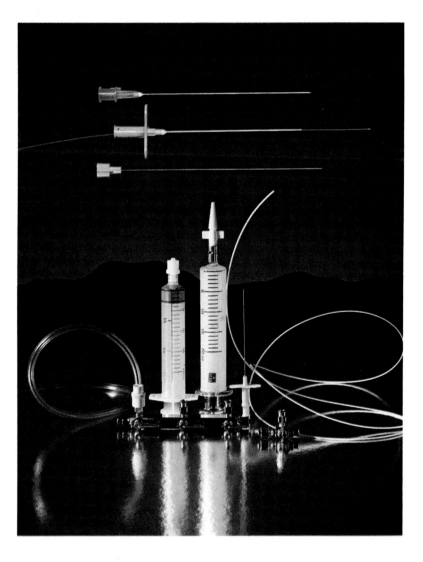

(Left) The message behind this advertisement is presented through the understated background—the dressing table of an elegant woman which holds, besides a man's cologne, the contents of his pockets. (Right) A piece of exquisite hand embroidery, a delicate pair of scissors— a most appropriate background for a product created especially for the women's market. Photos by Jerry Sarapochiello.

are based on different premises. But all have a need for illustration that is sound in design, quick to the point, and attractive, if possible.

If the illustration is technically inept, it fails to communicate and nobody gets the point. If it serves as a vehicle for a highly obtuse graphic exercise, nobody gets the point except its originators. If it is aesthetically sterile, it bores everybody, and nobody *wants* to get the point.

A successful, hard-working illustration starts with a good idea about the presentation of an advertising premise, and presents it in a clear, logical, eye-catching, and attractive way. There is a large

spot for beauty in advertising illustration, and its importance is based on simple human preference for love over hate, the beautiful over the ugly, the sweet over the sour. It doesn't matter either whether the picture is four-color or one, big or small, square or round. Catching the eye by means of color, design, size, or unusual technique can make a picture attractive. But it is content which keeps the viewer's attention and makes the illustration start to do its work.

Content is the fundamental idea of the picture and the story line used to carry out that idea. It is content that sets the mood; if the content is presented successfully, the sale should follow.

A classically shaped bottle softly backlit against a midnight sky: elegance, refinement, and a gentle aura of mystery. A view camera is almost essential for a photograph such as this. Photo by Jerry Sarapochiello.

Logic and Visual Appeal. To set a mood, an illustration must have a certain degree of logic. It should be simple enough to be understandable. And, above all, it should be visually pleasing to encourage the eye to linger.

The logic of a picture need not be an everyday obvious one. A bar of soap may almost always be used in a bathroom. This does not mean that the logic of illustration demands a bathroom setting. If the advertising appeal of the product is in the refreshing reward that comes with its use, a sparkling mountain stream surrounded by the cool greens of moss and ferns may say refreshment very appealingly. Such a setting forms its own suggestiveness and contributes to success because it sets a mood of refreshment.

On the other hand, the message about soap may be mainly its magnificent ability to create suds, in which case, an interestingly composed mountain of bubbles with the soap as its boulder may more di-

rectly make the point. The bubbles set the mood of soapiness.

Most good advertising illustration is comparatively simple. All elements in a picture should be there to make a contribution to the whole. The temptation to include extraneous material because of its appeal to the maker is ever present. Excluding it is the mark of an admirable, necessary discipline.

Establishing the Mood

Color and light are dominant factors in the establishment of mood. The photographer can influence these factors both while making the picture, and after the fact in the darkroom. The negative-positive way to color, in particular, offers extensive control of the image. The overall balance of the color print can be made considerably different than the original scene when that seems desirable, and the densities of parts of the image or the whole can be changed to lighter or darker than what might be considered normal.

Similar liberties can be taken with color transparencies by control during a duplicating step. Thus, to an appreciable extent, the photographer can overcome what might otherwise seem to be limitations of existing conditions in the establishment of mood. In the studio, obviously the photographer has complete control of both light and color, and the problems are reduced to skill and taste in using physical tools.

However, an advertising illustration must do more than not offend the eye. It must *illustrate,* which is to say, tell a story.

The composition of such a picture is governed by what is to be said. The background, or the environment in which the photograph apparently is set, can help with the important task of stopping the reader, as well as assisting in setting the mood and telling the story. The color to which the picture is keyed plays its part, as do the apparent time of day and level and contrast of overall lighting. As a matter of fact, emphasis, or punctuation by light, is one of photography's strongest devices.

Attention can be directed by the arrangement of models and objects, by their color, their lighting, their contrast, and by their sharpness as compared with their fellow models or objects. The aim of an advertising illustration is to direct the viewer's eye to a predetermined portion of the picture and to communicate an idea after it gets to the proper spot.

Execution of the Illustration in Advertising Photography

These are some of the principles, or basic methods, of photographic communication. But they must be put to effective use. When the advertising and illustrative idea is settled upon, there remains the execution of the illustration. Here, ideas are the photographic ones of what symbols or properties are to be used, the set in which they are to be arranged, the arrangement or composition itself, the lighting, the photographic equipment to be utilized, and other such matters. All of these are to present the product and/or idea with its best foot forward. And to do so in a way that the viewer will find attractive and understandable.

Elements of the Idea. There are two parts to the idea: what it says, and how it says it. What it says is an advertising matter predicated on product, merchandising aims, matters of the business world. How it says it is a graphic matter, the province of the art director and photographer. The frozen line of a layout provides scant room for development of the graphic idea. While the layout can communicate the advertising idea to the client and orient the photographer on direction and purpose, remember that the pencil is a shackle to the camera.

Technical Requirements. A photographer can follow a layout if it does not describe impossibilities of drawing and perspective. However, the photographer must have the technical ability to deliver forms exactly to specifications when that is essential.

For example, many advertising illustrations are composed of elements from two or more photographs. When negative-positive materials are used, it is a simple matter to adjust the final size of each element during enlarging. But if, as is frequently the case, color transparencies are being made, then every element must be photographed *in the camera* at exact size. Furthermore, they may have to be photographed on the same piece of film, which involves the additional problems of multiple exposure calculation and absolutely precise placement within the frame. Full technical mastery of the medium is only a starting point for an advertising photographer's success.

Visualizing the Final Illustration. The execution of an illustration does not always follow a direct, preplanned route. Subject matter tends to have a will of its own, and often it almost literally de-

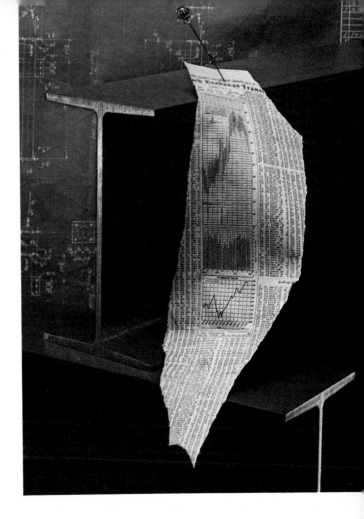

A steel I beam and stock market quotations make a timely and artistic allusion to the steel industry as big business. Photo by Henry Ries.

mands to be handled in ways that were not anticipated. Furthermore, ideas in the execution of an illustrative idea tend to develop from a train of thought in the same way as the original advertising idea. One thing leads to another, as it so often does elsewhere, and the final result may well be quite different from that originally envisioned—and considerably better.

A photograph for advertising use is usually only a steppingstone to the printed reproduction that actually carries the message to the public. Sometimes the picture is expected to tell all of the message, or a large part of it. Almost always it occupies most of the space. Always it is expected to stop the passerby and interest him or her. Therefore, it is not enough to judge the photograph simply as an end in itself.

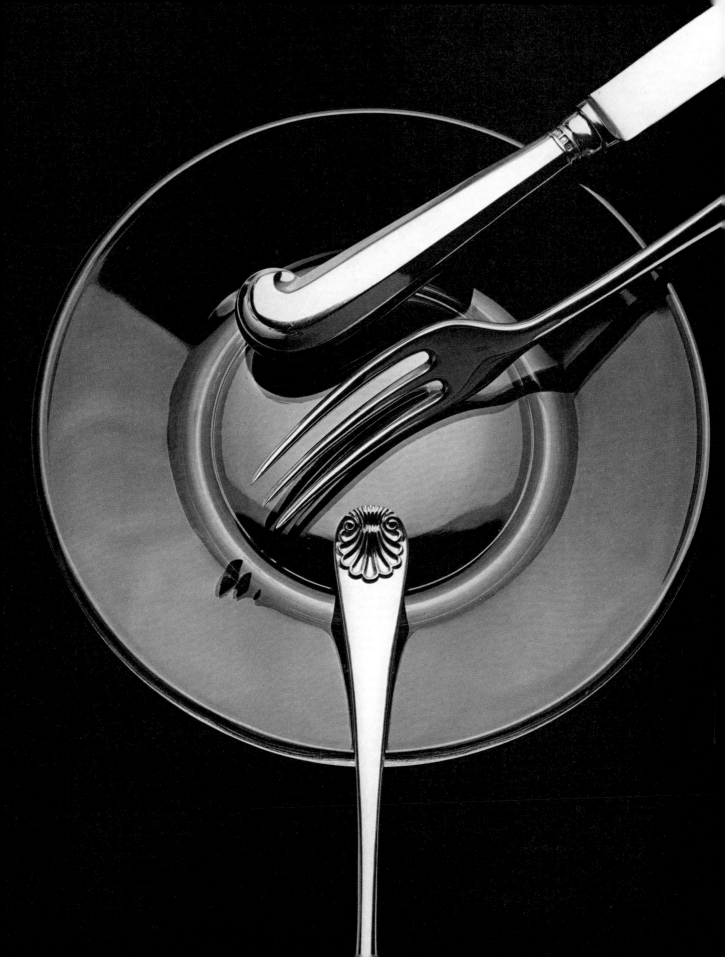

A small original that is to be reproduced in a large size must be examined accordingly. Does it just look sharp or is it really sharp? Will it come apart when enlarged? Will the enlargement be too great for the original?

Highlights that catch the eye and distract attention from the subject matter will catch the eye and distract even more when the picture is enlarged. Shadows that are annoyingly lacking in detail in the original will probably be more annoying in reproduction, and subject matter that seems to recede into the background will recede even farther on the printed page.

Because photography is such a versatile medium, and because so many effects can be achieved by judicious manipulation of the medium, any objective evaluation must take into consideration the purpose and story line of the picture. These are significantly affected by the degree of technical quality in the photograph.

Photographic Quality

Sharpness and tone separation are the two major indicators of photographic quality. In fact, the ability to render detail sharply and to separate tone gradations from the deep shadows through brilliant highlights are the two unique properties of the photographic process.

In judging sharpness, the sharpness of the main subject is considered. It is seldom desirable to have background and subject equally sharp, since a softness in the background emphasizes the sharpness of the subject. Closely allied with sharpness is texture, the rendering of which is a function of the way in which the subject was lighted originally. If the subject was smooth, had a surface pattern, or was rough, a technically fine photograph should show that it was.

The dark, or shadow, areas of the scene should have sufficient tone separation to show detail, and the highlights should show tones ranging from just off-white for the brightest downward. Most important is the subject of the photograph, and its tones should have enough separation or contrast to demonstrate its shape.

The effect of correct placement of tones in a photograph is to achieve a proper contrast or ratio of lights to darks. A flat photograph lacking in contrast is one that is dull to look at, while a photograph having too great a contrast is ugly and harsh. As a matter of fact, quality in a photograph is most obvious when the photograph is poor. When there is good quality, each characteristic of photography is doing its part, and the viewer sees only the subject

Illustration Problems and Solutions

Catalogs. The success of the large mail order catalogs in moving goods is well known. Their use of photography is exemplary and worthy of close study.

Illustration in catalogs, brochures, and other sales literature must, of course, be descriptive. It must be honest, but flattering, and should have the attributes of advertising illustration—it should sell the idea and the product. It is not enough to simply show a highly retouched shape in silhouette, or squared off in a rectangle of nothing.

The product is always front and center on a mail order catalog page. It is presented at its best and with as much technical photographic perfection as possible. The picture is the product, and no effort is spared to present it appealingly with an aura of quality. Current productions utilize a more illustrative treatment. Furniture and other household goods are shown in room settings, and the models displaying clothes are shown on location in interesting settings. Photography for mail order catalogs is becoming less catalog and more space advertising in character.

The illustrative problem in an industrial catalog is somewhat different from that in many consumer catalogs. The specifications and technical characteristics of the product are of first interest to the reader. In many cases, he already knows what the product looks like. This would certainly be the case with twist drills and reamers. Yet imaginative photography can dress up the catalog to advantage and, more importantly, contribute to the word picture of quality, reliability, and other adjectives loved by catalog writers.

The production problems in putting together a large mail order catalog are immense. Every possible means of making the operation economically efficient must be utilized both for the photographic and photomechanical steps.

(Left) Cover photo for a department store catalog advertising a white sale. Photo by John Pemberton. (Right) One of a series of point-of-sale posters for Howard Johnson. Photo by Albert Gommi.

Posters. A really great poster needs nothing but a word to say it all, and there are times when it doesn't need that. It is the ultimate of what an advertising illustration can be, for it can stop the eye with its design, set the mood with its content, and start the sale with the desire it creates. The photographer must be aware of these three elements.

The essence of poster art is speed of communication, which suggests that photographs created for posters be simple ones. This is particularly true for outdoor advertising where the potential customer is passing by at varying rates of speed, usually fast. The message and design can be more complex where the poster is used at point-of-sale, for here the customer is contained within a store and therefore movement is restricted.

• *See also:* ADVERTISING AGENCIES; BUSINESS METHODS IN PHOTOGRAPHY; FASHION PHOTOGRAPHY; GLAMOUR PHOTOGRAPHY; MODEL RELEASE; PHOTOMECHANICAL REPRODUCTION METHODS.

Further Reading: Croy, Otto R. *Graphic Effects by Photography.* London, England: Focal Press Ltd., 1973; Hammond, Bill. *How to Make Money in Advertising Photography.* Garden City, NY: Amphoto, 1975; Jenkins, Nicholas. *Photographics: Photographic Technique for Design.* New York, NY: Van Nostrand Reinhold, 1973; Reedy, William A. *Impact—Photography for Advertising.* Rochester, NY: Eastman Kodak Company, 1973.

Advertising Photography

Aerial Fog

Fog in a developed emulsion is non-image-forming overall density that can degrade the printing characteristics of a negative or the visual quality of a positive. A print from a fogged negative commonly shows lighter-than-normal dark areas with decreased contrast. A fogged print commonly shows grayed highlights with decreased contrast. In both cases, fine details may be obscured in these areas.

Development produces a certain amount of chemical fog, usually at an acceptable or non-image-degrading level. Excess density can be created by letting an emulsion that is wet with developer come in contact with the air too often or for too long. This aerial fog may result from extra activity as the air oxidizes the developer, from staining caused by oxidation by-products, or from a combination of the two. Aerial fog may be prevented by keeping the emulsion submerged in the developing solution except when it is absolutely necessary to remove it, for example, when lifting sheet film or turning over a print for agitation and by the use of restrainers or antifoggants in the developer formula.

• *See also:* ANTIFOGGANT; DEVELOPMENT; FOGGING.

Aerial Perspective

Aerial perspective is the impression of depth, distance, and space created when haze decreases the contrast and color saturation, lightens the tone, softens the outlines, and obscures details of distant objects. As things appear lighter and less sharp, we judge them to be more distant; the effect increases with distance because the amount of haze between lens and subject also increases. More haze than is visible to the naked eye may be reproduced in the final picture because invisible scattered ultraviolet energy also affects the emulsion, causing lighter tones in black-and-white pictures and excess bluish or bluish-violet tones in color pictures. The effect can be controlled or reduced by using a yellow, green, orange, or red filter with panchromatic black-and-white film. It may be almost completely elimi-

nated by use of an infrared film and filter combination, if the changed tonal representations that infrared film produces are acceptable.

Skylight or haze filters for natural color films reduce excess bluish tones caused by haze scattering the long wavelengths of visible and ultraviolet light; they do not materially penetrate the haze or reduce the overall effects of aerial perspective. A special infrared color film that produces false color reproduction can be used to penetrate the haze materially.

• *See also:* ATMOSPHERIC HAZE; FILTERS; INFRARED.

Aerial Photography

Air-to-ground pictures and airborne views of clouds, sunsets, and atmospheric effects can readily be taken with ordinary films and equipment during commercial flights, as well as during lightplane or helicopter flights made specifically for photographic purposes.

Types of Aerial Photographs

There are two types of aerial photos: verticals and obliques. Verticals are taken with the camera aimed straight down, and with the film parallel to the ground; obliques are taken at an angle. Vertical aerial photography, used for mapping and other photogrammetric and photointerpretive studies, requires specialized equipment and highly sophisticated techniques. The following material deals with oblique aerial photography only and pertains to still photography. However, much of the data and many of the techniques can be applied directly to motion-picture photography as well.

Commercial Flights

Although you have no control over the route or altitude, there are a number of things you can do to improve your picture-taking opportunities during a commercial flight.

Select a seat near a window, preferably on the shady side of the plane. You will have a better view of the ground if you are seated in front of or well behind a wing.

Set the camera controls before takeoff. If the camera is automatic, or has no settings, just shoot when the time comes. On an adjustable camera, set

The best opportunity for shooting familiar scenes from an airplane comes just after takeoff and just before landing, when the aircraft is at lower altitudes than during the flight.

the focus at 15 metres (50 feet). This will keep the wing fairly sharp, keep any dirt on the window out of focus, and keep the image of the clouds and ground sharp. Set a still-camera shutter at 1/250 sec. (or the closest speed the camera has) and set the lens opening to go with that speed as given in the film instruction sheet. For shooting movies during take-off, use 24 or 32 frames per second, if possible. But if the movie camera has only one speed, use it.

When the plane leaves the ground, start shooting anything that looks interesting—runways, skyscrapers, farms—almost anything looks unique from this viewpoint. Observe two important precautions:

1. Do not brace the camera against the window; vibration may blur pictures.
2. Make sure the lens is not obscured by part of the window frame. With a non-reflex viewing camera, the viewfinder may see out the window, while the lens cannot.

When you are up high—more than a mile—things look brighter. Use a lens opening one stop smaller than you'd use on the ground (f/11 instead

of f/8, for example). Try to include the wing in the foreground to add depth and interest to your pictures. Lots of pictures of the ground from around 9000 metres (about 29,500 feet) will be, frankly, rather dull. When you shoot pictures of the ground from great heights, you may run into a haze problem —color images look bluish from the scattering of blue light and ultraviolet radiation. A skylight filter over the lens will help a little. If you use a polarizer over the lens to darken the sky, it may interact with polarizing characteristics of plastic window material or glare-reducing window treatments. The result may be out-of-focus color bands in color pictures. Check carefully for this problem through the camera's reflex viewing system, or remove the filter and rotate it 180 degrees as you look through it and the window.

Pilots often make a special effort to identify and fly close to famous places like Niagara Falls and the Grand Canyon. Have your camera ready. Other good subjects to look for are farms and woods early or late in the day when shadows are long and the light is a warm orange; snowcapped mountains; city skylines at takeoff and landing; and ships, rivers, and harbors.

Flights for Photographic Purposes

When you have specific subjects to photograph, or when detailed views and particular features must be shown, you need a private flight specifically for photographic purposes. Usually this means renting or leasing a small aircraft and the services of a commercially licensed pilot.

Your choice of aircraft, equipment, and film will be determined by the photographic project. Ask yourself:

Why are aerial pictures being taken?
What do you need to show?
What will the photographs be used for?
What comparisons must be made?
In what form will they be used (slides, murals, 8″ × 10″ prints, illustrations in a report, color, black-and-white, etc.)?
When must they be available?
Where is your subject?
How much area will you need to cover?
What time of day will present the best lighting for the subject?
From what direction are you likely to have the best view?
Approximately what altitude will be best?
What terrain features or navigational hazards are in the general area?

When you have the answers to these questions, you can actually begin your mission.

The Aircraft

Good aerial photographs can be taken from almost any aircraft ever made. However, there are some generally accepted preferences. In fixed-wing aircraft, a high-wing, relatively slow-flying plane is generally preferred. A high wing presents less obstruction to view in level or nearly level flight than low-winged aircraft, and a slow plane helps keep problems due to movement to a minimum. Many of the high-winged aircraft have large windows that open, providing a good area for viewing the subject; also, they can be flown safely with a door removed. (The FAA publishes information on aircraft approved for flying with the door removed.) Often, low-winged craft do not have a window that can be opened, and they tend to have higher minimum flying speeds than high-winged craft. Some rental

Aerial photographs can be of considerable interest and appeal on the basis of their aesthetic value alone. Photo by Ralph Amdursky.

services have planes that have been specifically modified for aerial photo work.

Helicopters. A helicopter can offer several advantages for aerial photography, although the rental cost may be four or five times greater than for a low-powered, fixed-wing aircraft.

The ability to hover is not necessarily a major factor in choosing a helicopter for aerial photography. While hovering, a helicopter sets up fairly severe vibrations that contribute to unsharp photographs, and extended hovering is hard on both the aircraft and the pilot. The engine tends to overheat, and the pilot is busier than when he has additional lift and better control with forward speed. Turbine powered helicopters create less vibration than piston engine types.

The greatest advantages of helicopters are the ability to get in and out of places that may be inaccessible to fixed-wing aircraft, and the ability to attain low altitude more safely. The FAA restricts fixed-wing aircraft to a minimum altitude of 300 metres (1000 feet) (vertical distance) from any structures in congested areas, and 150 metres (500 feet) in the open country. However, no such restriction is imposed on helicopters by the FAA. Of course, local restrictions may apply in some areas. Additionally, with the door removed from a helicopter, you have even fewer obstructions in your view than in any fixed-wing craft.

Working with a Pilot

Use a commercially licensed pilot. Avoid the temptation to use a friend or acquaintance who holds a private license. He or she may be a good pilot, but generally speaking, you are better off with a pilot who flies professionally and gets more experience. You should concentrate on getting good aerial photographs and depend on a skilled commercial pilot to concentrate on safety and flying.

Before getting in the aircraft, try to brief the pilot as fully as possible on the project. This will make both your jobs easier and will save you flight time and cost over your subject.

Study maps of the site—air, road, and topographic—when available. Try to determine some landmarks that can be seen easily from the air. Things do look different from above, and it is easy to become disoriented. With your maps, your information, and your pilot's experience, determine if there are any navigational hazards or problems in the area. Decide approximately what safe, legal altitude will be likely to yield best results. Based on your study of the subject, tell the pilot approximately what primary and secondary angles you prefer to shoot.

Establish a set of hand signals with which you

Because of the angles available to the airborne photographer, feelings of sweep and space are particularly easy to convey. Photo by Ralph Amdursky.

Aerial photography can be particularly effective in documenting some types of air and water pollution. The weather was exceptionally clear on the day this photo was taken of air pollution at an industrial site. Photo by William Watson.

can help direct your pilot. Most photo planes tend to be too noisy for convenient voice communications, and hand signals are usually the best way to communicate. The pilot's view will be considerably different from yours, and he will be trying to put you in the best position. As a result, he may not have a very good view of the subject himself, and of course, he will not be looking through a viewfinder, either.

Weather

When you have aerial assignments, call the airport near the close of the day to get the weather prediction for the following day. (Or have your pilot check the forecast. Usually, he has access to more detailed information than you can obtain.) If adequate weather conditions are predicted, you can then make flight arrangements.

Good weather conditions are considered to be clear with a breeze (to help blow off smoke and smog) and visibility of 24 kilometres (approximately 15 miles) or more. Minimum conditions for acceptable quality are considered to be scattered clouds and about 16-kilometre (approximately 10-mile) visibility. Less clear conditions may yield photos of some value for record or study purposes, but they are likely to be of marginal quality.

If weather conditions are poor, shoot low* obliques from fairly low altitudes. This will help to minimize the effects of haze and smoke.

Cold weather and flying with the aircraft door

---

*A low oblique aerial picture is one that is shot downward at a small angle from the vertical.

Aerial Photography

off make a chilling proposition. But don't shy away from cold-weather flying. Often, cool, clear days provide the smoothest flying conditions possible. Bumpy flying caused by thermals is less of a problem than on hot days.

Selecting a Camera

The best camera to use for oblique aerials is probably the professional camera that is most familiar to you. There is little or no advantage to using an aerial camera for oblique aerials at altitudes lower than 1500 metres (about 5000 feet). You are probably most familiar with a conventional camera, and generally, films for it are easier to obtain.

For low-level oblique photographs, aerial films are not likely to yield results any better than conventional films, and in some cases results may not be as good. You can process your own film or have it processed through your normal source, whereas most sizes and types of aerial films are likely to require special processing equipment or different processing chemicals.

The end size requirement of your photographs will dictate the choice of camera. There is much to recommend a medium-format camera such as a 120/220 roll-film camera or a camera with a 70 mm roll-film back. These cameras are easy to handle in confined spaces; they are small enough to be convenient; and with modern films, carefully processed and printed, almost any size enlargement can be made. If you prefer 35 mm cameras, acceptable results can be obtained with them. They offer compactness, a wide variety of interchangeable lenses, and ease of handling. A 4 × 5 camera represents the upper limit of practical size for oblique aerial use.

When using a bellows-type camera, be sure to avoid getting it into the slipstream of the aircraft, where the wind can distort or rip the bellows. For protection, you can make a simple, three-sided windscreen out of light aluminum sheet, and fasten it over the bellows. Secure it to the camera by drilling holes in the windscreen to go under the nuts that lock the rising-front standard of the camera. With any camera, use a neck strap or wrist strap to be sure that you can't lose it. It is a federal offense to drop anything from an aircraft.

Films and Filters for Aerial Photography

Black-and-White Films. Kodak Tri-X pan films or Tri-X pan professional films should receive first consideration. These films are fast (even when haze-control filters are used), have excellent exposure latitude, have fine to very fine grain that will permit excellent enlargements, are readily available, and are conveniently processed.

For very low light levels, some faster films such as Kodak Royal-X pan may be useful.

Black-and-white prints from color negatives are usually practical, but when you are sure that only black-and-white prints will be needed from an aerial assignment, black-and-white film is recommended, because haze control and contrast control are more difficult to achieve with color films.

For most low-altitude oblique aerials, use a yellow filter such as the Kodak Wratten filter No. 15. Near or above a 1500-metre (about 5000-foot) altitude, use a red filter such as Kodak Wratten filter No. 25. If haze is particularly bad, use the No. 25 filter at lower altitudes. With Kodak Tri-X pan or Tri-X pan professional film and a No. 15 filter, use a filter factor of 2.5 or open the lens 1⅓ stops. With the same film and Kodak Wratten filter No. 25, use a filter factor of 8 or open up 3 stops.

Because subject contrast is almost invariably lessened in aerial views, black-and-white films must be developed for longer than normal times to build up contrast to normal levels in the negative.

Infrared Films. Black-and-white infrared film provides higher contrast than panchromatic film, and it offers a unique ability to record far more detail through haze than the eye can see. It should always be used when assignments must be flown under haze conditions. However, infrared film cannot penetrate haze that is primarily composed of smoke such as that common over industrial areas.

The greatest use of infrared film in oblique aerial photography occurs when extreme distances must be covered as a result of high altitude or a high angle of view (high oblique). Prints from infrared negatives show blue sky and water as almost black. Growing crops and deciduous trees appear white or very light because of infrared reflectance by chlorophyll in the leaves. Most evergreens have low infrared reflectance and consequently appear darker than deciduous growth.

Kodak high speed infrared film is available in magazine, roll, and long-roll sizes. All sizes of high speed infrared films must be loaded in cameras in

An area south of Syracuse, New York, photographed on a Kodak aerial color film.

total darkness. Some Kodak high speed infrared film is available in sheet-film sizes.

When infrared film is used, the blue and ultraviolet radiation must be filtered out by using a filter such as a Kodak Wratten filter No. 25, No. 29, or No. 70. The visually opaque No. 87, 88, and 89 filter series are especially designed for infrared photography. For maximum haze penetration, use a No. 89B filter.

Color Negative Films. These films can be used to make color or black-and-white prints, slides, or large transparencies. Because photographers seldom know all the potential uses for their photographs, color negatives are often preferred. Unless haze is particularly bad, color films can yield excellent black-and-white prints. Color negative films have greater exposure latitude and more versatility than films for slides or transparencies, and they offer a great degree of control over color balance and density during printing. Kodacolor and Kodak Vericolor films are available for 35 mm and roll film cameras. Vericolor film is also available for sheet film cameras.

Reversal Color Films. Kodak Ektachrome and Kodachrome films are excellent for making oblique aerial slides and transparencies. Kodak high speed Ektachrome films for daylight are particularly use-

ful for late-afternoon or dusk photographs when the light level is low.

Haze is a very important factor with both color negative and color reversal films; it can affect color balance and saturation as well as contrast. If any haze is apparent, or if you are taking high obliques, use a Kodak skylight filter No. 1A. At higher altitudes, and when haze is a problem, use a Kodak Wratten filter No. 2B. With positive transparency film, it is possible to get a warm (slightly yellow) cast when the No. 2B filter is used from low altitudes—particularly when little haze is present. If you have an HF-3 aerial filter, you can use it in lieu of the 2B; the characteristics are the same. At high altitudes, a No. 2E or No. 3 filter will give slightly increased haze penetration and a more warming color effect.

Contrast enhancement is possible from Kodak Ektachrome films. Push-processing will increase image contrast and permit the use of a higher exposure index. If you must take aerial color photos under bad haze conditions or from very high altitudes, you can improve the contrast somewhat by having an internegative made on Kodak Ektacolor internegative film. Have the internegative made by a photographic laboratory that normally makes color internegatives.

Infrared Color Films. The emulsion layers of

infrared color film are sensitized to green, red, and infrared radiation instead of the usual blue, green, and red light. The resulting transparencies display colors that are false for most natural features.

These films emphasize differences in infrared reflectance between live, healthy vegetation and visually similar areas. They have become especially useful for a variety of forest-survey and crop-survey projects such as the early detection of disease and insect outbreaks.

In the spring and summer, healthy deciduous trees photograph magenta or red, and healthy conifers photograph reddish to bluish purple. Dead or dying leaves that have turned red or yellow still retain some of their infrared reflectivity. Red leaves photograph yellow, and yellow leaves register white.

Infrared color films may be beneficial in calling attention to the effects and extent of pollution, the effects of overfertilization on streams and lakes, and so forth.

Kodak Ektachrome infrared film is available in magazines and rolls. Kodak Aerochrome infrared film is available in rolls. This film may be loaded into 15 ft. cassettes by the user, but the cassette *and the camera* must be loaded in total darkness.

Expose infrared color films used for aerial color photography through a Kodak Wratten filter No.

12. A recommended starting point (with a No. 12 filter) is EI 100, for meters marked for ASA exposure indexes.

Many modern, professional lenses have a separate mark for infrared focusing. You can ignore it and use normal focusing with infrared color films.

There may be several methods and processes available for processing some of these color-infrared films in equipment such as stainless steel reels, rewind equipment, or modern continuous processing machines. However, to offset the different color balances that may be produced by these different processing methods and processes, a camera filter(s) change may be necessary during exposure. Therefore, exposure and processing instructions should be read carefully prior to using the film.

Camera Lenses

Most aerial photographs can be taken with normal-focal-length lenses. However, the use of wide-angle lenses provides two advantages:

1. The effect of image motion is less so that the pictures appear sharper.
2. The pictures can be taken from lower altitudes, which almost always improves the image contrast.

The same area as in the photograph on the opposite page, exposed on a Kodak aerial infrared film. Plants containing chlorophyll appear red or magenta on this film, which is used for making forest inventories, detecting plant diseases, and identifying water pollution.

The aerial view of this football stadium is much more interesting and aesthetically appealing than a ground-level shot would have been. Although the scale changes from top to bottom in this oblique photograph, the overall symmetrical effect shows planning and design details not readily obvious from the ground. Photo by Ralph Amdursky.

It is exceedingly difficult to get sharp pictures with telephoto lenses. The effects of the plane's vibration are very severe with such lenses. If it is necessary to use a telephoto lens, shutter speeds of 1/1000 sec. are recommended.

Taking the Photographs

Exposure. Make exposure readings before take-off to determine what the proper exposure for ground photography would be. (Be sure to allow for filter-factor correction.) In most cases, for low-level aerials, use about the same exposure in the air as you would use on the ground. When you are airborne, take a meter reading from about the altitude at which you will be working. At low altitude with little or no visible haze, the exposure reading should be very close to the ground exposure; set the camera about halfway between the two readings. If there is noticeable haze, or if you are working from a higher altitude, the airborne meter reading is likely to be significantly higher than the ground reading. If this is the case, set your camera nearer to the ground reading, because the meter is probably biased by light reflected by haze and may not give a true read-

Aerial Photography

ing of your desired subject. Bracket exposures by at least one stop when possible.

Shutter Speed and Lens Aperture. Since depth of focus and depth of field are insignificant factors in aerial photography, you can concentrate on the significant problem of stopping motion. Set the focus at infinity. Set the aperture at wide open. There is no need to stop down to obtain depth of field, since the entire scene is effectively at infinity. You may prefer to stop down one or two stops if your lens performs best when stopped down slightly. Then make necessary exposure adjustments by varying the shutter speed. With the lens wide open, you will be able to use the fastest shutter speed that conditions allow.

Making the Exposure. As you approach your subject, check to see that you attain a viewpoint that places the shadows in position for the best modeling, and that your altitude and position are correct for the best view. Using hand signals, direct the pilot to place the aircraft in the best position. Best results are usually achieved when the pilot reduces throttle, banks the aircraft slightly, and slips it toward the subject. This keeps down engine vibrations and minimizes image movement by reducing forward motion. When subject movement is toward or away from the camera, the effect of movement is less than when the movement is at 90 degrees to the camera. Most pilots who have flown many photo assignments are aware of the advantages of the side-slip technique, but discuss it with your pilot in advance.

At particularly low altitudes, this technique cannot be used safely, since the aircraft needs room to recover. From very low altitudes, it is usually best to reduce throttle and apply several degrees of flap to reduce the airspeed even more. How much, if any, will depend on several factors. Under gusty conditions, the flaps may cause too much buffeting, which could contribute more to unsharpness than would using increased speed without flaps. You can minimize motion by panning the camera with the subject. Be careful to avoid getting wings or struts in your photos. When you are concentrating on your subject, it is easy to look past such obstructions and not even see them.

Keep the camera from touching any part of the aircraft. If the camera is in contact with the craft, it will pick up engine vibrations, and even with a fast shutter speed you will get unsharp pictures. Also, keep your body, from the waist up, from contact with the aircraft so that you will act as a shock absorber for vibrations.

Always use a lens shade to eliminate contrast reduction caused by lens flare. Use a screw-on type or tape the lens shade in place so that the wind cannot pull it off.

Determining Scale in Aerial Photographs

It is reasonably easy to determine scale in a vertical aerial photograph; it is somewhat more difficult in an oblique view because the scale changes from

VERTICAL SCALES (1000 ft. altitude)*

Focal Length of Lens		Negative Scale Film Actual Image Size	Ground Area Covered† (in feet) 35 mm Format	2¼" × 2¾" Format	4" × 5" Format
50 mm	1.97 in.	1 in. = 508 ft.	455 × 710	—	—
80 mm	3.15 in.	1 in. = 317 ft.	295 × 435	715 × 870	—
100 mm	3.94 in.	1 in. = 254 ft.	240 × 350	570 × 700	—
127 mm	5.00 in.	1 in. = 200 ft.	—	—	800 × 1000
135 mm	5.32 in.	1 in. = 189 ft.	175 × 255	425 × 520	755 × 945
150 mm	5.91 in.	1 in. = 169 ft.	160 × 230	380 × 495	675 × 845
163 mm	6.42 in.	1 in. = 156 ft.	—	—	625 × 780
200 mm	7.87 in.	1 in. = 127 ft.	120 × 175	290 × 355	510 × 635
250 mm	9.84 in.	1 in. = 102 ft.	95 × 140	230 × 280	410 × 510
305 mm	12.00 in.	1 in. = 83 ft.	80 × 115	185 × 230	330 × 415

*To find scale or coverage at other altitudes, multiply by factors of 1000. (For 500 ft., multiply by .5, for 2000 ft., multiply by 2, etc.)
†Rounded to nearest 5 ft.
The metric equivalents for this table are as follows: 1 ft. = .3 m; 1 in. = 25 mm.

the nearest portions to the more distant portions (that is, from the foreground to the background). Once scale is established, you can determine the true size of any object in the photograph with a fair degree of accuracy.

Scale in Verticals. To determine scale on a vertical view, use the ratio of the focal length of the lens to the altitude at which the picture was taken:

$$\text{Scale} = \frac{\text{Lens Focal Length}}{\text{Altitude of Aircraft}}$$

The preceding table permits rapid calculation of scale and area coverage in vertical views.

If the altitude is unknown, scale can be determined by comparing the length of the known object to its length on the photograph:

$$\text{Scale} = \frac{\text{Object Length in Photo}}{\text{True Length}}$$

Scale in Obliques. In an oblique photograph, the scale of the picture decreases from the bottom (nearest the camera) to the top (farthest from the camera). The approximate scales for aerial oblique photographs can be seen in the accompanying diagram.

• *See also:* INFRARED PHOTOGRAPHY; PHOTOGRAMMETRY, AERIAL.

Further Reading: Brock, Gerald C. *Image Evaluation for Aerial Photography.* Belmont, CA: Pitman Publishing Corp., 1968; Heiman, Grover, Jr. *Aerial Photography: The Story of Aerial Mapping and Reconnaissance.* New York, NY: Macmillan Publishing Co., 1972; Newhall, Beaumont. *Airborne Camera: The World from the Air and Outer Space.* New York NY: Hastings House, 1972.

In an oblique photograph, the scale of the picture decreases from the bottom to the top.

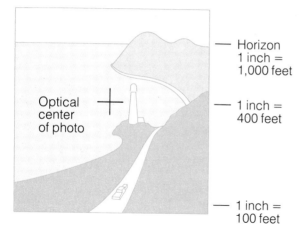

The position of the optical axis of a camera equals the camera-look angle in an oblique aerial photograph.

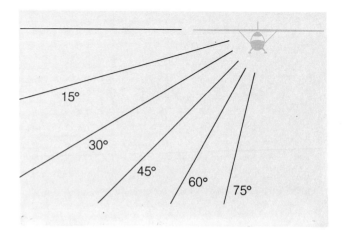

Aerial Photography

Aftertreatment

Altering a negative or print after processing to correct errors or to change the appearance of the image. Various methods are used to add or remove image elements, to change tone or color, and to adjust contrast. Physical methods of image alteration include painting, dyeing, scraping, abrading, airbrushing, and penciling. Chemical methods include reducing, intensifying, bleaching-and-redeveloping, and toning. Optical aftertreatment consists of rephotographing the image using filters in order to change contrast, density, or color rendition. Print finishing procedures such as ferrotyping, texturing, mounting, and matting deal with presentation of the final picture; they are distinct from aftertreatment, which affects the character of the image itself.

• *See also:* AIRBRUSH; BLEACHING; INTENSIFICATION; REDUCTION; RETOUCHING; SPOTTING PRINTS; TONING.

Ag

Chemical symbol for silver (Latin "argentum")

White metallic element, atomic weight 107.88. Combined with other elements, it forms many salts, of which bromide, chloride, and iodide are light sensitive and form the basis of modern photography. Silver bromide, silver iodide, and silver chloride are called silver halides. While other metals, notably iron and lead, are known to have light-sensitive salts, none of them have the requisite sensitivity for other than very limited photographic purposes.

The silver halides are sensitive to ultraviolet radiation and blue light. They can be made sensitive to other colors of light and to near infrared radiation by the addition of certain dyes. Silver bromide with traces of silver iodide to form imperfect crystals is the most sensitive of the silver halide combinations. The addition of certain other chemicals, such as sulfides and noble metal salts, during the manufacture of film emulsions increases the basic sensitivity considerably, forming the basis of today's very fast films.

Agencies, Picture

Picture agencies supply photographs and other images to editors and publishers, art directors, illustrators, artists, advertisers, and other users of visual materials. Agencies have major areas of interest or specialization that may be classified as news, feature, general stock, special interest, and historic. All agencies maintain a library of pictures. News agen-

Do not ignore the small wonders of nature when choosing subjects for photographs that might interest an agency. This tropical flower, for example, could go in a travel ad.

cies also transmit pictures by wire, radio, or facsimile to clients—primarily newspapers and magazines —to overcome the limits of time and deadlines.

How Agencies Work

To obtain pictures, a user generally contacts one or more agencies to make his or her needs known and to arrange to examine whatever material is available in the relevant categories of each collection. Established clients may be provided with a selection of pictures by mail, but in most cases the user or picture researcher must go to the agency to make a personal selection. When a preliminary choice has been made, pictures are taken on approval so that a final decision can be made during a specified holding period. Pictures held beyond that specified time are subject to a holding fee, regardless of whether they are subsequently used. For those pictures that are chosen, a reproduction or use fee is charged. The user does not actually buy the picture, but in effect rents it by purchasing the right to publish or otherwise use it in a specified way for a stated period.

Rates and Rights. Charges vary with the kind of rights obtained and the nature of the picture. The charge for commercial or advertising use is many times the charge for educational or textbook use of the same picture. Charges for color photographs are generally three to five times greater than those for black-and-white pictures of the same subjects, but in the area of pictures for advertising, black-and-white rates are approaching those for color. Rights are generally for one-time use within a year. Exclusive rights guarantee that no one else will be allowed any use of the picture for a stated period (commonly one, five, or ten years) or in a specified area (e.g., the U.S., Europe, the world). Such rights are extremely expensive, because they remove a picture from income-producing circulation. All pictures must be returned to the agency immediately after use. High penalties are charged for damaged or lost items to cover the expense of replacement or to compensate for lost sales of irreplaceable images.

Silversmiths of this man's caliber are rare, even in Taxco, Mexico. Examples of their work are of interest, and care should be taken to display them properly. A little extra effort will produce pictures that can be used in a variety of ways.

These glowing flower fields of the lush Vale of Kashmir attract the eye. This photograph could be ideal for an agency that deals with travel clients.

The Right Agency

The work of an agency—promoting and selling pictures—requires a very different kind of talent and effort from that of taking pictures. Photographers place their work with an agency to gain the advantage of a combination of specialists: themselves on the one hand and the experienced agency staff on the other. Most importantly, placing pictures with an agency gets completed work out of the photographer's files and into a location where it can potentially earn income, while leaving the photographer free to concentrate on taking new photographs.

News Agencies. A photographer must consider carefully the nature of an agency when he approaches it to submit pictures. A news agency does not need to see an extensive portfolio; a sampling of pictures that shows the ability to produce strong images of events and personalities under a variety of conditions will be enough. The news agency primarily wants to know: What do you have of what has happened *just now?* The agency wants pictures fast, and it wants solid, accurate information for captions and identification. It is up to the photographer to get to an event, shoot it, and get to a telephone to deter-

Top-quality photographs of rare and significant events, such as the arrival of the Tall Ships in New York Harbor for the Bicentennial celebration, have not only immediate news value but historical value as well. Operation Sail photos were used for a number of promotional purposes and as models for paintings, etchings, metal castings, and other commemmorative objects.

mine if the agency wants the pictures. Then the film must be delivered immediately. To save time, the agency will process and print the pictures. Payment is usually a flat fee for each picture accepted; the size of the fee depends on the importance of the event and the uniqueness of the pictures. A photographer who has exclusive coverage of a major event or disaster can often negotiate between two or more agencies for the highest payment, but he must act rapidly because the news value of a photograph or event can die fast.

The Importance of Quality. In submitting work to other kinds of agencies, speed and personal contact are not of great importance. An initial visit may be helpful in getting accepted, but many photographers deal with agencies in major cities almost entirely by mail. What is important is the depth and quality of the work submitted, especially in seeking acceptance. If the work seems at all interesting, the agency will want to see as much as possible in order to select those pictures which have the best sales potential and which fill in or strengthen their collec-

Agencies, Picture

tion in various areas. Thus, a photographer should have a brief but strong portfolio or slide presentation to catch interest, followed by a significant quantity of well-produced work.

No agency can use technically poor photographs. Unspotted prints, bad exposure, weak composition, even in just a few pictures, will affect the evaluation of all the work and can result in complete rejection. Similarly, trite, unimaginative pictures, or those which imitate what has already been done—

and overdone—will lower the estimation of a photographer's worth. Agencies need pictures of new subjects, but they also have a continuing need for genuinely new pictures of familiar subjects to keep their collections fresh and to replace some of the most-used pictures before they become clichés.

Most of all, an agency wants to see pictures that fit into their coverage. A sports agency will gladly look at hundreds of good pictures of skiing or sailing, but not of sunsets or nature close-ups. A pho-

The beauty of this unusual landscape photograph is in the unique subject and the composition that combines the dome-shaped houses in the middleground and the higher curves of the Himalayan foothills in the background. Such photographs are ideal for use in textbooks and general information encyclopedias because they show, in a striking manner, the way people live in exotic areas of the world.

(Above) Lighting is an important factor to consider when taking quality photographs. The silhouette effect adds to the beauty of this image of a thistle.

Feature Agencies. Feature agencies handle picture stories and essays about people, their customs and activities, and individual pictures that emphasize personality, "human interest," or out-of-the-ordinary characteristics. Famous or unusual places around the world and animals are also important feature subjects. Good feature pictures deal with contemporary topics that sustain interest for a much longer period of time than news events.

Special interest agencies concentrate on providing great depth of coverage within a narrow subject range. Because they attract knowledgeable buyers who have well-defined picture needs, such agencies are excellent outlets for photographers who are specialists in such things as sports, nature, astronomy, science, art, architecture, and many other areas.

(Below) The crystallized gold mineral seems enriched by the faded blue background. Photo by Joel E. Arem.

tographer will greatly strengthen his presentation by investigating an agency's coverage and needs beforehand and editing his pictures accordingly. A large general stock agency offers the greatest scope, because it is essentially an all-purpose library of pictures in almost any conceivable category. But, because of its breadth, the general stock agency receives the greatest amount of work to consider and the greatest amount of subject duplication—sunsets and babies, for example. The necessary emphasis on handling volume may result in an individual photographer's work not receiving as much attention or promotion as it would at a smaller, more specialized agency.

Historical Agencies. A contemporary photographer generally will be least concerned with an agency that concentrates on historical material. A possible exception is the case of a photographer who comes into possession of historical pictures and makes modern copies of them, or a photographer who takes some pictures that an agency might purchase because of their possible eventual historical interest. A number of historical agencies are based on the accumulated negatives of major commercial or portrait photo studios that flourished earlier in the century but later ceased to be active. Of course, the files of news picture agencies become increasingly important sources of historical pictures with the passage of time.

Agency Requirements

When an agency decides to take a photographer's work, it may ask for black-and-white prints if only a few pictures are involved. Usually, however, the agency will want negatives and contact sheets so that file prints, extra copies, and special

(Above) This picture of a Fiji fisherman was taken at 5 a.m., just when dawn was breaking. The setting and lighting combined to produce a technically exact and unusually beautiful photograph. Daybreak and sunset produce particularly striking photographs with dramatic lighting and colors.

(Below) White calcite appears three-dimensional against black background. Choose background colors and texture with great care—these design elements can make all the difference. High quality is essential for agency sales. Photo by Joel E. Arem.

orders can be supplied quickly and efficiently. If the photographer retains the negatives, sales may be lost if prints can't be supplied when required. Few agencies handle color negatives or color prints; the requirement is overwhelmingly for color slides or transparencies. The photographer must be prepared to turn over his originals to the agency. Duplicates, or copy slides, always have less quality than the originals, and even though the difference may be slight, only the best looking pictures will sell. Many photographers make two color exposures of everything they especially like: one for themselves and one for the agency.

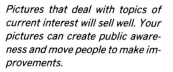

Pictures that deal with topics of current interest will sell well. Your pictures can create public awareness and move people to make improvements.

Information. Pictures are not enough. An agency must have information that identifies the subject, date, and location of every picture. Technical photographic data are seldom required, but everything that provides background information or further explanation is valuable in promoting and selling the pictures. Photographers who place a great deal of work with agencies keep complete records with details of everything they shoot. Many find a miniature tape recorder an ideal accessory in the field for this purpose. Each photographer must find a method for retaining the pertinent data.

Picture Agency Details

Releases. From the agency standpoint, there is one question of more importance than any other about every picture in which people appear: *Is there a model release?* A picture cannot be sold for commercial or advertising purposes unless the people appearing in it have signed a release specifically permitting that use of their images. If a picture is used without permission, the photographer, the agency, and the user are open to legal action. The costs and penalties often amount to tens of thousands of dollars. The problem is so serious that many picture buyers now also insist on model releases for pictures that will be used only for editorial or educational purposes. It is the responsibility of the photographer to obtain the releases—when the picture is taken is the best time—and to supply copies to the agency as required. He or she must also make sure that the agency knows exactly which pictures are covered by releases and which are not.

Contracts. When taking pictures from a photographer, an agency contracts to retain and sell them for at least one and often five or more years. The photographer agrees not to sell copies of those or essentially similar pictures to others during that period and for one year more to protect a user who might purchase the rights to a picture just before a contract is dissolved. Most agencies take work on a consignment/commission basis; no payment is made to the photographer until a picture has been sold.

For agencies interested in either travel or general-interest subjects, a photograph such as this one of a magnificent tiger may be easy to sell.

Often payments are slow in coming to photographers, because payments to agencies are slow. Sale prices are established by the agency, which has the most complete knowledge of the current market conditions.

Depending on the extent of the services provided and the contract terms, an agency will take a 40 to 70 percent commission on each sale. This is not excessive when one considers that the agency must maintain and staff an office and library, have prints made, provide filing, identification, and captions,

This photograph might interest an agency specializing in science, nature, or general-interest subjects. Possibilities for the sale of quality photographs are almost limitless.

distribute and retrieve photographs, attend to all financial details of sales and payments, and monitor customer activities to guard against loss or improper use of pictures. In addition, some agencies have an editorial staff that creates and sells stories and essays from submitted work. And some staff members act as agents to secure assignments for their leading photographers.

Cooperative Agency. A large number of photographers find it very profitable to deal with an agency on the aforementioned terms, recognizing that continued sales of completed work can help bridge the gaps when current work is scarce. Other photographers feel that the same advantages can be obtained under their direct control in a cooperative agency. A cooperative is owned by its member photographers who share the operating expenses. Profits are divided according to the proportion that each photographer's sales contribute to the total agency income.

A few photographers with a large backlog of pictures in a specialized area successfully operate their own stock picture services. However, this demands that they devote a significant amount of time to publicity and promotional contacts and to the details of record keeping, mailing, and finances—or that they hire someone to do it for them. They feel that the advantage of this over an agency is that their work does not get mingled with that of many other photographers and is thus less likely to appear anonymously or with only an agency credit.

Personal Agent. A photographer may prefer an association with an individual rather than an agency. A personal representative, or agent, offers intensive, specific attention to the promotion of a photographer's work. The "rep" usually has extensive contacts with editors and other picture buyers and up-to-date knowledge of their needs. With a personal rep, emphasis is on current production; the problem of unexploited previous work may remain unsolved. More importantly, relatively few people have the experience, judgement, and energy required to be successful as photographers' representatives. Those who do are naturally interested only in photographers of proven ability and professional excellence. While an agency may draw on the output of 25, 50, or even 100 photographers, a personal representative's income depends on the two or three individuals with whom he is associated. Because personalities, career aims, working methods, and a variety of other factors must mesh smoothly, the photographer/representative relationship may be as intricate and personal as a marriage. The rewards can be immeasurable, but it makes great demands on both partners.

• *See also:* LEGAL ASPECTS OF PHOTOGRAPHY; MODEL RELEASE; SELLING PICTURES.

Further Reading: Ahlers, Arvel W. *Where and How to Sell Your Photographs,* 8th ed. Garden City, NY: Amphoto, 1977; Harter, Walter L. *How to Shoot and Sell Money Making Pictures.* Garden City, NY: Amphoto, 1972.

Agitation

Agitation is the moving of processing solutions over and around films and prints, or the moving of films and prints in the solutions, to provide even processing. In the case of developers, agitation, among other things, helps control contrast. The purpose of agitation is to provide a continual flow of fresh solution to the emulsion, and to remove the waste products of the chemical reaction taking place so that the reaction can progress at a uniform rate across the surface of the emulsion. Proper agitation creates a relatively random movement of the solution, which prevents the streaking that a too regular pattern of flow can cause. Agitation must also be done in a manner that can be repeated consistently so that variation in processing results is kept to a minimum.

Types of Agitation

Agitation may be continous or intermittent. Continuous agitation is used in trays for both films and papers, and it is the type of agitation provided in many types of processors. In a tray, the sensitized surface is moved through the solutions by rocking the tray or interleaving the sheets of material. In some tube or drum processors, the material rolls through the solutions inside the tube or outside the drum during rotation. In other types of tube processors, photographic paper is curled inside the tube with the back of the paper against the inner surface of the tube. The tube is rotated so that the solution moves over the emulsion surface of the paper. In continuous web processors, film in long rolls is moved through the solutions, its path being determined by rollers or belts. In processors designed for rapid processing, the solution may be sprayed against the emulsion as the sheets move through the processor. In laminar-flow agitation, the fresh solution is moved continuously past the emulsion in a thin layer.

Intermittent agitation of roll films in small tanks is accomplished in one of several ways. In tanks that can be sealed, the tank is inverted several times during the agitation cycle. Another good method is to move the tank across a flat surface in a figure-eight motion. Some small tanks are equipped with reel stems by which the reel can be twirled during processing. This method may be too regular and lead to uneven development. Small-tank agitation usually consists of 5 seconds of agitation once every 30 seconds.

Both roll and sheet films can be processed in large tanks. Hand agitation consists of lifting the films up out of the solution and tilting them in alternate directions. The cycle usually is about 6 seconds of agitation once every minute. "Dip and dunk" processors, often used by photofinishers, provide an automatic large-tank process. In addition to the agitation provided by lowering the films into the tanks and raising them, agitation is provided by gaseous-burst equipment.

A gas distributor (a sparger), which is a sloped tube with small holes in it, is located at the bottom of the tank and connected by a hose to a gas supply. A timer releases bursts of bubbles at intervals. In rising to the surface in random paths, the bubbles stir the processing solution, thereby causing agitation. Nitrogen gas is used in developers because it is inert and does not cause oxidation. Oil-free compressed air can be used in most other solutions, such as stop baths and fixers, and is essential for certain bleaches used in some color processes to keep the bleach in condition.

Agitation is one of the four variables that affect contrast in film development. In order to obtain consistent negative contrast, the agitation must be consistent, film to film or batch to batch.

When films are first lowered into a developing solution, bubbles (often called air-bells) form on the surface of the film. If allowed to remain on negative materials, these bubbles cause circular areas of low density that cause dark areas on the prints. To remove these bubbles, small tanks are tapped several times on a flat, firm surface just after the film is inserted into the developer. In large-tank development, the racks or hangers are tapped sharply several times against the top edge of the tank.

While development is nearly always stopped before it is complete, to maintain a consistent negative contrast other solutions must work to completion. Proper agitation (along with care to avoid overuse of solutions) is necessary in the fixer for permanence of the image. Proper agitation in the stop bath helps ensure complete neutralization of the developer in order to avoid contaminating the fixer.

Agitation in the wash following fixing is usually provided by the proper water flow—usually a rate that completely replaces the water once every 5 minutes for black-and-white materials and color films. For color papers, the water may need to be replaced twice every 3½ minutes.

The design of washers should be such that the flow does not allow dead spots in which the heavier-than-water fixer can accumulate. Films should be supported in reels or hangers so that the water can flow between the film surfaces, and so that the films cannot touch each other. Print washers should have enough turbulence to keep the prints moving, but not enough to damage the prints or to splash excessively. The number of prints in a washer should be kept to no more than the capacity of the washer so that they do not stick together. When prints do stick together, the agitation needed for proper washing is prevented.

• *See also:* DEVELOPERS AND DEVELOPING; GASEOUS-BURST AGITATION; MACKIE LINE.

Airbrush

An airbrush is a miniature spray gun, about the size of a fountain pen, operated by compressed air. It is widely used to retouch photographs because color can be applied in a smooth, continuously variable way, creating an appearance similar to actual photographic tone.

Applying Color

The amount of color sprayed on the image is controlled by a button on the airbrush; the area covered depends upon the distance from the nozzle to the surface being painted. Fine lines are produced with the airbrush held very close to the surface. At a maximum practical working distance of about four inches, the cone of spray covers an area about two inches broad. Tonal effects are built up by repeated applications of color. The airbrush must be kept moving as it sprays in order to avoid puddles and splotchy color.

Color Materials

Airbrush colors are commonly diluted with water, but other solutions may be used if they are compatible with the material being painted. Dyes, inks, and oil colors are all suitable. Ground pigments must be finely sifted to ensure that no oversize particles will clog the airbrush, especially the minute orifice through which the spray emerges.

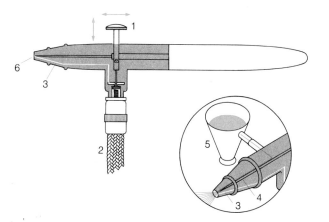

An airbrush is operated with one hand. Pushing down the button (1) lets air from a small compressor or pressure tank pass from the connecting hose (2) into the air channel (3); pressure is 30–50 psi. Air escaping through the tip of the nozzle creates a partial vacuum in the color channel (4), pulling liquid out of the color cup (5). The size of the tip opening varies with the position of the needle tip (6), which is controlled by moving button (1) backward or forward. The amount of color sprayed out in a cone-shaped pattern varies with the size of the tip opening; the width of the area covered varies with the distance from the tip to the surface being sprayed.

Airbrushing is one of the photographer's most useful tools. It is commonly used in portrait and figure photography to eliminate physical blemishes such as scars and wrinkles. It is also useful for repairing damaged negatives and transparencies. Above, heavy scratches damaged an outdated transparency, resulting in photo at left. When properly removed by airbrushing, as in photo at right, neither original damage nor repair should be visible.

Transparent colors are used to subdue portions of a print or transparency and to adjust contrast or coloring without obscuring the details of the image. They are used on negatives to add density so that the treated area will print lighter. Opaque colors are used to obscure and eliminate image areas or details and to add new elements. Colors or gray shades must be carefully matched and all effects subtly blended into the surrounding image. The artist should have a duplicate uncorrected image for comparison as he or she works. Special opaque colors are available to match light tones in prints made on papers that have fluorescing whitening agents (so-called "brighteners") incorporated in their bases.

Masking

Areas that are not to be sprayed are protected by a variety of masks or stencils.

Stencils. Hand stencils are cut from flexible card or from celluloid or plastic (such as clear scrap sheet film). The latter two materials keep the image visible during work. If placed directly against the print, a stencil will produce a revealing hard edge. When held a short distance from the surface and moved slightly during spraying, a soft, blended edge results.

Fixed Masks. Fixed masks are made with frisket materials. Frisket paper is thin, strong tissue with a mild adhesive on one side. It is pressed in place over the face of the print, and a fine-blade, extremely sharp knife is used to trace around all the areas or objects to be treated. The cut frisket is easily lifted away, leaving a protective mask over the other areas. The mask is then peeled off after work is completed.

Liquid frisket is a thin, rubber-cementlike solution that is painted onto the image. It is especially useful when object edges and outlines are too varied or irregular or when areas are too small for easy cutting. Edges are painted first with a fine-tip brush, then the enclosed, large areas are quickly covered with a broader brush. Liquid frisket dries quickly; like a film of rubber cement, it can be removed by rubbing with the fingertips or with a soft eraser.

Removing Color

Color accidentally sprayed onto an area can be removed with a variety of erasers or with swabs or blending stumps moistened with water or the appropriate color solvent. Edges can be softened or blended in the same way.

Airbrushing Procedures

Film materials are airbrushed on the base side only; a retouching ground may first be applied to promote adhering of the sprayed color. Prints are treated on their emulsion surfaces. In the case of a unique or valuable photograph, a copy print is made for treatment, or the airbrushing is applied to a transparent acetate overlay. Usually the treated print is rephotographed, and prints or reproductions are made from the resulting copy negative. The airbrushed print itself is seldom presented for viewing because the surface quality of the sprayed color is different from that of the emulsion, and this is noticeable under most conditions. The difference is not evident in the copy print. Airbrushed images should be clearly marked on the back or on protective sleeves or envelopes to prevent anyone from trying to clean them with water or other solutions.

Uses of Airbrushing

Airbrushing is commonly used in a number of ways. You can enhance exterior photographs by adding clouds to the sky and by subduing or eliminating unwanted surrounding elements. Catalog and advertising photographs are routinely cleaned up and improved by the elimination of glare, wrinkles, and other imperfections, and by the addition of such things as wisps of smoke or steam and highlight gleam or sparkle. Airbrushing is the most subtle way of retouching portraits. It is extremely valuable in covering cracks, tears, stains, and other damages when copying and restoring old photographs.

• *See also:* RETOUCHING.

Further Reading: Croy, Otto R. *The Complete Art of Printing and Enlarging,* 13th ed. Garden City, NY: Amphoto, 1976; ————. *Retouching,* 4th ed. Garden City, NY: Amphoto, 1964; Floyd, Wayne. *How to Retouch and Spot Negatives and Prints,* 2nd ed. Garden City, NY: Amphoto, 1968; Lootens, Joseph Ghislain. *Lootens on Photographic Enlarging and Print Quality,* 8th ed., ed. Lester Bogen. Garden City, NY: Amphoto, 1975; Ruggles, Joanne and Philip. *Darkroom Graphics.* Garden City, NY: Amphoto, 1975; *Guide to Retouching Negatives and Prints*, 3rd ed. Garden City, NY: Amphoto, 1972.

Albada, Liewe Evert Willem van

(1868–1955)
Dutch officer, optician, inventor

Albada was a major general in the Dutch army and an instructor in the advanced military school in The Hague. He is especially known for his invention of the Albada Finder used on many cameras. In this finder, a reticle plate or the rear surface of the front finder lens carries a reflective frame outline, which is mirrored in the objective lens of the finder. The eye sees the film coverage frame superimposed over the subject being viewed.

Albada finder

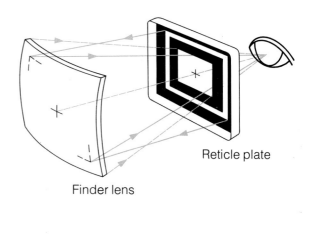

Reticle plate

Finder lens

Albumen

Albumen is a complex protein compound that is the major constituent of egg whites. In a clarified form, it dries to a colorless transparent film that is a strong adhesive. This property led to its being used in the 19th century to coat glass plates with light-sensitive compounds for negatives and to produce a glossy-surface paper for prints.

The albumen-on-glass negative was introduced by Abel Niépce de Saint-Victor in 1848. It was soon replaced by the more versatile, less fragile, and faster collodion wet-plate process. However, albumen paper was the standard photographic printing material from the time of its invention in 1850 by Louis Désiré Blanquart-Evrard until the 1890s. It could be used as either a printing-out or a developing-out paper. Although modern gelatin-emulsion papers are far better suited to present-day photographic purposes, albumen paper may be prepared for experimental use in the following way.

Separate the yolks from the whites of several eggs and measure the quantity of egg whites. For each 30 ml of this crude albumen, dissolve 0.7 grams of ammonium chloride in distilled water (11 grains of chloride for each ounce of egg whites). Use only as much water as required to dissolve the chloride.

Stir the chloride solution into the egg whites and beat the mixture to as complete a froth as possible. Let the froth stand in a clean place until it liquefies again. Beat to a froth a second time and let stand to liquefy.

Pour the albumen into a shallow tray and carefully remove any surface bubbles; use the edge of a piece of stiff paper or a card to scrape the bubbles to one side and lift them off. Hold a piece of high-quality rag-content paper by the ends so that the center hangs down in a U-shape. Lower the center of the paper onto the surface of the egg-white solution, and then lower the ends, taking care that no air is trapped under the paper.

Let the paper float on the albumen for about three minutes. Then lift it off, drain the excess, and place it to dry on a flat surface. The albumen side must face upward, and it must be protected from air-borne dust.

When the paper is completely dry, place the albumen side down against a ferrotype tin or a sheet of glass, place a protective piece of paper over the back, and heat the paper with a hand iron set at about 120–140 F. This will produce a high gloss and will help set the albumen so that it will not be affected by later solutions. Keep the iron moving over the paper to avoid scorching the paper or discoloring the albumen.

Paper prepared this way may be kept indefinitely; it must be sensitized for use. A plain silver-acid solution is easiest to prepare, but an alcohol-ammonia-silver solution will produce a greater sensitivity.

Plain Silver Solution

Silver nitrate	59 ml	(2 oz)
Distilled water	355 ml	(12 oz)
Nitric acid		2 or 3 drops

Dissolve the silver nitrate in the water, and then add just enough acid so that the solution turns blue litmus paper red. Float the prepared paper, albumen side down, on this solution for about five minutes; drain and dry in the dark.

Alcohol-Ammonia-Silver Solution

Silver nitrate	59 ml	(2 oz)
Distilled water	237 ml	(8 oz)
Ammonia (see instructions below)		
Grain alcohol	30 ml	(1 oz)

Dissolve the silver nitrate in about 175 ml of water. Separate about 60 ml (2 oz) of this solution and slowly add ammonia to it. A precipitate will form. Continue to slowly add ammonia while stirring until the precipitate dissolves. Then add the alcohol and the remaining silver nitrate solution. Float the albumen surface of the prepared paper on this solution for about one minute; then drain and dry in the dark.

A rather dense and contrasty negative is required for printing. Make a contact print by exposure to sunlight or to an ultraviolet lamp, using a frame that permits inspection during the process. Although prints may be developed in a gallic acid solution (modern developers are not usable), it is more practical to print-out the image in order to determine proper exposure.

Print to a somewhat darker image than desired; it will lighten during fixing. However, to improve image color, wash the print and treat it in a gold toning solution before fixing. Work in subdued artificial light or under a red safelight.

Gold Toning Solution (Kodak gold protective solution GP-1)

Water	750.0 ml	(25.0 oz)
Gold chloride (1% solution)	10.0 ml	(0.3 oz)
Sodium thiocyanate (liquid)	15.2 ml	(0.5 oz)
Water to make	1.0 litre	(34.0 oz)

Add the gold chloride stock solution to the first volume of water. Mix the sodium thiocyanate *separately* in 125 ml (4 oz) of water. Then add the thiocyanate solution slowly to the gold chloride solution, stirring rapidly. Treat the washed print for up to 10 minutes in the toning solution, or until the desired image color is achieved.

Wash the toned print thoroughly. Then fix in a 30 percent plain hypo solution (300 grams of sodium thiosulfate in water to make 1 litre); do not use an acid fixer. Wash the fixed print thoroughly and dry without heat.

Alcohol, Denatured

Quakersol, shellac solvent, etc.

A mixture of ethyl alcohol with small amounts of methyl alcohol and certain petroleum derivatives, to render the mixture unfit to drink so that it can be sold without payment of beverage taxes. It may be substituted for pure ethyl alcohol in most photographic applications.

Alcohol, Ethyl

Alcohol, ethanol, grain alcohol, rectified spirits, spirits of wine

When denatured with methyl alcohol alone, ethyl alcohol can be used for preparing collodion, as a solvent in highly concentrated developers, and for rapid drying of negatives.
Formula: C_2H_5OH
Molecular Weight: 46.07

Colorless liquid with a slight aromatic odor. It is inflammable and volatile and mixes in all proportions with water, ether, and chloroform.
NOTE: "Absolute" alcohol is free of water and is used for drying and chemical analysis. The term "proof" or "proof spirit" indicates a mixture of alcohol and water. The percentage of alcohol is one-half the proof figure. A 100-proof mixture contains equal parts of alcohol and water, and thus is 50 percent alcohol. 80 proof is 40 percent alcohol. Absolute alcohol is 200 proof.

Alcohol, Isopropyl

Dimethyl carbinol, isopropanol, rubbing alcohol

A useful substitute for grain (ethyl) alcohol where only solvent properties are of interest, isopropyl alcohol can be used to prepare highly concentrated developers. It is also useful in certain developers to control the penetration of the solution into the emulsion.
Formula: $CH_3 \cdot CH(OH) \cdot CH_3$
Molecular Weight: 60.06

Clear, colorless liquid with a mild odor somewhat resembling that of acetone. It mixes with water, other alcohols, and ether, and is inflammable. The chemical grade sold for mixing formulas is from 99.5 to 100 percent isopropyl alcohol. "Rubbing alcohol" is diluted with water and may contain 80 percent or less of isopropyl alcohol.
CAUTION: While isopropyl alcohol can safely be allowed to come in contact with the skin, it is poisonous if taken internally.

Alcohol, Methyl

Carbinol, methanol, wood alcohol

Used mainly as a denaturant for ethyl alcohol, methyl alcohol is also useful as a solvent and in preparing highly concentrated developers. Its use in drying film should be avoided, because it attacks some film base materials. Unless specifically called for, it should be avoided in favor of denatured alcohol. Denatured alcohol is a much less toxic liquid.
Formula: CH_3OH
Molecular Weight: 32.04

Clear, colorless liquid, burns with a blue flame, mixes with water and ether.
DANGER: Methyl alcohol is very toxic; breathing the fumes can cause illness and even death. If drunk, even a small quantity of methyl alcohol will attack the optic nerve and cause blindness; larger quantities are usually fatal. Handle this liquid with extreme care.

Alkali

An alkali is an oxide or hydroxide of one of the alkali metals, chiefly sodium and potassium. Alkalis are water-soluble bases; they react with acids to form neutral salts. They are soapy to the touch, turn red litmus blue, and concentrated, are corrosive.

Alkalis and alkali-like compounds are essential to photography, because most developing agents become active only in alkaline solutions. As alkalinity increases (from 7 to 14 on the pH scale), most agents become more active and development progresses at a faster rate; thus, the function of the alkali in a developer is to be an activator or accelerator. High-energy high-contrast developers use strong alkalis such as sodium or potassium hydroxide. Most normal negative and print developers use sodium carbonate; others use potassium carbonate or sodium metaborate. Fine-grain developers use borax (often in combination with boric acid), trisodium phosphate, sodium sulfite, or low concentrations of sodium carbonate or metaborate.

Solutions of the strongest alkalis change pH greatly with small changes in alkali concentration; developers of this sort quickly lose activity as they are used. Long-life developers employ alkalis that have a high buffering action. That is, they act only a little at a time and have a great reserve of alkalinity to maintain solution pH at a certain level over a long period. Sodium and potassium carbonate, trisodium phosphate, sodium metaborate, and borax plus boric acid all have high buffering action.

A film developer with a high concentration of sodium carbonate may produce pinholes in the image when followed by an acid stop bath. The acid-carbonate reaction forms carbon dioxide, which can cause ruptures as the bubbles escape to the surface of a thick emulsion. Most proprietary film developers do not contain sodium carbonate. Use a water rinse instead of a stop bath to avoid pinholes.

Alkaline Salts

Alkaline salts (basic salts) are sodium or potassium salts other than the hydroxides or carbonates, hav-ing a solution pH of 8 or above, and hence are basic in reaction. They are used in photography as accelerators, where the greater activity brought about by the true alkalis is neither necessary nor desirable. These salts include the borates, such as sodium tetraborate (borax), sodium metaborate (Kodalk balanced alkali), and sodium carbonate.

Alum, Chrome

Chrome alum, potassium chrome alum, potassium chromium sulfate

A powerful hardening agent for gelatin, often used in stop baths and fixing baths for tropical or high-temperature processing. Ordinary ammonium alum, sold in pharmacies for household and medicinal uses, is not used in photography because of the tendency of ammonium salts to cause fog. The alum used in photography is either chrome alum or potassium alum.
Formula: $K_2Cr_2(SO_4)_4 \cdot 24H_2O$
Molecular Weight: 998.84

Dark violet-red crystals or light violet powder freely soluble in water. The solution is violet in color, but in the presence of a sulfite, as in a fixing bath, it turns dark green. The color has no practical significance in such a case. When a solution of chrome alum is used as a stop bath and hardener, contamination with carried-over developer causes it to change color to a yellowish green and it then ceases to harden. Chrome alum hardening baths and fixing baths do not keep well and should be prepared shortly before use.

• *See also:* ALUM, POTASSIUM.

Alum, Potassium

Alum, alum meal, potassium aluminum sulfate

A good hardening agent used in hardening baths and hardening fixing baths. Potassium alum is also in the hypo-alum toning bath for prints.
Formula: $K_2Al_2(SO_4)_2 \cdot 12H_2O$
Molecular Weight: 474.39

Large, colorless crystals or white, crystalline

powder freely soluble in water. It decomposes in alkaline solution, so it must not be added to hypo until the acid and the other ingredients are fully dissolved.

• *See also:* ALUM, CHROME.

Ambrotype

The ambrotype was devised in 1851–52 by Frederick Scott Archer, inventor of the wet collodion process, and Peter W. Fry. Its name comes from James Ambrose Cutting, who patented the process for portraiture in England and the United States in 1854.

This partially mounted ambrotype shows how the negative image appears positive when backed with black. Photo courtesy of George Eastman House.

The ambrotype is a positive-appearing variant of the collodion "wet plate" process. A dark, slightly underexposed negative image on glass was bleached to become whitish gray. It appeared positive when the glass was backed with black, which created the dark areas of the picture where the plate was transparent and mid-tones where the emulsion had varying density. Physically tough, the image could readily be colored by hand or stencil methods. It was preserved with the same decorative mat and frame, cover glass, and padded case as the more expensive and difficult daguerreotype, which it quickly replaced for portraiture.

• *See also:* ARCHER, FREDERICK SCOTT; COLLODION.

Amidol

2, 4-diaminophenol hydrochloride, Acrol, Diamol

A very powerful developing agent that can work without an alkali activator; sodium sulfite, used as a preservative, is sufficiently alkaline to activate it. Amidol was formerly very popular because it produced excellent, rich blue-black tones on bromide enlarging papers. It does not work well with modern chlorobromide papers and has fallen into disuse.

Formula: $(NH_2)_2C_6H_3OH \cdot 2HCl$
Molecular Weight: 197.07

Fine crystals, white to bluish gray, soluble in water. Amidol deteriorates rapidly in solution, even in the presence of sodium sulfite, and therefore always is mixed immediately before it is to be used. The used solution should be discarded immediately after use.

Ammonium Chloride

Muriate of ammonia, sal ammoniac

A neutral salt which when added to a fixing bath causes it to act much more rapidly. Rapid fixing baths are useful for negatives but have little value for prints because paper emulsions are thin and fix rapidly with standard solutions. In addition, rapid action leads to overfixing, which bleaches image highlight detail and forms compounds that are virtually impossible to remove from the emulsion. At one time, ammonium chloride was used as a "hypo eliminator." It was claimed that it caused the hypo to wash out of emulsions and paper bases more rapidly, but this was never proven, and its use for this purpose has been abandoned.

Formula: NH_4Cl
Molecular Weight: 53.50

White, odorless granules or powder; dissolves freely in water, in ammonium hydroxide, and also in alcohol.

Ammonium Persulfate

An oxidizing salt that dissolves silver, so is used as a reducer for excessively dense negatives. It has the unusual property of being able to remove more silver from dense areas than from the thinner image areas, thus reducing both density and contrast in a given negative. This makes it useful for treating over-developed negatives, which tend to be both dense and excessively contrasty.

Formula: $(NH_4)_2S_2O_8$
Molecular Weight: 228.21

Colorless crystals or white powder freely soluble in water. Ammonium persulfate decomposes in hot water, hence it should be mixed only in cold water. It also decomposes in moist air, so it should be stored in tightly closed bottles. Buy it in small quantities so that it may be used before it spoils. The mixed solution for reduction does not keep; it ceases to act in a short time. If a great deal of reduction is needed, it may be necessary to treat the negative in successive fresh baths of ammonium persulfate.

Ammonium Thiocyanate

Ammonium sulfocyanide

Sometimes used as a fixing bath for films at very low temperatures, such as in the arctic when processing at zero and sub-zero temperatures. Used at higher temperatures, it attacks the gelatin of the emulsion.

It is also used in some gold toning baths. It can be used in developers for reversal processing, but potassium or sodium thiocyanate is preferable for this purpose.

Formula: NH_4SCN
Molecular Weight: 76.12

Colorless crystals that tend to absorb moisture from the air, hence should be kept in tightly stoppered bottles. Very soluble in water; freely soluble in alcohol.

• *See also:* POTASSIUM THIOCYANATE; SODIUM THIOCYANATE.

Ammonium Thiosulfate

Ammonium hyposulfite

A very rapid fixing agent sometimes used in fixing baths as a substitute for sodium thiosulfate. (*See:* SODIUM THIOSULFATE.) A 15–20 percent solution of ammonium thiosulfate fixes as rapidly as a 35–40 percent solution of sodium thiosulfate.

Formula: $(NH_4)_2S_2O_3$
Molecular Weight: 148.20

Colorless crystals soluble in water, insoluble in alcohol. It is sometimes sold as a 60 percent solution in water for convenience and because of its better keeping qualities.

• *See also:* SODIUM THIOSULFATE.

Anaglyph

An anaglyph is a stereoscopic image pair, printed in complementary colors (usually red and green, sometimes magenta and cyan), in superimposition. When viewed through a pair of spectacles having one red lens and the other green, each eye sees only one of the two images, but the two images are perceived as one three-dimensional black-and-white image. The system can be used only for black-and-white pictures. The system was used through the early 1960s in the production of 3-D motion pictures, and today, the system is sometimes used in textbook illustrations.

• *See also:* STEREO PHOTOGRAPHY.

Anamorphic Systems

Anamorphic systems are lens or prism systems that have different magnifications horizontally and vertically. Such systems are used in the making of "wide-screen" movies. The unit used on the camera compresses the recorded image laterally so that a wide area is recorded within the normal frame width. When the compressed image is projected through a similar optical system, it is spread to fill a wider screen, with all objects in the scene restored to their normal proportions. As an example, the image of a circle will be an ellipse, with its long axis vertical, on the film; when projected, the image is restored to its normal circular shape, while the entire frame area is widened.

The best-known version of the anamorphic motion-picture system is *Cinemascope,* introduced by Professor Henri Chretien. Other versions include Panavision and a number of private systems in which the camera records on a wider-than-normal film, and a compressed print is made in an optical printer fitted with an anamorphic lens system. Projection, in the latter case, is done with any lens system suitable for Cinemascope.

• *See also:* CHRETIEN, HENRI.

Anastigmat

An anastigmat is a lens of several elements, usually in symmetrical or triplet arrangement, in which all aberrations including astigmatism are corrected to a relatively high degree. The anastigmat camera lens design first became possible with the invention of new optical glasses in the late 19th century. The first anastigmat was introduced in 1889–90 by Zeiss; it was called the Protar lens and was designed by Paul Rudolph.

The word anastigmat is usually applied to camera lenses. Such lenses have flat fields when focused on distant subjects, but as they are focused on very close subjects, the field curves, making it difficult to obtain images that are sharp in the center of the field and at the corners simultaneously. Virtually all modern lenses of good quality are anastigmats. En-

larging lenses and macro lenses are corrected to give a flat field at relatively close distances. They also must be corrected for astigmatism, although they may not be specifically called anastigmats.

• *See also:* ABERRATION; LENSES; OPTICS.

Andresen, Momme

(1857–1951)
German photographic scientist

As a director of the Agfa Company, Dr. Andresen did a great deal of research on the subject of developers and development. He introduced developing agents such as para-phenylene-diamine in 1888, Eikonogen (sodium 1-amino-2-naphthol-6-sulfonate) in 1889, and para-aminophenol in 1891. He wrote many books and articles, and in his book *Das Latente Lichtbilde,* published in 1913, he expressed the opinion that the abundance of developing agents then available was neither necessary nor even desirable for practical photography.

Animal and Pet Photography

Animals as photographic subjects fall into three groups:

1. Pets and domesticated animals, including farm stock and those trained for show or performance.
2. Undomesticated animals and sometimes semitame animals found in controlled environments or protected habitats such as parks, zoos, or preserves.
3. Animals in the wild.

Pets and Domesticated Animals

The first group is relatively easy to photograph. For the most part, surroundings can be chosen for their photographic advantages—the home or studio in the case of pets. The animals are usually trained to some degree or accustomed to handling. They can be tethered, corralled, or otherwise controlled. Many pets and domesticated animals may even be posed with ease.

Fast reflexes are needed to capture an appealing moment such as this. Rubbing a bit of food on the ears may have helped make such a moment more predictable. Photo by Walter Chandoha.

Undomesticated and Semitame Animals

Animals roaming free in habitats and parks tend to be accustomed to the presence of people. This makes it fairly easy to get close enough for good pictures so long as the posted safety precautions are followed explicitly; undomesticated animals are not consistent in reaction or behavior.

Animals in zoos are frequently in confinements that offer relatively clear views. In the majority of cases, it is possible to find viewpoints that avoid the problem of cage bars or fencing in the foreground of the picture, although the surroundings may not appear completely authentic. Animals in exterior compounds can be photographed without permission. But inside bird, reptile, and monkey houses, and similar locations, it is important to inquire whether flash may be used. Some creatures react strongly and violently to sudden light; others ignore it completely. There is usually no objection to existing-light photography.

Animals in the Wild

Animals in the wild pose special photographic problems beyond the basic task of getting to them. Tracking and stalking skills are at least as important as photographic technique, and a broad familiarity with the species being sought is required. Some approaches are discussed at the end of this article.

Kinds of Animal Pictures

Pet Portraits. Pet owners most frequently want pictures that capture the personality of the pet. They want portraits in the fullest sense of the word—not necessarily posed views, but pictures that show the individual's distinctive features and traits. Generally, this means a close shot with the animal's face and expression as the center of interest. The situation is usually secondary.

Pictures of Show Animals. The intention of this type of photograph is to exhibit perfect types—the individual as a superb example of the breed rather

Patience is especially necessary when photographing small creatures in the wild. As they are quite unpredictable, a long wait is usually required for one really good shot. Electronic flash is useful for bringing out details and texture. Photo by Herb Taylor.

than as a distinct personality. With trained animals, two rather formal show views are usually required. The first is a picture taken directly from the side to show head and tail carriage, proportions and overall conformation, and stance in the prescribed show position. The second is a head-on view to show face, symmetry of head, breadth of chest, and shoulder and leg formation. Often, a three-quarter front view is also desired as a formal portrait. The trainer or handler will know how to pose the animal; the photographer's job is to record it well. Untrained show animals such as cats may be photographed somewhat less formally on a cushion, for example, but again, the intent is to show the perfection of their development.

Identification Pictures. Photographs for identification or to show examples of various species are the kind of single pictures most often taken in the wild. The problem is to get a clear view of a representative individual that shows color, size, and attitude in a typical habitat. Pictures showing such

things as living and feeding habits and rearing of young generally must be done as a series of many different views—distant, midway, and close. This often requires extensive photography on several occasions to make the series complete and authentic.

Action Photographs. Animals in action—playing, working, racing—make up another large class of picture subjects. Here the problems are basically those of any kind of action photography. (*See:* ACTION PHOTOGRAPHY.) The photographer needs experience and an understanding of the action in progress to sense the moment a picture should be taken; he needs equipment adequate to the task; and he needs a fast reaction time in the face of unpredictable events.

Equipment

Cameras. Formal poses of trained animals and pictures of small animals in restricted or controlled locations may be taken with large-format cameras, if desired. But for the most part, animals must be photographed during movement or at momentary intervals of rest. This calls for a versatile, fast-operating camera that is easy to handle. A range-finder or sports finder may be valuable for some action pictures. Otherwise, through-the-lens reflex viewing is preferable, and it is essential when using telephoto or zoom lenses. In very close work, reflex viewing overcomes parallax, the problem of the different viewpoints of a separate lens and viewfinder system.

If the image will fill the frame, 35 mm cameras are excellent for color slides as well as black-and-white pictures. But if much enlarging must be done to get a final image of adequate size, a camera that uses 120/220 or 70 mm film will give better quality results.

Lenses. A lens of moderately long focal length —say 90 or 100 mm with a 35 mm camera—is the best choice for most work. As in human portraiture, it will fill the frame at a convenient working distance with an image free of the distortion that is apparent when a camera is moved close enough for a big image with a normal- or short-focal-length lens.

Very long focal lengths should be avoided as much as possible because although from the same camera position they give a larger image, there is less depth of field than with a shorter focal length. This is a critical factor in full views of large animals or head shots of long-nosed animals such as horses or collies.

Zoom Lenses. A zoom lens is especially valuable for animal photography outdoors, whether in the wild or in the yard where pets are frolicking. It permits maintaining a desired image size rapidly without having to constantly run after the subject. A lens that zooms from a normal focal length (or slightly shorter) into the telephoto range is more useful than one that zooms from the normal to the wide-angle range. However, "zooming long" presents the problem of getting to a focal length that cannot be held sufficiently steady by hand for sharp images at the shutter speed in use. The same problem arises with the extreme focal lengths often required for photography in the wild. A tripod, gun-stock, or shoulder support becomes an essential piece of equipment in such cases.

Films. Standard panchromatic and color films are well suited to all kinds of animal photography. Fast films will usually solve three problems:

1. A shutter speed of 1/125 sec. or faster is necessary to overcome subject movement.
2. A fast shutter speed is also required to avoid camera movement problems with long-focal-length lenses.
3. As small an aperture as possible is necessary to provide adequate depth of field.

Special Equipment. Remote-control camera attachments, motor-drive film advances, self-triggering devices, and similar special equipment can be very helpful in field photography.

Lighting

Outdoors. Existing light is the rule when taking pictures outdoors; flash fill is sometimes needed in close-up, backlit situations, especially for color photography. Flash is also useful for some remote-control setups in the field; it is essential for most night photography.

The absence of a busy background helps emphasize the detail and beautiful colors of this parrot. Kodachrome 25 film, 1/500 sec. at f/4. Photo by Herb Taylor.

(Left) It is unlikely that this almost classic pose of a cat and a fishbowl came about as a result of happy coincidence. Knowledge of the animal's habits and careful preplanning are responsible for the effectiveness of this photograph. (Right) If you are separated from an animal by bars, move in as close as possible and aim through the bars. If there is no way to avoid the obstruction, try to aim so that the bars don't cover the animal's face.

Indoors. Obviously, there must be enough light for adequate exposure at a shutter speed that will stop movement; few animals can be relied upon to hold still exactly when required. Bounced or reflected main light eliminates many shadow problems and usually covers an area large enough so that it is not critical for the animal to remain in a single spot. However, the lighting must also provide modeling that makes the subject appear three-dimensional. This generally requires a main light source from one frontal angle and a fill-in source of less intensity from another angle. Daylight coming through a window or skylight can be used to an advantage. It can provide excellent modeling and is usually sufficiently bright to provide adequate exposure levels.

Backlight or strong sidelight is essential to emphasize the texture of fur or to pick out a distinctive feature such as a cat's whiskers. Flat frontal lighting is unsuitable in almost all cases because it destroys both modeling and texture.

Indoor Lighting Equipment. Indoors, direct or bounced electronic flash provides the greatest freedom for shooting and overcomes many problems of subject movement. Continuous light sources may be used equally well, but care must be taken that those with high heat output—such as tungsten-halogen, or so-called "quartz," lights—are not close enough to singe fur or cause discomfort. Some animals will bask contentedly in the warmth of a light, and this provides an easy way of controlling them, even if the major illumination for the picture comes from other sources.

Exposure

While the choice of shutter speed and aperture will be influenced by concerns of subject and camera movement and the need for depth of field, the most important factor in determining exposure is the color of the animal. Under identical lighting, a black cat, a tawny dog, and a white rabbit each require a somewhat different exposure for best results. It is essential to take a meter reading directly from the subject whenever possible. Meters calculate an exposure that will render any tone or color as a middle gray in black and white. To avoid overexposing dark-colored or black subjects, it is necessary to give one or two stops less exposure than the meter indicates; to avoid underexposing light-colored or white subjects, it is necessary to give one or two stops more exposure. In color photography, the exposure should be that called for by a meter reading of the most important tone in the picture—the head or body of the subject.

A camera exposure system that reads through the lens or a separate narrow-angle or spot-reading meter will give excellent results in almost all cases. The use of a gray card with a reflected-light meter, or an incident-light meter with appropriate adjustments for subject brightness, works well with cameras that do not have built-in meters.

Settings

Exterior. Outdoors, three factors must be considered when choosing the location for an animal photograph: background, light, and distractions.

Background. The background should be appropriate to the animal and the activity. Its tone or color and its texture must contrast well with the subject's fur, feathers, shell, or scales. In addition, the background should not be so detailed or "busy" that it detracts from the subject.

Light. The direction and quality of the light will determine the contrast and the textural feeling of the picture. Direct sun from a frontal angle is brightest, but it creates maximum contrast with shadows that may be overly harsh. Especially in color photography, it is helpful to use the sun as a backlight (with a deep lens shade to avoid unwanted glare and reflections) and to illuminate the front of the subject with

electronic flash. Open shade avoids contrast and shadow problems, but the soft, even light of open shade may not bring out the texture of the animal's coat sufficiently.

Distractions. A location as free as possible from distractions is important. Children playing, a cat, a bird, or any number of extraneous factors may so distract the subject that photography becomes impossible. In the wild, such things are completely out of the photographer's control; the problem is to ensure that the photographer will not be the disturbing element.

Interior. In a home or furnished interior, unnecessary furniture should be cleared from the area chosen for photography, with special attention paid to breakable items.

The Interior Setting. In a studio or other specially set-up area such as a basement or garage, seamless paper, painted flats, rugs, blankets, or any number of things can be positioned to form a setting. Whatever is used, it must contrast well in tone or

(Left) Knowledge of the mating habits of birds is useful to the photographer. A peacock fans out his tail to attract the female. (Right) Avoid photographing animals in bright overheard sunlight; shadows can obscure detail.

Animal and Pet Photography

The most effective portrait photographs are those in which the subject has direct eye contact with the viewer. A close-up lens at the animal's own level is most useful here. Photo by Walter Chandoha.

color with the animal, and it must be of a different, unobtrusive texture. The nature of the subject and the fragility of the entire setup must be considered. An uncontrolled puppy, a startled cat, or a mischievous monkey can shred seamless paper and wreak havoc with light stands and tripods in a matter of seconds.

Restricting Movement. There must be room for the animal to move, but not an excessive amount of space. Cats and dogs will want to wander out of the camera area. Choosing a corner will help limit their roaming, but the space must not appear cramped or confining in the picture. Working too close to any wall may create the problem of shadows on the background, especially with on-camera flash.

A table provides a controlled area for many small animals. They may venture to the edge, but probably they will not try to jump down to strange territory if there is nothing to attract their attention below. The simplest way to avoid their jumping down is to provide something that will attract their attention on top of the table.

Boxes vs. Cages. Cages pose the problem of bars or wires. A large, white box with one glass end can be substituted for picture purposes. If the back is a single piece of curved material, the vertical lines at the corners will be eliminated, as may be seen in the accompanying illustration.

Photographing Through Glass. The standard method of keeping fish within camera range in a small aquarium is to insert a sheet of glass just a few inches behind the front glass to create a narrow corridor. The second sheet of glass will be invisible under water. (See illustration.)

When photographing into any glass enclosure, the camera must be at an angle to the front glass in order not to include the camera's reflection or the reflection of any lights in the final picture. Dark material should be set up as well to eliminate reflections of the tripod and of the surroundings. (See the accompanying illustration.) If it is absolutely necessary to shoot head-on through a sheet of glass, a large, black curtain with a slit or a jet-black card with a hole just big enough for the lens to look through must be placed in front of the camera, or the lens must be pressed directly against the glass.

Point of View

As explained previously, formal photographs of show and exhibition animals may require specific viewpoints. Otherwise, it is up to the photographer to find the best angle from which to picture the subject. It is generally best to photograph at or near the animal's own level, so long as this does not bring distracting background elements into view or cause a horizon line to cut through the subject. A high viewpoint makes animals appear stunted and out of proportion.

Close-ups show distinctive markings, the texture of the coat, and the animal's expression; full shots reveal shape and proportion. Size is indicated by the inclusion of some reference point such as a bit of natural surroundings or, with a very small animal, a hand perhaps gently holding the subject.

Motion. Animals in motion can be caught with a fast shutter speed; a head-on view minimizes the movement at the moment of exposure. However, this makes everything in the picture sharp and static. To emphasize speed, with a race horse, for example, the camera can be panned in a side view and the exposure made during the camera movement. The result will be a sharp image of the animal against a background blurred by the motion. The fast-moving feet of the animal may also be slightly blurred, enhancing the feeling of motion.

Controlling the Subject

Some animals are fully trained to commands; the owner or handler can control them as required. Other animals can be controlled only to a small degree, and some—especially cats, among common pets—are completely independent.

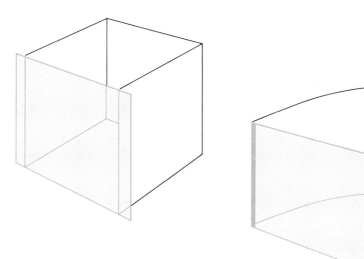

A three-sided box with a glass front confines small animals for photography. Walls can be a light color, or covered with a variety of materials. Flexible material, curved and taped to the edges of the glass, provides a background with no vertical corner lines. The open top can be covered with wire mesh when necessary. An open bottom permits easy use of any ground material: grass, gravel, blanket, and so forth. The enclosure can be used equally well indoors and out.

Animal and Pet Photography

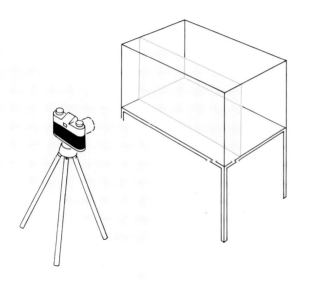

A sheet of glass inserted in an aquarium forms a narrow corridor to keep fish within the focused range of the camera. The camera should be positioned behind dark material through which a hole has been cut. The dark material eliminates reflections of camera tripod, photographer's body, and other elements.

Tropical fish in an aquarium display exquisite jewel-like colors. To keep fish within camera range, insert a sheet of glass several inches behind the front glass to create a narrow corridor.

Adjustment Period. It is important to allow plenty of time for the animal to become accustomed to the photographer and equipment, and to the location, if it is strange. Even just shifting furniture and setting up lights may make a familiar environment different enough to require investigation. Dogs and, in particular, monkeys will want to examine everything new. The camera lens should be capped throughout this period to avoid moist smudges and noseprints, and the tripod should be guarded against being overturned.

Maintaining the Position. A major problem is keeping animals within the intended camera range. A familiar blanket or cushion will often help keep a pet in one place. Mice, hamsters, rabbits, and reptiles will remain in a warm location—under a spotlight or infrared lamp, for example. Anything that holds an animal's interest will also serve to hold it in one spot. A toy or something new to examine will interest cats, as will a sock with a bit of catnip tied in the toe. Food is an obvious device: tidbits to nibble, some closed in a box, a bit smeared on a paw or behind the ears of a companion animal will all attract attention. It will also generate some activity and help prevent the photographer from becoming a distraction.

Create Alertness. Most animals become sleepy after feeding; this may subdue an especially frisky

subject, but it may also produce no action or alert expression at all. Alertness and a sense of liveliness are important in most animal pictures. They are revealed by an erect head, perked ears, attentive eyes. A click, a snap of the fingers, a whistle or the tinkle of a bell, and many other sounds will almost

Small kittens and puppies tend to be very active. Isolating them on a table or chair will usually keep them within camera range. Especially when photographing more than one animal whose behavior can be unpredictable, an assistant is almost essential. He or she can position the subjects, allowing the photographer to concentrate entirely on catching the right moment. Photos by Walter Chandoha.

always catch momentary attention. But no device can be repeated indefinitely. A familiar voice may evoke a response, but the photographer should watch carefully early in the session to see whether the presence of a pet's owner attracts too much attention or causes the animal to keep moving toward the owner. One solution is to include the owner in the picture, but then the photograph is no longer about the animal as an individual. It becomes a picture of a relationship, and the human personality may become the dominant interest, especially if the owner is a child.

Considerations with Specific Animals

Cats. The eyes and whiskers of a cat are its most important features in a close shot. Fur may also be distinctive, as in the case of an angora. Cats may squint to watch a camera as it comes close, and bright light will cause the eyes to "iris down" to

narrow slits. This may look more natural than the round black spots of wide-open pupils.

Cats are climbers and leapers. A table or platform can be a valuable prop. Create an interest there, and a cat will jump up to investigate. This produces three picture possibilities: the crouch to leap, in the air, and landing in an alert position. When a cat is playing with something on the table, pulling the toy off the table and onto the floor will generate a pause at the edge to watch and then a jump down to follow. Generally, table height should be low to encourage a downward jump but high to create a more graceful upward leap.

Just after napping and before eating, cats will often stretch and sharpen their claws. A patch of rug or a cloth-covered scratching post will direct such activity. After eating, cats spend a good deal of time cleaning themselves, which keeps them in one spot and fully preoccupied.

Many housebound cats have a daily "mad time" when they chase frantically about, apparently spooked by their own shadows, invisible creatures, or things too small to be seen. Whatever the cause, it is a fine time for action shots. Electronic flash is essential.

Dogs. The photographer cannot both control a dog and take pictures; a helper should look after keeping the animal alert and within camera range. In familiar surroundings, a dog is less likely to wander or to feel the need to explore.

As with all animals, groom the subject and groom the location before beginning to take the pictures.

Before meals, a dog is alert and will obey commands in return for tidbits of food.

Puppies are unpredictable action subjects except when they are full of food, and then they are sleepy. If not yet housebroken or if easily overexcited, they are also the cause of frequent delays to mop up or to replace seamless paper.

Horses. These are basically patient creatures, but they may shy and run off when startled by sudden noises or quick movements. Talking in a steady, normal tone has a calming effect. Carrots, lumps of sugar, or handfuls of oats are traditional rewards. A loose rubber band slipped over the tongue will occupy a horse's complete attention for a long time, but the expressions that arise may be very odd.

Rabbits. As with all sleek-furred animals, sidelighting is required to prevent the coat from looking like a tight, smooth skin. An open sky background is unnatural for rabbits; a suggestion of foliage is better. A bit of chopped parsley will keep them nibbling contentedly in one spot. Two rabbits will usually huddle closely, side by side.

Shelled Creatures. Turtles, snails, and other animals with shells need dampening to create highlights on their coverings. Crosslight will bring out both the texture and the color of the shell. Only patience will bring out the head after it has been withdrawn into the shell for protection.

Use caution when photographing dangerous species, even in controlled habitats. You may have to wait until the animals are in good positions to be photographed, but the picture results will be well worth the wait.

Photographing Animals in the Wild

The first requisite for photographing animals in the wild is knowledge. The photographer must be thoroughly familiar with the species he or she wants to capture: its movements, feeding habits, range, its strengths and weaknesses. If the photographer does not have this knowledge, an experienced guide who does must be relied upon. Otherwise, it will take weeks to get pictures that should require only days, or the quarry may not be found at all. The greater the potential danger—with snakes, bears, or rhinos, for example—the greater the need for professional guidance.

Equipment. Versatile, lightweight equipment and long telephoto lenses are invaluable. Special equipment to arrange "traps" that cause an animal to take its own picture when seizing bait can be improvised, but they should be thoroughly tested before trekking into the field. Such pictures offer no guarantee of a satisfactory pose; they may record only a startled expression or the back of a head.

A long lens will help you capture a bird of prey on film. It will also emphasize the fine detail of the feathers.

is excellent for the open plains, but in mountains or forests, you can only get a bit closer before you must follow on foot. When suitable, following by vehicle provides the greatest coverage of territory without fatigue, and it provides far more safety than being on foot.

Working from a Blind. This method ties the photographer to one location and essentially one viewpoint. It is necessary to find a waterhole, den, or habitual feeding point. A suitable spot can be baited repeatedly so that an animal builds up an expectation of finding food there. The blind should be positioned on the first baiting so that it, too, becomes a familiar part of the surroundings. An elevated blind, perhaps established in a tree, provides safety and minimizes the likelihood of detection. However, this position of a blind creates a downward point of view that is not desirable if you are too close to the subject. Using a longer lens at the same height but at a greater distance will minimize the visual problem of the vertical angle.

Bait. The bait must be appropriate to the subject. A snake or an owl will come after a live mouse but not a dead one. Crisp greens (but not domestic iceberg lettuce) will interest a rabbit but not a fox, who will come after raw meat bits, eggs, or even bread and milk. Young plant shoots and a salt block will attract deer; almost any plate scraps will interest porcupines and skunks. A bit of research will reveal ways to lure almost any animal to within camera range. The photographer's task is to be in position (however long the wait) and alert for the picture opportunities when they arise.

• *See also:* ACTION PHOTOGRAPHY; NATURE PHOTOGRAPHY; ZOO PHOTOGRAPHY; BIRD PHOTOGRAPHY.

Further Reading: Bauer, Erwin A. *Hunting with a Camera: A World Guide to Wildlife Photography.* New York, NY: Winchester Press, 1974; Bennett, Edna. *Nature Photography Simplified.* Garden City, NY: Amphoto, 1975; Chandoha, Walter. *How to Photograph Cats, Dogs, and Other Animals.* New York, NY: Crown Publishers, 1973; Hodgson, David. *All About Photographing Animals and Birds.* Levittown, NY: Transatlantic Arts, Inc., 1975; Stagg, Mildred. *Animal and Pet Photography Simplified.* Garden City, NY: Amphoto, 1975.

Many setups can be monitored from afar with binoculars, and the camera and flash can be fired by remote control—a switch and wire at moderate distances or a radio device from farther away. This technique also requires a motor drive to advance the film and cock the shutter and battery-powered flash units. The setup must be protected from the weather, and the equipment must not operate or recycle so noisily that it frightens off the subject.

Finding the Subject. There are three basic ways of going after animals in the wild.

Stalking. Following on foot is probably the least effective method of finding an animal because of the great effort over a long period of time that it demands. With some species, it may be impossible to get within camera range on foot or to remain downwind to avoid detection by scent.

Following by Vehicle. This method of tracking the subject is limited to certain kinds of terrain. It

Animal and Pet Photography

Animation

In every age, artists have recognized that color and form are not enough for a complete representation of life. Even the Stone Age artist felt the urge to make pictures move, but could not. It was not until 1831, when Frenchman Joseph Plateau made the first animated cartoon, that pictures actually did begin to move.

One of the beauties of animation is its remarkable flexibility; it can do almost anything. Animation techniques are equally applicable to character or technical animation. In fact, not only is animation an entertaining change of pace in the world of theatrical motion pictures, but in certain applications, it is downright indispensable. Without animation, how could one effectively show the rearrangement of molecules that takes place in a chemical reaction? How could one show the details of large office-management systems, sales reports and charts, production and maintenance procedures? With animation, it is possible to travel to the nucleus of a single atom and watch it split, to simulate intricate space flights and maneuvers, or to create the means of extracting unknowns from highly complicated mathematical formulas. In each of these cases, animation can provide maximum effectiveness by enabling an audience to focus on a specific subject without the distraction of conflicting elements that surround it.

Principles of Animation

Means by which motion pictures record and reproduce images of moving objects are quite well known. The motion-picture camera records on a strip of film a series of still pictures at a rate of 18 frames per second (silent speed) or 24 fps (sound speed). As a result, a continuous action is converted by the camera into a series of individual stills placed in order on the film. The positions of objects in motion will vary slightly from frame to frame throughout the progress of the movement. Then, when projected in rapid succession, this series of still pictures seemingly recreates the movement of the

objects that were filmed. This effect occurs because of persistence of vision, which causes the eye to retain for a brief instant the images that are presented to it; the eye fuses each preceding image with the one being presented, and the illusion of pictures that move is created.

Illusion of motion is obtained in exactly the same way in animated pictures as it is in regular filming and occurs during projection as the series of pictures on the film is presented to the eye. However, although regular and animated films create their illusion of motion in the same manner, the photographing of animated motion pictures is an entirely different matter.

In ordinary filming, it is relatively easy to record a scene involving moving objects simply by pressing the shutter release and causing the camera mechanism to record a sequence of pictures at regular intervals throughout the scene. Not so in the animated film. The scene must be filmed *one frame at a time,* while the positions of objects that will

An animation artist at work. Attention to detail is most important. Photo courtesy Hanna-Barbera Productions.

ART — JOB No. J8 — ILLUS. No. V24	ART — JOB No. J8 — ILLUS. No. V25	ART — JOB No. J8 — ILLUS. No. V26
CONTINUITY	CONTINUITY	CONTINUITY
Later artist actually did draw from these images, and made many pictures with their help. Eventually someone (Daniello Barbero, patriarch of Aquileia) (in 1568)	replaced the pinhole with a lens--an old man's reading glass, which formed an image in the same way, but made a much brighter image.	Other men wanted to get a breath of fresh air, moved out of the box, made the box smaller, and even put a mirror inside to bounce the light to the top of the box, so that an artist could sit comfortably and draw.
ART — JOB No. J2 — ILLUS. No. V41	ART — JOB No. J2 — ILLUS. No. V42	ART PHOTO — JOB No. J2 — ILLUS. No. V43
CONTINUITY	CONTINUITY	CONTINUITY
They even had to have a tent, an instant darkroom as part of their camera equipment.	People had to keep still.	But there has been progress, first in the area of creative invention and later in the laboratories they founded.

Storyboards provide the opportunity to visualize the production in rough form prior to filming. The individual drawings remain free to be positioned and studied simultaneously whenever necessary.

"move" on the screen are altered slightly between frames. There must be separate drawings or setups for each of the items that move—in each of their various positions—throughout the desired cycle of movement.

Planning the Animated Film

Animated films require more precise preparation than most live-action motion pictures. The fact that the movement within the scene is created by the artist or the camera operator (or both) makes detailed planning, in many ways, more important than any process that follows, for it is in this stage that the policy governing the entire production is established. Since the amount, tempo, and quality of each movement must be controlled exactly, mistakes at this point can result in additional costs at every stage of production; hence, the need for careful, thoughtful preparation.

The amount of detailed preliminary planning in simple animation is largely dependent upon how precisely the movements must be timed to synchronize with the narration or to fit a predetermined schedule. In situations that demand precise timing, it is best to use an exposure sheet. As a rule, the more elaborate the animation is, the more detailed the preliminary planning must be.

Initial phases of animated-script preparation are much the same as those of conventional-script preparation. They may include the development of the basic idea or story, the adaptation of it to a specific film treatment, and the preparation of the shooting script. The latter, while often permitting a certain amount of flexibility during filming, is quite detailed as to the scenes, camera directions, and dialogue.

For regular cel animation,* the problems of planning action are in the hands of the animator and the artist. The camera operator's responsibility is to follow faithfully the directions on the exposure sheet. In animating puppets or other three-dimen-

---

*Each frame of an animated film is photographed from a drawing. So that a new drawing will not have to be made for each frame, the background is usually drawn on a white card; white moving objects are drawn on cels (cellulose acetate overlays) in several layers. See further details later in this article.

Animation

sional objects, the duration and artistic quality of the action are the responsibility of whoever prepares the exposure sheet and moves the puppet or object between successive exposures. As is true with other skills, a genuine feel for animation and the ability to handle it well are developed best through practical experience.

The Storyboard. A storyboard is a device that will hold a series of drawings (not unlike a comic strip) arranged in a sequence to illustrate a story or situation. The individual drawings remain free to be positioned and studied simultaneously whenever necessary. Storyboards, which are commonly used in connection with filming, usually contain rather crude drawings that are intended to convey an idea rather than display any artistic merit. (Where necessary, drawings are more finely drawn, with details sharply indicated to show exactly what is expected in the finished film.) Under the rough sketch of each scene is provision for the applicable narration or dialogue to be written or typed.

Storyboards also serve a useful function in selling a prospective client on a proposed film treatment, even though he or she may have had no previous experience with film production and therefore might have difficulty envisioning how a motion picture will appear from simply reading the customary shooting script.

The Exposure Sheet. The exposure sheet (sometimes called a camera or "X" sheet) is the most important item in the final preparation for animated film production, because it contains the information and instructions required for each step that follows in the production sequence. The sheet is the culmination of all previous planning and is, in reality, the camera operator's shooting script, accounting for *every frame* of animation, for it indicates the camera and artwork movements, the exact order in which the cels are to be photographed, and the length of time each cel, background, and element is on the screen. Exposure sheets also include a description of the sound and the action taking place and other information pertaining to the scene.

Sheets of this type are commercially available, or they can be printed locally to meet the requirements of your production unit. Exposure sheets intended for regular cel animation contain columns for each cel involved in a scene and give a diagram of the cel numbers required in the particular sandwich of cels

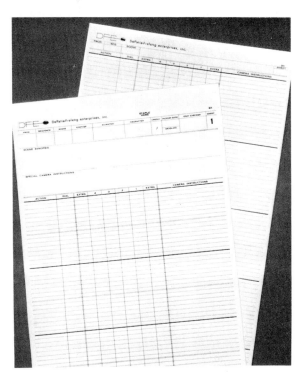

Exposure sheets account for every frame of animation, including a description of the sound and the action taking place. Photo courtesy DePatie-Freleng Enterprises, Inc.

for each frame throughout the film. (*Every* cel and background must be numbered sequentially according to their place in the planned animation. The correct position of each cel in relation to its background should be indicated in multicel levels. For example, the cels of the first scene to be photographed can be numbered 1c, 1b, 1a, and 1 to indicate their relative proximity to the background. The next would be labeled 2c, 2b, 2a, and 2, and so forth. Backgrounds can be labeled separately, according to the order in which they will be used. It is mandatory that only one system be chosen for numbering the cels and backgrounds.) In addition, there are columns for action, dialogue, scene background, and camera instructions. Each sheet usually provides the detailed instructions for a few seconds of film running time.

The main body of the exposure sheet is divided horizontally and vertically by a series of parallel lines. Each horizontal line represents one frame of film. There are usually 80 horizontal lines on a page, representing 2 feet of 16 mm film or 5 feet of 35 mm film. The vertical lines divide the sheet into columns in which are specified the moves to be made on the stand, and the cels and backgrounds to be exposed.

The exposure sheet for the animation of three-dimensional objects, including puppets, does not need to be quite as elaborate as the one in the accompanying illustration. The scene being filmed is not a composite of a number of drawings that carry the entire action, but is a single setting in miniature in which all portions of the action are accounted for in a single take. Consequently, the columns for extra cels would be superfluous. But if superimposed titles or multiple exposures are required, adequate space for them should be provided in the simpler exposure sheet.

Planning Action. The planning of action in an animated sequence has several aspects that should be considered.

Timing. Most important is correct timing. The animator must keep in mind that an animated action should take the same or a lesser amount of time than the same action would take if it were done live. For accuracy, the animator should clock several times a real-life movement that is similar to the desired animated one and then average the timing for that ac-

tion. This procedure will show how many frames to allot to a particular movement. As an example, suppose that it is discovered that in normal walking the average man takes about 10 steps in 5 seconds. This is approximately ½ second per step, or in terms of animation, it would require 9 frames (silent speed) or 12 frames (sound speed) to animate one step. It becomes obvious, then, that fast action will require fewer frames in taking than will action that moves slowly.

The speed of the subject's movement will determine the number of drawings needed. For example, a 2-second movement can be animated with 24 drawings (photographed on twos, sound speed). However, if the same action is slowed down and done in 4 seconds, 48 drawings will be required for its animation.

In some instances, the literal presentation of actual speed will appear wrong on the screen. This problem will occur if two objects are depicted to move parallel to each other across the screen. When each object is animated at the same speed, the object in the foreground will appear to be moving much faster than the one in the background. Only by proportionately exaggerating the speed of the distant object and understating the speed of the near one can they be made to appear synchronized.

How fast to make a subject move across the

TYPICAL RUNNING TIMES OF FILMS

Film Format	8 mm		Super 8		16 mm	
Projection Speed in Frames per Sec.	18	24	18	24	18	24
Inches per Sec.	2.7	3.6	3.0	4.0	5.4	7.2
Film Length and Screen Time	Min. + Sec.	Min. + Sec.	Min. + Sec.	Min. + Sec.	Min. + Sec.	Min. + Sec.
Feet 50	3 42	2 47	3 20	2 30	1 51	1 23
100	7 24	5 33	6 40	5 0	3 42	2 47
150	11 7	8 20	10 0	7 30	5 33	4 10
200	14 49	11 7	13 20	10 0	7 24	5 33
300	22 13	16 40	20 0	15 0	11 7	8 20
400	29 38	22 13	26 40	20 0	14 49	11 7
500	37 2	27 47	33 20	25 0	18 31	13 53
600	44 27	33 20	40 0	30 0	22 13	16 40
700	51 51	38 53	46 40	35 0	25 56	19 27
800	59 16	44 27	53 20	40 0	29 38	22 13
900	66 40	50 0	60 0	45 0	33 20	25 0
1000	74 4	55 33	66 40	50 0	37 2	27 47
1100	81 29	61 7	73 20	55 0	40 44	30 33
1200	88 53	66 40	80 0	60 0	44 27	33 20

RUNNING TIMES AND FILM LENGTHS FOR COMMON PROJECTION SPEEDS

Film Format	8 mm (80 Frames per Ft.)		Super 8 (72 Frames per Ft.)		16 mm (40 Frames per Ft.)	
Projection Spd. in Frames per Sec.	18	24	18	24	18	24
Running Time and Film Length	Feet + Frames	Feet + Frames	Feet + Frames	Feet + Frames	Feet + Frames	Feet + Frames
Seconds 1	0 18	0 24	0 18	0 24	0 18	0 24
2	0 36	0 48	0 36	0 48	0 36	1 8
3	0 54	0 72	0 54	1 0	1 14	1 32
4	0 72	1 16	1 0	1 24	1 32	2 16
5	1 10	1 40	1 18	1 48	2 10	3 0
6	1 28	1 64	1 36	2 0	2 28	3 24
7	1 46	2 8	1 54	2 24	3 6	4 8
8	1 64	2 32	2 0	2 48	3 24	4 32
9	2 2	2 56	2 18	3 0	4 2	5 16
10	2 20	3 0	2 36	3 24	4 20	6 0
20	4 40	6 0	5 0	6 48	9 0	12 0
30	6 60	9 0	7 36	10 0	13 20	18 0
40	9 0	12 0	10 0	13 24	18 0	24 0
50	11 20	15 0	12 36	16 48	22 20	30 0
Minutes 1	13 40	18 0	15 0	20 0	27 0	36 0
2	27 0	36 0	30 0	40 0	54 0	72 0
3	40 40	54 0	45 0	60 0	81 0	108 0
4	54 0	72 0	60 0	80 0	108 0	144 0
5	67 40	90 0	75 0	100 0	135 0	180 0
6	81 0	108 0	90 0	120 0	162 0	216 0
7	94 40	126 0	105 0	140 0	189 0	252 0
8	108 0	144 0	120 0	160 0	216 0	288 0
9	121 40	162 0	135 0	180 0	243 0	324 0
10	135 0	180 0	150 0	200 0	270 0	360 0

screen so that the action will appear realistic is a matter of experience—apparent accuracy is sometimes the result of unnatural distortion. Remember that the closer the action is to the camera, the larger the subject will look on the screen and the less time it will take to travel a specific distance. On the other hand, the farther the movement is from the camera, the smaller the subject will appear and the longer it will take to complete a move.

Acceleration and Deceleration. If the action is to have a living quality, it is not sufficient simply to ascertain the number of frames necessary for a particular action. Careful attention must be given to acceleration and deceleration of motion at the beginning and end of the movement. For the purpose of illustration, assume that a puppet figure is going to be animated to throw something. To divide the number of frames necessary for the duration of the movement into the distance from one extreme of the action to the other, and to change the figure position by this amount from frame to frame is not enough.

This method will produce a stiff, mechanical action. An analysis of the movement in real life will disclose that a throw starts relatively slowly and builds up to faster and faster motion until the completion of the movement, with a deceleration of speed or action to the stop at the end. In planning action of this sort, it may take many frames to get the arm back ready for the throw, but only two or three to make the throw. The speed and style of the acceleration and deceleration will depend upon the personality and character of the object being animated.

The following figure represents the acceleration and deceleration of a puppet action. The numbered white lines show the positions in animating an arm of the puppet. Ten frames are required to move the arm from the old man's side. In frames 1, 2, and 3, the movement is slight. It increases in frames 4, 5, 6, and 7, and begins to decrease again through frames 8, 9, and 10. This shortening and lengthening of a movement lends a more lifelike quality to the action.

A Movieola film-editing machine.

The beginning animator can analyze frame by frame live-action motion pictures of people and/or animals to determine the number of frames it takes for them to perform action. (A film-editing viewer is helpful for this work.) Indeed, even professional animation studios sometimes resort to shooting key live-action scenes with real actors in order to have an accurate record of the frame-by-frame variations that comprise a specific bit of "business."

Where it is desired to have a character speak in realistic fashion (in close-ups), it is often helpful for the beginner to take live-action shots of a person speaking the intended words. This serves to show what lip movements must be accounted for when drawing the facial expressions.

Artistic Expression. In addition to the considerations of timing, and acceleration and deceleration of action, there is the need to study the *quality* of the action. For example, since cartoon characters are basically caricatures of people—fat people, thin people, tall people, and short people—each with individual characteristics, most animated cartoon actions are exaggerated. The gestures, postures, and features are overdrawn in terms of the nature of the

In this photograph of puppet animation, the numbered white lines indicate the ten frames required to move the man's arm.

distortions inherent in the cartoon characters. The amount and type of exaggeration depend upon the characters involved.

Style of action is determined also by the type of art treatment the scenes receive. With *simple* treatment, objects are shown without detail, in silhouette, or they are reduced to symbols and have little or no perspective. Figures are usually flat, featureless, and unmodeled; backgrounds, such as water and sky, are toned areas on paper. *Average* treatment depicts objects fairly realistically and in perspective, but some points are simplified or omitted. Figures have some modeling and detail. This method is widely used, since drawings of unembellished objects can be repeated quickly and economically. The *detailed* treatment renders objects with great particularity, nearly photographic in quality. Figures are highly modeled and portrait-like in character. Backgrounds are illustrated in perspective and have trees, roads, houses, figures, cloud shadows, textures, and other details. Obviously, this latter method is time-consuming and comparatively expensive to produce.

Movement Cycles. The movement cycles used most often in the animation of figures are the *walk,*

the *strut,* and the *run.* When animating these or other movement cycles, an important rule to remember is that the slower the movement of the character being animated, the more upright the position should be. For instance, a walk is always slower than a run; in a walk the body may lean forward in the direction of travel, but it is relatively upright when compared with one that is running.

In most movement cycles, the animated character should face the direction opposite to the one in which the background is moving. Backgrounds can be made to move by using an animation stand, on which two sets of traveling pegbars (see the accompanying figures) are mounted on mobile tracks in the tabletop. The movable tracks on both top and bottom enable the animator to mount a background from one side and cels from the other; each can then move independently. Thus, a subject can be made to appear as if it is moving across a static background or a changing background.

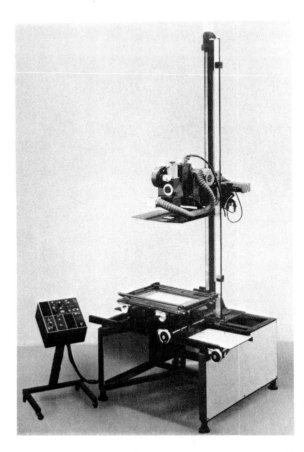

(Right) Animation stand provides accurate control of camera and art movements. (Below) Close-up shows pantograph, field guide, platen, registration pegs, pegbar-track controls. Photos courtesy Oxberry Div., Richmark Camera Svce., Inc.

This camera is equipped with a solenoid for single-frame filming.

To create a changing background, the pegbar holding the background is moved while the pegbar holding the subject is held stationary. The illusion created when the film is projected is that the subject is moving across a changing landscape.

When two or more characters are walking or running in a scene, and each of the characters is on a separate cel level,* the animator should continually check their actions and positions in relation to each other, as well as to the background. Such checking also enables the animator to match the characters with any objects on, or portions of, the background.

Equipment for Animation Filming

Camera. Several factors should be considered when a camera is being chosen for animation filming. First, the camera should be equipped for single-frame exposures. Many motion-picture cameras have a single-frame release or can be adapted for this work by the attachment of special motors. (The cost of such installation should be determined

---

*The use of multicel levels is standard practice by professional animators. When cycles are used for repeated action, or when one subject is held while another is moved, it may be necessary to photograph several layers of cels simultaneously.

prior to the camera purchase; it can exceed the cost of the camera.)

Ideally, the single-frame device in a camera should give uniform exposures from frame to frame. However, most spring-wound cameras do not meet this condition exactly; differences in spring tension throughout the stages of winding, in addition to varying amounts of friction within the mechanism, preclude absolute accuracy. Sometimes the manner in which the release lever is depressed will affect the shutter timing or the stability of the camera in single-frame work. The use of a solenoid to trip the release lever will yield better results than releasing by hand.

An accurate means of viewing the precise field that is being photographed is necessary for the critical focusing and framing at the short distances encountered in most animation work; therefore, a reflex or rackover viewfinder is of prime importance. Such a finder permits viewing of the subject through the camera lens without exposing the film.

Animation Stand. The successful production of sophisticated animated films requires accurate control of the movements of the camera and the artwork, since the slightest inaccuracy will be greatly magnified when the film is projected. Consequently, of prime importance in this level of animation work is the animation stand. Stands can range from the highly precise and often elaborate piece of equipment, such as the Oxberry or the Richmark, to the custom-built variety constructed for a specific class of work.

Professional stands are sturdy and precise. They provide an exact means of holding a camera in a vertical plane (pointing straight down), and have the facility for moving the camera up and down to any desired height over the copy area. (Stands can be, and often are, built to operate in a horizontal plane; this will be discussed later.) Although it is possible to accomplish certain types of animation through the use of a tripod, an animation stand helps to assure an improved quality in all phases of the work and effects important economies in production time. The advantage of camera-in-motion techniques, such as zooms, pans, or tilts, can easily be achieved with most animation stands, and with such apparatus, a number of animated effects can be obtained without the need for a large number of additional drawings.

There are many excellent animation stands available commercially, but their cost may be higher than can be justified on the basis of production volume. If the equipment budget is limited, consider building a stand tailored to specific needs. Satisfactory stands have been constructed by ingenious operators, some of whom have successfully modified lathe beds to suit their purpose. A drawing of an animation stand used by Stockdale and Company, Salt Lake City, Utah, is shown in the accompanying figure. It can be fabricated from materials that are readily obtainable and will require a minimum of machine-shop work. Being extremely flexible, the stand can be used either horizontally or vertically; it can be made large enough to accommodate the animation of small- and medium-size objects, and precise enough for use in photographing small titles.

If necessary, the copy area for ordinary title work can be nothing more than a flat-topped table. In animation work, however, it is customary to have a glass platen, mounted on a compound table, that can accommodate the largest field size to be used.

Construction diagram of an animation stand.
1. *The main frame members are made of channel aluminum.*
2. *A 10-foot steel tape is used to regulate the height of the camera carriage.*
3. *The drawing of the working-table surface shows the threaded bracket that couples to knob 8 and the guide channels that regulate the "north-south" table movement. The top of the table is fitted with a standard Acme peg for cel registration.*
4. *Sash weights are used to counterbalance the weight of the camera carriage.*
5. *End brackets are equipped with bearings that permit tilting the camera track from vertical to horizontal.*
6. *The camera carriage is equipped with rollers that fit on either side of the track flange to permit up-and-down fingertip movement.*
7. *The adjustment knob and screw control "east-west" table movement.*
8. *"North-south" adjustment knob and screw.*
9. *The mounting base.*

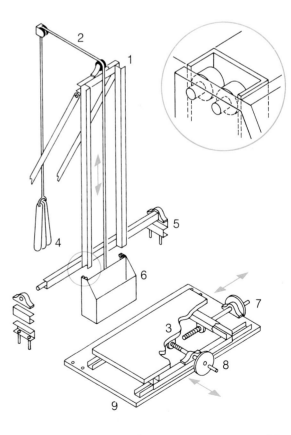

The usual table has registration pegs and provides for movement in a north/south–east/west direction. Some tables also have a large ring-gear arrangement that permits the tabletop and platen to be rotated a full 360 degrees.

Cel Animation

Perhaps the best known of all animation forms is cel animation. Essentially, it is a series of drawings made on sheets of clear cellulose acetate (termed "cels") on which the figures are drawn in slightly different positions that progress through the desired movements as each cel is placed in register under the camera. (The amount of movement would be resolved in the planning phase of the operation.) The drawings are then photographed one frame at a time, with appropriate cel changes between frames. Filming is done on the animation or copy stand, which keeps cels and camera in correct relationship while filming is in progress. When projected, the animated characters or objects move with a lifelike realism that is still peculiarly their own and not an exact duplication of the movements they depict.

The popularity of this form of animation is evidenced vocally whenever the lead title of a cartoon appears on any motion-picture screen. The genius of the late Walt Disney, and others, has raised the standards of this art to a very high level. Of course, animating with cels is not restricted to cartoons. Many techniques and procedures in education, business and industry, science, and the arts are more easily and better shown through cel animation than would be possible by filming the real-life situation.

Held Cels. By using a *held cel* (a cel that is held still for several frames during some portion of an animated sequence), the animator can effectively avoid unnecessary inking and coloring. Those portions of a scene that will not move do not have to be redrawn for each new exposure; they can be used

Horizontal animation stand, built on lathe bed which is base for camera mount and track. By David W. Evans & Associates.

Photo below shows a black-lined acetate cel, before it has been painted on the reverse side (at left) and after it has been painted (at right).

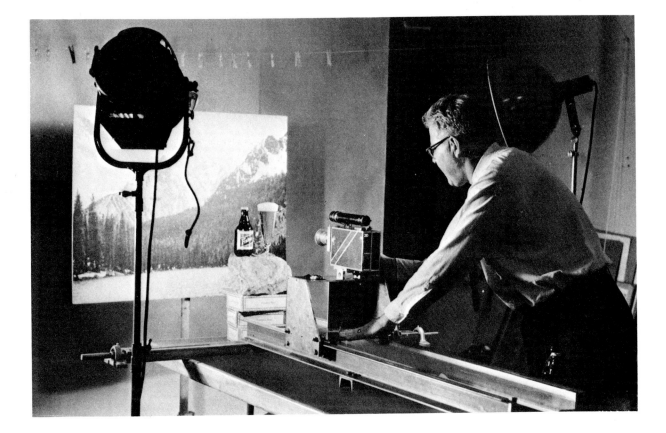

In this production setup for the animation of three-dimensional objects, the track-mounted camera can be used for either a simple zoom-in on the subject or for more elaborate single-frame animation. The same lighting system can be used for either technique. Photo courtesy of Stockdale and Company.

over and over until it is their turn to move. Only then do new drawings of these portions need to be made. Imagine, for example, an animated sequence in which a character stands still while speaking. The animator can make a separate drawing of the character's head and body and indicate on the exposure sheet that it is to be held for the length of time the character remains in the still position. Then the animator needs only to draw each new mouth action instead of the full head and figure.

Not only do held cels save work, effecting a great economy in the preparation of the artwork, but the results obtained through their use are much better than those achieved through retracings, where there is danger of jiggling ink lines.

Cel Levels. The number of *cel levels* (separate drawings placed on top of each other to be photographed at the same time) used over the background must be consistent throughout a scene. If certain cels are needed for only a portion of the action, they must be replaced with blank cels to maintain uniform density over the background of the scene. The maximum number of cels needed over the background at *any* point in the scene must be used to establish the cel level for the whole scene. Then, the complete cel "sandwich" should be compressed with a platen, or other suitable device, to prevent focus and shadow problems during filming.

Five-level scenes, or anything over that number, should be avoided, if possible. Although the cels are

After the background has been prepared, the first cel (left) is laid down. In this sequence, the first cel carries the action of the house. The next cel added (right) shows the people in the window, the objects in the foreground, and the legs of the man in the chair.

The third cel (left) adds the man's body and arms and the newspaper. The final cel (right) adds the man's head, completing the picture. The man's head carries most of the action in this sequence. Production economy is realized by redrawing only the head if it is the only part of the picture that moves. Sequence courtesy of Stockdale and Company.

transparent and only .005-inch thick, each one will tone down the background somewhat, and five cel levels will have a considerable effect. Thus, the artist must know before he or she paints a cel which level it is to be, and then choose a pigment whose hue is calculated to compensate for the level that the cel will occupy. (To help assure consistent results, some animation studios have more than 400 hues for color productions.)

Care of Cels. Cels prepared for animation must be handled with extreme care; the paint can be chipped easily, the plastic attracts lint and dust, and their surfaces are relatively soft, so can become scratched and marred. Cels should be handled by their edges, beyond the areas that will be photographed, and the place used for filming (and storage) should be as dust-free as possible. The use of a Kodak 2-inch camel's-hair brush and the Kodak static eliminator power unit, will help to keep the cels free from dust while in use.

In summary, cel animation is as versatile a form of motion-picture presentation as any currently available; virtually nothing is impossible. But, because of the amount of time and talent required, the cel approach to animation may be beyond the means of many motion-picture budgets.

Animating Three-Dimensional Objects

The successful animation of three-dimensional objects is largely dependent upon careful planning. Every aspect of the production should be anticipated in advance. Animation of this kind is not particularly difficult, and most of the problems encountered will be related to the size, weight, shape, and color of the objects being animated and the types of movements they are to perform. Proper timing—with regard to the nature and speed of the action—is important here, as it is with other types of animation.

Before resorting to the tedium of single-frame animation of a three-dimensional object, you should first consider trying to achieve the desired motion by means of *live-action photography,* which can entail the imaginative use of such devices as concealed wires and supports, moving backgrounds, puffs of compressed air, and so forth. Success in this effort will effect a considerable saving in production time and the results will usually be comparable to those results that are achieved by the process of single-framing.

Obtaining Rotating Motion. To obtain a rotating movement without single-framing, it is easiest to mount the object on a motor-driven turntable and then film the subject in a continuous run. The object can be made to appear as if it is rotating in mid-air by covering the turntable and background with black velvet.

This typical cel sandwich is purposely misaligned to show that each separate cel must be positioned correctly for the whole to work.

Puppet Animation

Animated puppets afford the charm of comic and semicomic characters. However, the puppet world is a solid one, with characters that move in space; no matter how imaginative the settings and the characters are, they have less freedom from the limitations of time and space than the wholly drawn creation, which exists only as lines and paint on paper or acetate. The wide variations of expression and chances for distortion of figure proportions for dramatic emphasis are the special province of the drawn figures in cel animation and cannot be duplicated in puppet animation.

Preliminary Precautions. When animating puppets, a number of preliminary precautions should be

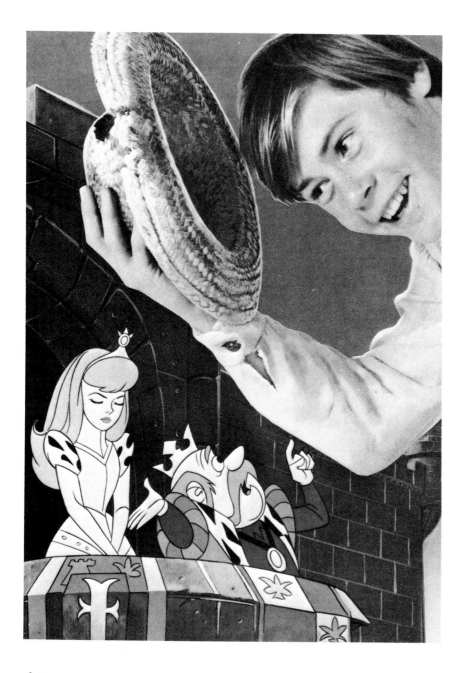

Animation combined with live action results in real people and animated characters performing in the same scene. Photo courtesy of Hanna-Barbera Productions.

Puppets have a charm that is peculiarly their own. Their three-dimensionality permits an endless variety of lighting setups and camera angles.

Animation

taken before the work actually begins. All items in the set, such as furniture, trees, fences, shrubs, and so forth, should be mounted rigidly in place. Otherwise, an accidental bump or jar when filming, however slight, could cause them to move and necessitate redoing the scene. To hold them firmly in place, pins mounted in the ends of the legs of furniture and in the bases of other items in the set can be pushed into balsa floors. In addition, a small drop of quick-drying model-making cement can be used and later cut away with a razor blade or knife if changes in set arrangement become necessary.

Procedure. To animate a movement, especially at the beginning of a scene, it is generally best to expose several frames to establish the position of the character before moving any of the limbs. The animator should remember that 24 frames can be exposed without moving the character, and that this will require only one second of elapsed screen time. Then, keeping in mind the idea of acceleration and deceleration (discussed in this article in the section "Planning Action"), the animator should move the limb slightly (for 7- to 9-inch figures, a distance of ⅛ inch will be sufficient) and make an exposure. Next, the limb should be moved about ¼ inch and another exposure made, and so forth. For relatively slow movement, ¼-inch intervals will work well; for extremely rapid action, such as throwing a punch or batting a ball, three or four frames can be used to start the action, then perhaps only two frames to complete it—one about a third of the way through the action and the other at the end. Three to six (or eight) frames could be used for the pause and holding the pose at the end of the action, with extremely small amounts of movement of the figure in between these actions.

Some actions that seem to be the simplest are the most difficult to animate. An ordinary step in walking or running is a good example of this. To do the job well, almost every part of the puppet's anatomy must be moved in coordination between successive exposures. This requires concentrated effort. Also, there is a tendency for general body gesture and attitude to become more bent and slumped over. Gravity, combined with handling, contributes to this.

The beginning animator should keep his or her initial animated puppet figures simple and stylized. It is a mistake to try to make them too lifelike; the results are likely to be somewhat ghoulish. If puppets are designed to look and act like the little jointed characters they are, the animated film will have a more refreshing and unique charm.

Making Puppets. Puppets can be made from a variety of materials, such as wax, rubber, wood, and clay. Another important consideration when making puppets is the size of the figures. Figures have to be made fairly small, if the studio is small and large sets are required; otherwise, there might be very little room left to accommodate the lighting equipment, in addition to the sets and the camera. Also, mechanical difficulties can arise if the figures are too large.

Paper Cutouts

Paper cutouts have been used to good advantage in certain types of animation. They retain much of the simplicity and economy of animated puppets, yet allow for some of the flexibility of expression inherent in cel animation. Like characters on acetate cels, paper cutouts perform against a painted background, and like puppets, their segmented bodies, arms, and legs can be moved between frames without the necessity of drawing new cels for each portion of a movement.

Graphs, Charts, Maps, Lines, and Arrows

A procedure that is simple, but effective, is the animation of graphs, charts, maps, lines, and arrows. This technique serves a vital role in documentary, travelogue, and educational films and helps to make palatable otherwise dull material.

Routes on maps can be made to trace themselves magically from point to point and give the motion-picture audience a sense of orientation as to the geographic locations of film sequences. Arrows can move in to point out crucial material. Business trends can be illustrated in a moving manner that gives a feeling of "It's happening now." In addition, educational films can be made to present complex processes in a simplified manner that can be understood readily.

Lines that seem to draw themselves are easy to create. One way that this can be achieved is to place a sheet of glass or acetate over the subject, draw the line one segment at a time, and make a single-frame shot of the line after each portion has been added. If the line is complex in shape or direction, it is better to do this in reverse (described in the section on scratch-off). The result will be that when the film is projected, the line will seemingly draw itself.

Special Effects

Animators learn to draw action effects mostly through observation and experience. Books offer pages of explanation about the technique, but to draw these actions realistically is something else again. The animators must carefully study everyday actions, for there are few set rules for them to follow. Although they have individual styles and draw similar actions differently, animators must adhere to the primary requisite that the action—regardless of the style—must look convincing and realistic when it appears on the screen.

Fades, Dissolves, and Wipes. Two of the most frequently used effects in motion pictures are the *fade* and the *dissolve*. The *fade,* as the name implies, refers to the appearance or disappearance of an image from the screen. The fade-out is used at the end of a scene or sequence and has a note of finality about it. The fade-in has a completely opposite effect and is used to introduce a scene or sequence. A *dissolve* is simply a superimposed fade-in and fade-out.

If prints of a film are to be made, you should obtain the services of a professional film laboratory; it is much better to use printer-made fades and dissolves than to attempt to make them in the camera. (An improperly made camera dissolve can ruin two scenes instead of just one.) After editing a workprint, indicate on the film where fades, dissolves, or other special effects should be. The lab will then take the camera original film and cause it to conform to the workprint. (*See:* A AND B ROLL EDITING.)

A *wipe* is a special effect in which a line seems to move across the screen, obliterating one scene and revealing another. Many wipes used for optical effects are actually mattes, originally photographed with an animation camera. The length and speed of the moving wipe pattern can be determined by the displacement of images between cels and the number of times each cel is photographed.

Many special lenses and prisms can be obtained to produce image rotation, flip-flops, multiple images, and other special effects. Innovative persons can create their own results by using prisms, mirrors, broken glass, ferrotype tins, and other items in front of the camera lens. The variety of wipe effects is limited only by the creative genius of the animator and his staff.

Animating Mouth Movements

Lip synchronization (mouth action) is as important in animation as is the accompanying action.

Wipes move across the screen, obliterating one scene and revealing another. Below, some commonly used wipe patterns; arrows indicate the direction of their movement.

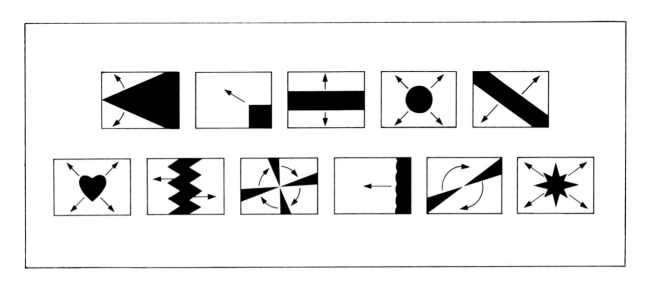

Certain mouth shapes are used to express key sounds in cartoon dialogue. Shapes for the vowels and "M," "N," and "W" are shown here.

Nevertheless, the rules governing the animation of mouth actions are few and simple; in fact, the simpler the animation of mouth actions, the better the results in most cases.

An experienced animator usually absorbs the overall feeling of the dialogue before deciding which words, syllables, or sounds should be accented. (Animators have learned that it is not necessary to put each vowel or consonant into lip-sync animation; as a matter of fact, it is almost impossible to animate an action for each syllable in a sentence, and it should not be attempted.) Looking at his or her reflection in a mirror while repeating the recorded dialogue will help the animator select—and later draw—appropriate expressions for complete sentences. After such decisions have ceen made, the next step is to pencil in roughly the key positions for the mouth actions to be accented. The in-between drawings will usually carry the balance of the animated dialogue. The accompanying illustration shows some mouth actions that are frequently used in animated cartoon dialogue. It should be remembered that sometimes facial expressions, as well as head, shoulder, arm, and hand movements, should be animated to complement the lip movements for synchronized-voice animation.

Using Close-Ups

Another technique that can be used to animate a subject is that of making close-up shots during photography. Examples would be a close-up shot of the head rather than an entire figure, or a close-up of hands holding an object or pointing out its features. This method—in addition to requiring the preparation of less artwork—results in the presentation of a "cleaner," less distracting image on the screen.

Cutaway and Reaction Shots

Showing the face of the person being spoken to (in a conversation between two characters) is much easier than animating the lip movements of the one speaking; this is called a reaction shot. Showing the item under discussion, rather than the character talking about it, is also a great saving in production time. The character can be used merely to get attention and start the scene. The continuing voice is an easy and natural bridge between an animated scene and the thing being discussed. The same principles apply when education or training is to be the end use of the film.

Shortcuts in Animation

One means of keeping animation costs down is to use animation shortcuts early in the production stages of the film. Although most of the animated actions will be the result of conventional animation processes, one can achieve many actions and movements with other methods that result in a saving of time and money. Through the frequent use of guides and gimmicks to satisfy the varied animation requirements, effects that seem to be fully animated can be obtained with surprisingly few drawings. As time- and budget-savers, the value of these techniques is practically incalculable and, in most cases, the savings will not be made at the expense of animation quality.

Limited Animation. Two principles that can lead to economy and effectiveness are creativity and simplicity. By combining them with the technique described here, the animators have at their disposal a versatile and vital tool.

In limited animation, single drawings are strategically placed in the animation sequence and projected for several seconds as stills. Such drawings must be carefully conceived to illustrate key ideas in the script, and each drawing must possess so much impact that viewer interest will not wane during its screening. After the still, an animated transition to the next scene takes place. This transition sequence can consist of several drawings (cels) that reshape the previous still picture into the one that will follow. Thus, the number of drawings needed can be reduced to approximately 20 percent of the number required for a fully animated sequence.

The costs for this technique can be less per minute than for shooting other types of animation. And, when well done, limited animation will be regarded by the viewer as a quality production, not as a substitute for total animation.

Scratch-Off. In full animation, it is possible that each frame of film will be different. As a result, the preparation of numerous cel overlays may be required (for example, every second of super 8 or 16 mm film can call for as many as 24 drawings; 1440 drawings for a one-minute film). It is easy to see why full animation is time-consuming and expensive!

Suppose, for example, that an animator wants to show water flowing through a pipe. Full animation will require, in addition to the base art, the preparation of many cel overlays. Each cel must contain a progressively longer black line to represent the water. The artist will have to prepare a whole stack of cels and then give them to the camera operator, who must photograph the base art in combination with the first cel, then with the next cel showing a slightly extended line of black, and so forth.

The same completely animated effect can be accomplished with one piece of base art and one cel overlay. To do this, it is necessary first to prepare the base art. Then, a cel overlay with the completed black line has to be made. Next, the film should be exposed using one of the two following procedures:

A. *For 35 mm and 16 mm cameras without reverse filming capability:*
1. Load the camera with 35 mm or 16 mm film, perforated on both edges.

2. Turn either the artwork to be filmed or the camera upside down.

3. Make a single-frame exposure. (This shot will be of the piping full of water, or in other words, the black line.)

4. Scrape away a small amount of pigment from the leading end of the black line.

5. Make another exposure.

6. Repeat steps 4 and 5 until the entire line has been removed.

7. Have the film processed and then turn the segment of film containing this sequence end-for-end during the editing operation.

NOTE: Basically, this technique can be used with film perforated on one edge, such as 8 mm and super 8. Because the procedure is more involved, however, you should consult a film laboratory before attempting to do it.

B. *For cameras with reverse filming capability:*

1. Set the camera for reverse drive and advance the film (without exposing it) the number of frames needed to cover the scene length.

2. Make a single-frame exposure. (This shot will be of the piping full of water; in other words, the last frame first.)

3. Scrape a small amount of pigment from the leading end of the black line.

4. Reverse the film one frame.

5. Make a single-frame exposure.

6. Repeat steps 3, 4, and 5 until all of the line has been removed.

Cutouts are made from thin illustration board rather than from a cel.

Cutouts can be moved by hand from one position to another.

In both of the cases described above, the result will be that when the final film is projected in the normal forward direction, the line will "grow" on the screen as effectively as though multiple-cel overlays had been used.

Progressive Disclosure. A method of concealing, then disclosing, something that has been part of the art all of the time is progressive disclosure, which often is combined with the technique of planned double exposure. For example, suppose that the animator wants to show a moving radar signal. The background must be rendered in dark colors, the signal in white. The background must be shot separately, then the signal arc double-exposed. In early frames, part of the arc will be concealed behind a black cel prepared with a fan-shaped opening. In later frames, the fan-shaped opening can be pulled back to disclose more of the arc. In this way, the radar signal arc not only moves across the background, but it grows as more and more of it is disclosed. Again, only a single art cel is required for the signal; the disclosure cel and double exposure at the camera are substituted for multiple-cel overlays.

Cutouts. When used as an animation technique, the cutout has many functions and, in certain instances, is almost indispensable. It is made from an animator's drawing and is inked and opaqued on thin illustration board instead of a cel. The illustration board, after the inking and opaquing processes have been completed, is cut out along the outer ink lines. Then the cutout is usually placed on the background and *held* in one position for the amount of film footage indicated on the exposure sheets. It can also be moved by hand, from one position to another, according to indications on an accompanying guide.

Often, the cutout can be used in place of a *held cel* and results in a great saving in the inking and opaquing processes.

Although cutouts are frequently used instead of conventional animation, they are not used at the expense of reduced quality in an animated action. The overall effect of some animated actions where cutouts are used is usually smoother than the action obtainable with other animation methods.

On Twos. Instructions to a camera operator to shoot *on twos* calls for him to expose two frames showing identical views before he incorporates any alterations. This practice doubles the scene's length and effectively halves the cost, yet detracts very little, if any, from the apparent smoothness of most types of action. Exposing on twos suffices for all but the slowest and the fastest actions in animation. The speed of the subject's move determines the number of drawings needed.

• *See also:* A AND B ROLL EDITING.

Further Reading: Andersen, Yvonne. *Make Your Own Animated Movies.* Boston, MA: Little, Brown and Company, 1970; Halas, John, ed. *Computer Animation.* New York, NY: Hastings House, 1974; Halas, John and Roger Manvell. *The Technique of Film Animation,* 4th ed. London, England: Focal Press Ltd., 1976; Heraldson, Donald. *Creators of Life: A History of Animation.* New York, NY: Drake Publishers, 1975; Lutz, E. G. *Animated Cartoons.* New York, NY: Gordon Press, 1976.

Anschütz, Ottomar

(1846–1907)
German photographer, experimenter, and inventor

Anschütz was an early worker in the photography of moving objects and one of the first to utilize the focal-plane shutter. He did serial pictures of men and animals in motion and, in 1887, devised stroboscopic viewers for the examination of these pictures. These devices may be said to be forerunners of the motion picture.

ANSI

American National Standards Institute (formerly, ASA: American Standards Association) is an organization that promulgates standards for the manufacture, testing, and evaluation of products. Photographic standards include such things as film sizes, sprocket hole dimensions and spacing, lens testing, shutter performance, specifications for standardized lens mounts, and hundreds of other topics.

Because of long-established usage, the designation "ASA" has been retained as a prefix in film speed ratings, and a parallel designation, "ASAP," has been adopted for paper speeds. Thus, a black-and-white negative film rated by the procedures set forth in ANSI Standard PH2.5 would be properly described as having an American National Standard speed of, say, *ASA 100.* Similarly, a paper rated by the procedures in Standard PH2.2 would be said to have an American National Standard speed of *ASAP 50.*

• *See also:* ASA, ASAP SPEEDS; BSI SPEEDS; DIN SPEEDS; GOST SPEEDS; SENSITOMETRY; SPEED SYSTEMS.

Antifoggant

An antifoggant is a compound that retards or prevents the formation of chemical fog during development of a photographic image. Its action prevents significant development of unexposed silver halides while the exposed halides are being developed. This action is at maximum effectiveness during the time normally required for an image to be properly developed. However, if an emulsion is left in a developer long enough, all silver halides, exposed and unexposed, will eventually be reduced to metallic silver.

When a compound that inhibits development in this manner is included as a basic ingredient of a developer, it is commonly termed a *restrainer;* when such a compound is added to an already compounded developer, it is called an *antifoggant.* The majority of normal- and high-contrast metol-hydroquinone developers contain the inorganic compound potassium bromide as a restrainer. Phenidone-hydroquinone developers require additional restraining action, which is usually achieved by using benzotriazole as well as bromide.

The two most widely used antifoggants are the organic compounds benzotriazole and 6-nitrobenzimidazole nitrate. They have different uses and are not interchangeable.

Benzotriazole (*Kodak* Anti-Fog No. 1)

This organic compound tends to suppress fog when added to a film or paper developer, and thus effectively increases contrast by producing relatively fog-free negatives and clean highlights in the prints. Benzotriazole is useful when films or papers tend to show fog from excessive age or unfavorable storage conditions, when long storage of films or papers has occurred between exposure and processing, and when forced development seems necessary. It is also useful in retarding fog during warm-weather processing, when it may not be possible to maintain the developer at 20 C (68 F).

Preparation. Kodak anti-fog no. 1 is supplied in both tablet and powder form. Add the tablets directly to the developer solution and stir until completely dissolved. They dissolve more rapidly if crushed. A 0.2 percent stock solution is normally prepared from the powder form. To make an approximately 0.2 percent stock solution, dissolve 2 grams of the powder in 1 litre (or 30 grains in 1 quart) of hot water.

Instructions for Use. The quantity of Kodak anti-fog no. 1 necessary to suppress fog depends on the activity of the developer. Add the tablets or stock solution as indicated in the table that appears below.

These quantities can be increased as much as 50 percent, if necessary, but any excess should be avoided.

Use of Antifoggant

Type of Developer	Tablets per quart of developer	Stock solution (0.2%) (in ounces) per quart of developer
Low-energy, such as Kodak developers D-76, DK-20, D-23, D-25, Microdol	1	1/2
Medium-energy, such as Kodak developers DK-50, DK-60a, D-61a (tray or tank dilution)	2	1
High-energy, such as Kodak developers D-19, D-52 (1:1), D-72 (1:1 or 1:2), Dektol (1:1 or 1:2), Selectol (1:1)	3	2

CAUTION: An antifoggant is not a cure-all and under normal circumstances is not required. Used carelessly or otherwise than as directed, it may produce a loss of emulsion speed and a tone change in prints.

6-Nitrobenzimidazole Nitrate (*Kodak* Anti-Fog No. 2)

This antifoggant tends to suppress certain types of fog when added to a film prehardener or film developer. It is useful against fog caused by aldehydes in prehardeners and developers, and is also effective against fog caused by aeration of developers. It is not interchangeable with benzotriazole.

Kodak anti-fog no. 2 is a specialized antifogging agent recommended for use in Kodak prehardener SH-5 and in the high-emulsion-speed developer Kodak developer SD-19a. In order to allow convenient measurement of the small quantities needed, Kodak anti-fog no. 2 is usually used as a 0.5 percent stock solution. To prepare a 0.5 percent stock solution, dissolve 1 gram of Kodak anti-fog no. 2 in 200 cubic centimetres (18 grains in 8 ounces) of distilled water.

• *See also:* AERIAL FOG; BENZOTRIAZOLE; DEVELOPMENT; FOGGING; 6-NITROBENZIMIDAZOLE NITRATE.

Aperture

Aperture is the iris diaphragm opening in a lens. In combination with the magnifying/reducing characteristics of the lens, the aperture determines the size of the bundle of light energy that reaches the film. The *relative aperture* is an indication of the light-transmitting power of various aperture settings. It is a ratio of the actual diameter of the opening to the focal length of the lens. Each setting is designated by an *f*-number, which is calculated by dividing the focal length of the lens by an aperture diameter. For example, if a 50 mm (2-inch) lens has a maximum diameter of 25 mm (1 inch), its relative aperture is $50/25$, or $2/1$, or 2. This is written "*f*/2." When set to the same relative aperture (*f*-stop or *f*-number), all lenses transmit the same amount of light, except for slight differences caused by transmission of the glass elements and variations in lens coating.

When a lens is focused to a distance greater than its own focal length from the film plane (as in close-up photography), the marked *f*-numbers are no longer accurate. Instead, the *effective aperture* must be calculated by dividing the focal length into the lens-to-film distance and multiplying the result by the relative aperture (marked *f*-number).

• *See also:* DIAPHRAGM; *f*-NUMBER; FOCAL LENGTH; *f*-STOP; RELATIVE APERTURE.

Apochromatic

An apochromatic lens is a lens that has been corrected for chromatic aberration of three principle wavelength groups, commonly red, green, and blue. As a result, virtually all visible light is brought to a common plane of focus, providing a sharper image (other things being equal) than that from a two-color corrected (achromatic) lens. Apochromatic lenses are essential where the most precise and sharp images of subjects are required, such as in large-format color photography, photomechanical repro-

duction, and the making of separation negatives.

• *See also:* ABERRATION; ACHROMATIC; LENSES; OPTICS; PHOTOMECHANICAL REPRODUCTION.

Archer, Frederick Scott

(1813–1857)
English photographer and sculptor

Archer invented the collodion wet-plate process in 1850. The process was the first practical method of producing lasting negatives on a glass base. Archer had been using the Calotype process, but wanted higher quality results than those produced in prints from paper negatives. He published the details of the collodion wet-plate process in *The Chemist* (London, March 1851) but never patented the process. It became one of the most used procedures in photography, and was still being used by photoengravers as recently as the late 1930s. He also discovered a method of stripping the collodion image from the glass base, a process used in photomechanical work.

• *See also:* AMBROTYPE.

The construction photograph, if it is to communicate something of the finished architectural design from an incomplete building, must be tightly composed to utilize whatever dramatic elements are on hand to distract the eye from the sense of incompletion. Photo by John Veltri.

Architectural Photography

Photographs of man-made structures are taken either for records or for illustrative purposes. Pictures that record planning (for example, models and site surveys), stages of construction, and detail and overall views of the completed building are required by architects, construction firms, and government agencies, such as inspection and building-survey departments. Illustrative pictures that concentrate on the finished appearance and function of a building are used by architects and designers, construction and landscape contractors, owners, publishers, teachers, and producers of educational materials. Manufacturers or suppliers of materials and equipment also need pictures showing their products in use in the building. The specific requirements of these potential clients are quite distinct, and the photographer must be sure to take the kinds of pictures that are wanted and needed.

Construction Pictures

Construction-record pictures may be used as a proof of progress from contractor to architect, or from architect to client. For accuracy, it may be necessary to take each succeeding set of pictures from the same original camera locations, and they should be made at useful intervals. Excavation, foundation, and roughing-in work produce visible changes quite slowly; a space of 10 to 14 days between pictures may be more than adequate. The remainder of the work may proceed more rapidly, so pictures will be required every three or four days. As a job progresses, additional viewpoints will probably be needed for adequate coverage. The photographer should establish these elements with the client before the job begins and should review changing requirements as the work progresses.

Illustrative Pictures

The uses of illustrative pictures can vary greatly. The architect may want pictures that concentrate on overall design to show to prospective clients, and pictures that show the functioning or other aspects of the building to use with professional associates. A landscape contractor will want a different kind of view of the finished project than will the manufacturer of the window units or the facing stone. The owner will want yet other kinds of exterior and interior pictures to attract tenants or buyers. A textbook publisher may want a single illustration that sums up the building, while a writer for an architectural magazine will want a series of pictures related to the points the article is covering. Educational clients

When photographing an angle view of two walls that form a corner, marked convergence of parallel lines on one wall is minimized by partial adjustment of the camera position to allow some convergence on both walls. The wall most nearly head-on to the camera should have the least convergence.

In doing a thorough photographic interpretation of a single subject, you will probably discover the strongest and most exciting views only after considerable study of the subject—preferably over a period of several days and under various lighting conditions. This building has a certain monumental quality. To interpret this quality, the photographer has chosen an almost abstract treatment of the subject as a structural shape. The apparent lack of human scale is also emphasized by the absence of human figures or human-scale objects such as trees or automobiles.

usually want color slides that concentrate on aspects of design.

Consultation with Client

With so many different possible requirements, consultation with the client is essential. There are two aspects of consultation—one regarding the picture content, and the other regarding business arrangements.

The discussion of picture content should cover:

1. What kind of building is involved: residential, institutional, or industrial?
2. What does the client want the pictures for: technical record, display, advertising, illustration?
3. What are the important construction aspects to be shown?
4. What are the important, unusual, or innovative design features of the building?
5. What are the absolutely essential views: exterior, interior, details?
6. What functions are to be shown: Will the predominant activity in the building be human (for example, bank, school, home) or nonhuman (factory, computer or telephone equipment center, and so forth)? Is it necessary (or possible) to show the building being used?
7. What additional features should be shown: landscaping, other decoration (fountains, sculpture, and the like), environment, facilities (parking space)?
8. What are the problems in the way of photography: ongoing construction, uncompleted portions, unwanted surroundings?
9. How is the building situated in relation to the site and to the sun?
10. What arrangements must be made for accessibility: clearance or permission, contact person, hours, and so forth?
11. What additional information is available about the building: plans, brochures, sketches, renderings?

The business discussion should establish:

1. The work the photographer is to do.
2. The schedule for performance and delivery.
3. The number of pictures involved and the number of copies of each.
4. The ownership of negatives or transparencies after completion of the job.
5. The costs and expenses included.
6. The billing or invoice requirements.
7. The schedule of payments.
8. An equitable method of changing, expanding, or terminating the job.

These details should be included in a purchase order, contract, or at the very least a letter of agreement between the photographer and the client.

Architectural Understanding

In his or her own approach to the job, the photographer must first understand the nature and unique qualities of the building. Then the technical approach for obtaining the required pictures must be planned.

Architectural understanding comes from at least three sources: background study—at the minimum, a course in architectural history or appreciation; discussions with the architect and with those who use the building; and personal investigation of the building. Things to consider include the following.

Relatedness to the Environment. Does the structure exist as a self-contained unit essentially unrelated to its surroundings? This is the case with many traditional two-story houses, office buildings, and industrial plants. If so, the pictures should concentrate on showing the building as a closed, freestanding object.

On the other hand, does the structure open itself to the environment, breaking down the sense of solid walls to let inside and outside space flow together? In this case, the pictures should reveal how the surroundings and the building merge. They should look to the interior from the outside and look out to the environment from within. Ranch-house, residential design and many modern service buildings project this feeling. Some high-rise office and apartment buildings incorporate both aspects. On the ground level, plazas and open design let inside and outside flow together, inviting traffic and use; as the building rises, a transition to a self-contained structure standing distinct and isolated in the air takes place, emphasizing the privateness of the space within.

Volume. A building encloses volume, which may appear to be either a solid mass or a volume of space. Is it essentially a cube, sphere, pyramid, or other solid that has had the necessary openings cut into it and the required spaces carved out? Or is it a collection of functional spaces marked off by the most flexible, and least limiting, sense of walls?

Texture. What is the texture of the building? Up close, texture is defined by the materials used: glass, rough or smooth stone, polished metal, wood. In an overall view, it is determined by the rhythm of de-

sign variations on the surface: the repeated pattern of windows, the overlapping of siding boards or shingles, the contrast between large areas of different materials or colors, the outward extension of repeated wings or ells.

Decoration. Is there a sense of decoration about the building, or is the surface neutral, expressing only the quality of the structural materials or the underlying structure? If there is a decorative aspect, has the architect constructed decoration or decorated construction? Is the decoration best appreciated in an overall massing of detail or by separate examination of the various elements?

Use of the Structure. Is the building designed on a human scale for human use? If so, it will be best to include some people in the pictures. In contrast, monumental structures, industrial buildings, and

Building's texture is shown in contrast of coarse, pebbly stone used in lower area and smooth, finished blocks of the tower. Note also play of light and shadow on blind windows.

the like will look more impressive without human beings in them.

These and similar considerations help define the intangible nature of a building. They will determine the emotional quality that the photographer aims for in the pictures.

The Technical Approaches

Other factors determine the technical approaches to the job, because they affect what pictures you can get, and how it is possible to get them.

Exterior Views. For exterior views, geography and the path of the sun in relation to the building are of utmost importance. Which sides are lighted at a given time of day in a particular month? Where do the shadows fall? In addition, what are the surroundings like? Is there unfinished construction or landscaping, or an obtrusive, unrelated building that must be concealed? What viewpoint will accomplish this? Is it possible to get far enough away for an undistorted overall view? Will it be necessary to get into or on top of a nearby building to achieve a certain view? How many camera positions will be required, at what times of day, and what focal length lenses must be used?

Interior Views. For interiors, the light and the working space are the prime concerns. To what extent can existing light be used? How much must be added? In black-and-white work, exterior and interior light usually can be combined without problems, but for color pictures, the differences in the color temperatures of various sources must be adjusted. The diffuse quality and discontinuous color of fluorescent lighting pose special problems.

Height and vault of the dome are given added three-dimensionality by the statue, photographed from below.

For interior views, some shift of furniture and lighting may be necessary to strengthen composition and record significant detail. Lila Schneider, designer. Photo by John Veltri.

Architectural Photography

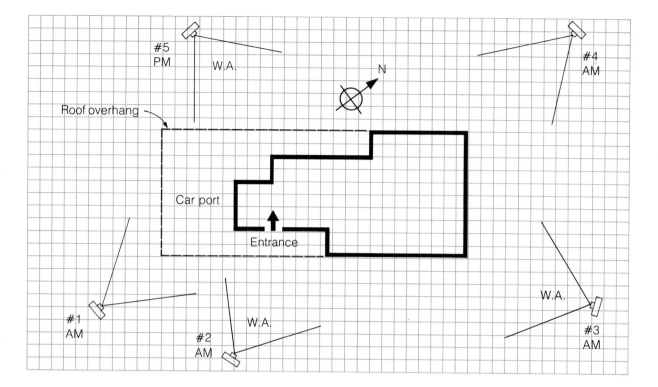

(Above) You can make rough sketches on graph paper similar to these drawings to help plan your exterior shooting. Distances or dimensions may be estimated, but overall proportions must be accurate to be useful. Locating north is essential for relating camera positions to the sun's direction and time of shooting. Camera positions and coverage can be accurately plotted with a protractor or normal angle-of-view guides. Notes should record the shot number, intended lens, and time of shooting. (Below) These symbols may prove convenient when drawing planning sketches. Other elements may be sketched and identified by notes.

Convenient plan symbols

Solid wall

Window in wall
or
window in wall.

Door, showing hinged edge, arc of swing.

Stairs. Arrow begins on floor level of plan. Note shows direction of travel.

Common double stair, one above the other.

Other elements can be roughly sketched in outline, identified by notes.

Electrical outlet

Available Space. Working space and maneuverability are important considerations. Is there enough room to set up a camera and lights to take in the desired area? With what lens? In working out interior and exterior coverage, it is extremely helpful to have plans of the building. While the photographer should be able to read a building plan, those used by the architect or contractor usually are far more detailed than the photographer requires and are certainly too bulky to use easily on the job. A small, simplified plan incorporating only photographically relevant information can easily be made from the full plan or from personal inspection of the building. (See the accompanying illustration.)

A protractor or a set of angles drawn on celluloid will show whether a particular lens will take in the desired area at a given camera distance, when used with an accurately proportioned sketch or plan. The

Architectural Photography

horizontal angle of view of the lens should be plotted; do not plot the angle that covers the diagonal of the film format (which is usually the angle given in lens specifications).

Camera Positions. In working out camera positions, it is important to remember that the pictures must convey a sense of three-dimensional volume. Flat, head-on views that show only a single, evenly lighted plane lack the dimension of depth within the structure. Volume is conveyed by angle views that show at least two planes (adjoining walls), and preferably three (two walls and roof or ceiling; or two walls and ground or floor) or four planes (two walls plus roof or ceiling and ground or floor). Flat views reveal symmetry, pattern, and overlapping forms in ways that angle views cannot. They tend to emphasize decoration or surface qualities, while angle views emphasize structure.

Equipment

Cameras. Serious architectural photography requires a view camera equipped with full front and back movements and capable of taking film sizes at least up to 4″ × 5″. (*See:* VIEW CAMERA.) A 35 mm camera is useful for slides and for some kinds of detail pictures, especially under difficult conditions during construction. However, even when equipped with a "tilt-shift" or "perspective control" lens (one with an adjustable front element group), the small-format camera is not adequate for the variety of problems that will be encountered. Nor can its small negative record the great amount of sharply detailed information that is commonly required in an architectural photograph. A 120/220 film single-lens reflex camera is also too limited, even those models with built-in bellows and a small lens-rise/-tilt capability. On occasion, a roll film, super-wide-angle, or panoramic camera may be required. Such a highly specialized instrument can often be rented when needed; it is not a necessary early investment.

The lens and back movements of a view camera provide the greatest control of image perspective and sharpness. The camera back should revolve at least 90 degrees to change easily between vertical and horizontal pictures, to help align straight lines in the subject with the picture edges, and to facilitate

Interior plans usually must be on a larger scale than exterior plans to include sufficient detail to permit accurate planning. Written notes and symbols record essential information.

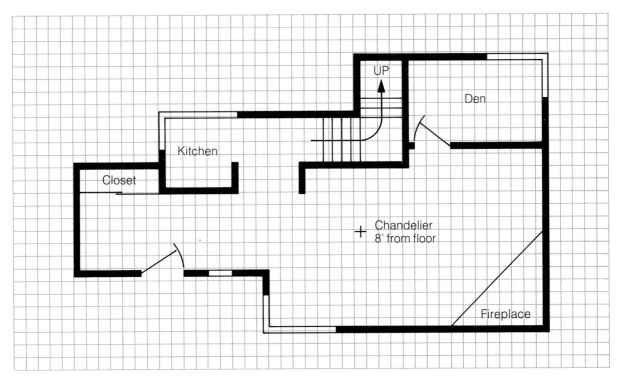

insertion and removal of film holders. Spirit levels on the camera are essential for accurate setting up; the circular, single-bubble type indicates both the horizontal and vertical leveling when the bubble is centered.

Tripod. A tripod is also essential. Architectural photographs are commonly taken at very small apertures for maximum depth of field; consequently, long exposures are the rule rather than the exception. The tripod must be a heavy-duty one that is absolutely rigid even at maximum extension, which should be about six feet high. Many photographers find a lightweight, two-wheeled, collapsible hand truck useful for transporting the equipment case, tripod, and a small, light stepladder on the job.

Lenses. Most architectural assignments require the use of more than one lens. A wide-angle lens will be most often used in interiors and will frequently be called on for exteriors as well. A normal-focal-length lens is preferable to avoid wide-angle "distortion" whenever possible, but it will not achieve the same degree of separation by making background elements smaller and seemingly farther away. A long-focal-length lens facilitates working from a distance and can provide close views of otherwise inaccessible details. All lenses should be good quality achromats with a wide circle of coverage to permit the maximum use of camera movements when required. A lens hood or an adjustable compensium (bellows shade) is required for exterior photography.

Spot Meter. A spot meter will overcome the problem of obtaining accurate luminance readings when the camera is a good distance from the building. Various models read a very narrow angle of light reflected from the building to the camera position, or an adjustable small-area probe reads selected portions of the image when inserted in place of a film holder in the camera.

Films and Filters

Fast films are seldom required for architectural subjects. The greater resolution and very fine grain

These three illustrations show the effect of varying the subject-to-camera distance. As the point of view is altered, the relationship of varying parts of the buildings are equally altered. Photos by John Veltri.

Architectural Photography

of medium- and slow-speed black-and-white emulsions are far more useful. Black-and-white infrared film provides extreme lightening of foliage and landscape; it is finding increasing use in architectural illustration because of the dramatic separation it makes between a building and the natural surroundings. Color films are chosen according to whether transparencies or negatives are required; they are also chosen to match the color temperature of the illumination.

Filtration with color films is generally limited to converting or balancing the light to match the emulsion in use. For illustrative pictures with black-and-white films, medium or deep yellow filtration is often used outdoors to emphasize clouds in the sky. A red or green filter provides significant darkening of a blue sky along with changed rendition of green foliage. A red filter will darken the greens; a green filter will lighten them. With tungsten light and a panchromatic film, a yellow-green filter provides the most accurate translation of various color brightnesses into equivalent shades of gray. For detail shots, filters may be chosen to increase color differentiation and emphasize such things as tile patterns

A large foreground imparts a greater sense of depth to a photograph. The preponderance of dark over light and a sky filled with clouds also contribute to the illusion. I.M. Pei & Partners, architects; Araldo Cossutta, Partner in charge. Photo by John Veltri.

Architectural Photography

Photograph at left, of United Nations tower, was taken at sunrise; photo at right was taken a half-hour later. Deep reddish tone of first picture has changed to a softer yellow tone. No filters were used. Harrison and Abramovitz, architects. Photos by John Veltri.

Architectural Photography

or wood grain. With both black-and-white and color films, a polarizer is effective in reducing or eliminating glare from windows, paneling, floors, or other smooth surfaces. It is also used to darken skies and to increase color saturation.

Techniques

The fundamental technique of architectural photography requires a mastery of view camera adjustments. In brief outline, the procedure for setting up is as follows:

1. Place the camera on a tripod at the desired distance and angle from the building, with all movements "zeroed" at their normal horizontal and vertical settings. The camera must be level.
2. Open the shutter and move the lens standard up, down, left, or right until all of the building is included within the picture area on the ground glass.
3. Examine the image for vertical distortion; tilt the back to make vertical lines parallel as desired.
4. Examine the image for horizontal distortion; swing the back to correct convergence. (Note that in an angle view of two walls that form a corner, swinging the back until it is parallel with one wall will eliminate all this wall's horizontal convergence, but may produce extreme convergence in the other wall. Usually a partial adjustment, leaving some convergence in the first wall, will produce a better result. The wall most nearly head-on to the camera should have the least convergence of the two walls in order for the image to look normal.)
5. Swing or shift the lens as needed to make final adjustments of the image placement within the picture area.
6. Focus on a point about one third of the way into the subject; stop down to working aperture; if necessary, tilt the lens to align the depth of field with the central plane of the subject.

Exterior Light. In exterior views showing two walls, the wall of principal interest should be more nearly head-on to the camera and more brightly lighted than the other, receding, wall. In direct sun, the brightness ratio of lighted side to shadowed side may be extreme; meter the two sides carefully to determine the range. In color photography, it is usually necessary to expose correctly for the bright wall and let the shadowed side go. Instead, it may be possible to insert a precisely cut neutral density filter in a mask box in front of the lens to reduce the intensity of the bright parts of the subject. In black-and-white photography, it is simple to expose adequately for the shadowed wall and reduce development to hold the highlight areas to a printable density.

As the sun's position changes from east to west during the day, its relative angle in the sky increases and then decreases. In addition, the maximum angle is higher in the summer months than in the winter months (in the northern hemisphere). For buildings with extreme roof overhangs, marquees, balconies, or other projections, it may be necessary to shoot in the early morning or late afternoon, when the low-angle light penetrates beneath the overhangs.

A wall facing north receives no direct sun at any time. If this is the principal wall, choose a time when it is relatively brighter than the adjoining wall to be shown, and increase development to increase the contrast range between the two.

Direct light from a raking angle reveals maximum texture. Head-on light eliminates the shadows that reveal surface variations, as does the diffuse light from an overcast sky or the light from the north sky.

Scale. When foreground elements such as framing foliage are included to give a sense of depth, their relative size affects the apparent scale of the building as well as the apparent distance to the building. A normal- or long-focal-length lens may be required to avoid the exaggeration that a wide-angle lens produces. Similarly, a building seems larger when the picture edges are close to its image and smaller when they are farther away, as is the case when a great deal of surrounding area is included.

Often it is valuable to show a parked car, a bicycle, or a figure or small group close to the building as an indication of scale. However, such an element must not look haphazard or messy, especially if the picture is going to be used as, for example, a formal illustration.

Double Exposure. A double exposure may be necessary to produce a picture of lighted exterior and interior. The exterior should be exposed late in the day so that shadows and overall light will seem appropriate, but while there is still sufficient light for good exposure. Interior lights should be off. The camera must remain locked exactly in place so there will be no out-of-register details when a second exposure is made after dark to record the now lighted windows and interior.

Double Printing. A stock of a variety of cloud negatives is very valuable; they can be double printed into otherwise clear skies when required.

The direction of the light in the cloud negative and in the building negative must be the same so that highlights and shadows correspond. A stock of foliage frames taken at various seasons is also valuable for adding apparent foreground elements. This technique is extremely useful to mask an unwanted building at the edge of the picture, foreground construction debris, and similar distractions. The kind of foliage should fit in with any actually photographed in the scene; pine trees and palms seldom grow together.

Time Exposure. To eliminate traffic and passersby, a long exposure may be divided into numer-

Scale of buildings is indicated by comparison with a recognizable object in the photograph, such as the bicycle in the foreground. Richard Snibbe, architect. Photo by John Veltri.

Architectural Photography

Architectural subjects include not only building facades, but also interior design. The sun filtering through the stained-glass windows reveals structure and the materials used. Kodak high speed Ektachrome film (daylight); 1/60 sec. at f/4.

ous short exposures taken at well-spaced intervals. A neutral density filter and a small aperture may be combined to require a time exposure. For example, a 40-second exposure divided into 2-second exposures taken over a period of 30 minutes or more can produce an "empty" view of a building on a well-traveled street. The technique works well inside or out, but care must be taken that standing vehicles, persons waiting in a lobby, and similar elements are not included in the same position in more than two separate exposures. Even when divided this way, a time exposure may require compensation for reciprocity failure and for the intermittency effect.

Color Temperature Balance. In interiors photographed in color, there is often the problem of balancing the color temperature of daylight coming through windows or other openings with the light from interior sources. An overcast day will minimize the daylight intensity, and its effect may be overriden with additional interior lighting. This may also be the case when the window area is relatively small, especially if the windows themselves are not included in the picture. However, the overall color balance must match from picture to picture in a set of photographs of the same interior spaces taken from various angles. It is possible to put large sheets of filter material over the windows to adjust the color temperature of the daylight. Rolls and sheets of plastic filter material are available from motion-picture and theatrical supply houses.

When the window area is large, the predominant illumination of the scene has a daylight color temperature. Then it is usually simpler to use an appropriate film emulsion and to equip interior lamps with blue "daylight" bulbs or to use electronic flash.

To photograph stained-glass windows from inside, the day must be overcast. Otherwise, the window light intensity will be so great that its details will be burned out if the interior is properly exposed, or the interior will disappear into blackness if the window is properly exposed.

Artificial Light. When artificial light is added to an interior, it should follow the natural illumination patterns. Often this may be accomplished by installing high-wattage bulbs in lamps. Separate lighting instruments must be carefully concealed and care must be taken to avoid multiple strong shadows, or glare from shiny floors, tabletops, or wall paneling. If electronic flash units are used, test exposures on instant print material are essential to evaluate light placement and balance. Generally, bounced light gives a more natural look than direct illumination.

Architectural Photography

Sense of depth is communicated by angle of view. High oblique shot of building model gives fine sense of three dimensions. Smotrich and Platt, architects. Photo by John Veltri.

If a central area is properly illuminated, dark areas may be brought up to an adequate brightness level by "painting" them with light during a time exposure. A light source is moved continuously to sweep across such areas, or a diffused flash may be fired one or more times. The supplementary light must not fall on the adequately illuminated portion of the scene, and the photographer or assistants handling the lights must not be lighted nor get between the lens and the area being "painted." The exposure of the dark areas can be determined by comparing a meter reading of the central area with a reading of the supplementary light. Total time, the number of flashes, or the distance should be adjusted so that shadow area detail will be made visible but will not rival the major portion of the picture in brightness.

Overall general illumination from ceiling panels or banks of fluorescent tubes is common in institutional buildings, office buildings, and stores. It is a soft, diffused light that creates no distinct shadows and reveals little texture. It may be necessary to add specific light sources to produce an appearance of dimension and surface in the photograph.

It is generally difficult to achieve accurate color rendition under fluorescent light. The filtration suggested for various color films will produce only an approximation of actual subject colors. Ring-around tests made with the film to be used and CC filters will find the closest balance possible. A three-color temperature meter is very useful in achieving color balance with fluorescent lights. The photographer must consult with the client, and perhaps show him or her examples of what is possible, to determine whether the results will be acceptable. If these results are not acceptable, the scene somehow must be illuminated with light of proper color balance.

Architectural Photography

Photographing a Scale Model

During planning, the architect may want a scale model of the project photographed so that he can see the various effects of sunlight at different times of the day and year. The photographer must place a single, strong light source in appropriate positions, which may be determined from an almanac, or by consulting a local planetarium, science teacher, or astronomy hobbyist.

When a model shot is to be used for display or presentation, clouds and foliage will add a sense of reality. The best clouds may be obtained by photographing the model outdoors. However, the weather may not cooperate, or the model may be too large or fragile to move with ease and safety. In this case, double printing from stock negatives will produce the required result.

• *See also:* CAMERA MOVEMENTS; MODEL AND MINIATURE PHOTOGRAPHY; VIEW CAMERA.

Further Reading: De Mare, Eric. *Architectural Photography.* New York, NY: Hippocrene Books, 1975; Molitor, Joseph W. *Architectural Photography.* New York, NY: John Wiley & Sons, 1976; Schulman, Julius. *Photographing Architecture and Interiors.* New York, NY: Whitney Library of Design, 1962; Veltri, John. *Architectural Photography.* Garden City, NY: Amphoto, 1974.

Detail of a model of a resort complex is dramatically lit to give depth and mood to the image. David Todd and Associates, architects. Photo by John Veltri.

Archival Processing (B & W Films and Papers)

Developing, fixing, washing, and drying all affect the stability and keeping qualities of photographic images. These simple steps are based on certain principles that must be observed, or the removal of all harmful residues may not be complete. Generally, processing for permanence does not require any different methods or additional steps in the process other than those normally used; careful, systematic work is the keynote.

In some kinds of photographic work, the stability of prints is not important; they are used and discarded immediately afterwards. "Stabilized" prints—that is, prints in which the silver halide is converted to compounds that are only temporarily stable—are intended for such use. Negatives, on the other hand, should always be fixed and washed properly. There have been many cases where a seemingly unimportant negative has become valuable after a time, due to unusual circumstances. If time is important, negatives can be refixed and rewashed after the prints have been made.

For most purposes, fixing and washing should be carried out according to the recommendations given by manufacturers of sensitized materials or the recommendations given later in this article. Negatives and prints processed in this way can be expected to keep for many years under normal storage conditions. Photographs intended for permanent records should be processed to achieve a condition known as archival permanence. This condition implies total removal of chemical residues harmful to the photographic image or its support.

Note that as used in photographic practice, the words "stable," "permanent," and "archival" are relative or comparative terms. They should not be taken to imply indefinite resistance to the effects of destructive agencies.

Causes of Deterioration

Small amounts of hypo (sodium thiosulfate or ammonium thiosulfate) remaining in a photographic material after processing eventually combine with the silver of the image to form silver sulfide. The result of this reaction, as seen in a black-and-white negative or print, is a stained and faded

Photo by Victor Skrebneski.

Archival Processing

picture. Stability is also impaired by traces of complex silver compounds (products of the fixing reaction) that remain in the material due to a curtailed fixing time or to an excessive amount of silver compounds in the fixing bath, a condition that exists when a fixing bath has been used beyond its useful capacity.

A further cause of deterioration in negatives and prints is exposure to unfavorable atmospheric conditions. The photographer has little or no control over this aspect of stability, but he should be aware that the effect of residual hypo and silver is greatly accelerated by high temperature coupled with excessive humidity, as well as by sulfurous matter and harmful gases in the air. Photographs intended for use in tropical climates or in industrial areas should therefore be processed for maximum stability.

In addition, the particular granular structure of a silver image has a bearing on its tolerance to residual chemicals. For example, fine-grain negatives and prints on warm-tone papers are more susceptible to attack by hypo than are coarse-grain negatives and prints on cold-tone papers. As a practical matter, however, it is easier to process all materials to a high standard of stability than to select a particular film or paper for special treatment. The purpose of fixing is to dissolve the undeveloped, light-sensitive silver halides from the emulsion. The products of this reaction are complex silver compounds. As more material is fixed in a bath of hypo, the concentration of these silver compounds in the hypo solution becomes greater. When the concentration reaches a certain critical level, some relatively insoluble silver compounds are formed; these compounds cannot be removed by washing. Moreover, as the concentration of silver in the fixing bath increases, so does the time required for complete fixing. As a practical matter, this means that you should test your fixing baths frequently to make sure that they are not used when the amount of silver they bear has reached the critical level. See the testing procedures given in this article.

Fixing

To make a negative or print as stable as possible, two conditions must be met:

1. All of the undeveloped silver halides in the emulsion must be dissolved by the fixing solution so that the silver compounds thus formed can be removed from the material by washing.
2. Both the fixing chemicals and the soluble silver compounds must be removed from the emulsion and its support by thorough washing.

Fixing Time. A single sheet of film or paper fixes in a relatively short time in a fresh fixing bath, because fresh solution is in contact with the whole surface of the material throughout the immersion time. When a batch of prints or negatives are fixed together in a tray, a different condition exists. The sheets of material adhere to one another and so prevent access of fresh solution to the surfaces. For this reason, photographic materials must be agitated and separated constantly throughout the fixing time. The effect of lack of agitation is often seen as a stained patch in the center of the negative or print, indicating that solution reached the edges of the material but failed to reach the center of the sheets. This bunching of negatives and prints during fixing is one of the most common causes of deterioration.

Each fixing time recommended by Kodak includes a safety factor that helps to compensate for the difficulties in fixing material in batches and for the slowdown of the fixing reaction by a buildup of silver compounds in the hypo solution. The fixing times recommended should not be exceeded, particularly in the case of paper prints. The reason for this will become apparent later in this article.

Practical Limits for Concentration of Silver in Fixing Baths. As stated previously, when the concentration of silver in a fixing bath reaches a certain level, insoluble silver compounds are formed that fail to leave the material in washing. A higher concentration of silver can be tolerated in a fixing bath for negatives than in one for papers. This is because chemical solutions are not absorbed by the film base. Removal of residual chemicals is therefore relatively simple. The maximum amount of silver that should be allowed to accumulate in a bath used for negatives is about 6 grams per litre of hypo solution. As a general rule, this concentration is reached when a film takes twice the time to clear that the same film would take in a fresh bath.

In fixing papers, the situation is more complex; chemical solutions are absorbed by the paper base and the baryta coating on the paper, as well as by the emulsion. As a result, residual chemicals are much more difficult to remove by washing. Experiments have shown that not more than 2 grams per litre of silver can be tolerated in a fixing bath used for papers. Obviously, when a single fixing bath is used for prints it must be tested frequently; otherwise, the permissible level of silver can easily be exceeded without the knowledge of the operator. A more certain method of fixing prints is to use the two-bath system described later in this article.

Fixing Negatives. A few negatives can be fixed in a tray if they are separated and handled carefully. In batch processing, the best method is to use suitable film hangers suspended in a tank. In this way, the films are always properly separated. Fixing is carried out with the minimum of handling, and consequently, less damage.

About one hundred 8″ × 10″ films can be fixed in a gallon of hypo solution. However, if you have failed to count the number of films processed, you can check the condition of the fixing bath by observing the time the film takes to clear. If it takes twice the time to clear that the same film would take in a fresh bath, the solution should be discarded. Remember that some types of film take much longer to clear than others; therefore, the same film must be used to check the clearing time in both the fresh bath and the used bath. Whether it is exhausted or not, a tank of hypo should be discarded after one month of use.

Fixing Prints. Prints are usually fixed in a tray and often in fairly large batches. Consequently, precautions must be taken to be sure of complete fixing if the prints are to be stable.

Always use trays or tanks that are large enough to permit easy handling of the prints. For example, not more than twelve 8″ × 10″ prints can be fixed properly in an ordinary 16″ × 20″ processing tray.

It makes no difference whether prints are placed in the fixer face up or face down; they cannot be left unattended for any length of time no matter which side is up. Bubbles form under a print that floats face down; consequently, some areas are only partially fixed. The effect may not be apparent in a black-and-white print, but it will be seen as circular, purplish stains in a print toned by one of the sulfide processes. A print that floats face up exhibits the same effect, but the purplish stains are irregular in shape.

Exhaustion Life of a Paper-Fixing Bath. The useful life of a print-fixing bath is shorter than a bath used for fixing negatives. There are two reasons for this:

1. Due to the absorbent nature of paper, silver compounds are difficult to remove from the material by washing.
2. There is always a carry-over of stop bath or rinse water to the fixer; thus the hypo solution is diluted and its working strength reduced.

This situation cannot be corrected by increasing the fixing time, because there is a significant relationship between fixing time and washing time in print processing. The recommended fixing time is 5 to 10 minutes for conventional papers, 2 minutes for water-resistant papers. Times in excess of 10 minutes permit the hypo solution, and the silver compounds it bears, to penetrate conventional paper fibers, as well as the spaces between the fibers. Paper in this condition is difficult to free from residual chemicals by washing. After a period of keeping, the effect can be seen as an overall yellow stain that extends through the paper base. It becomes apparent immediately if the print is toned by one of the sulfide processes.

Fixing Prints in a Single Bath. As successive sheets of paper are fixed in a bath of hypo, the quantity of silver in the solution builds up. When prints are fixed, a critical concentration of silver is reached after comparatively few sheets of paper have been fixed. The recommended number of 8″ × 10″ prints per gallon of solution (or the equivalent area in other sizes) is 100 for commercial processing. However, if prints with the minimum tendency to stain are required, the bath should be discarded after only thirty 8″ × 10″ sheets of paper per gallon have been processed. The above figures give only an approximate estimate of the condition of a fixing bath, because the

Photo by Karl M. Rehm.

Archival Processing

amount of silver compounds added to the solution by a print depends on how much of the silver halide in the emulsion was developed to metallic silver. Obviously, less silver halide would be left in a very dark print than in a very light one. See the testing procedures in this article.

Two-Bath Fixing. If space permits, it is always preferable to use the two-bath fixing method in print processing. This method is much more efficient and effects a considerable economy in chemicals. The prints are fixed for 3 to 5 minutes in two successive baths. The major part of the silver halide is dissolved in the first bath, and the remainder is dissolved or rendered soluble by the second bath. To operate a two-bath fixing method, follow this procedure:

1. Mix two fresh fixing baths and place them side by side.
2. Fix the prints for 3 to 5 minutes in each bath.
3. Discard the first bath when two hundred 8″ × 10″ prints per gallon of solution have been fixed.
4. Substitute the second bath for the one you have just discarded; the second bath has now become the first one.
5. Mix a fresh bath and place it beside the first one.
6. Repeat the above cycle four times.
7. After five cycles, mix fresh chemicals in both baths.
8. If five cycles are not used in one week, mix fresh solution in each bath at the beginning of the second week.

Washing

In photographic processing, the purpose of washing is to remove the fixing chemicals and silver compounds that remain in the material. Washing negatives and water-resistant papers is a fairly simple operation because chemicals are not absorbed by the base materials. Under suitable conditions, film emulsions are freed from residual chemicals after 20 to 30 minutes of washing. Water-resistent papers are freed of fixer and silver compounds in 4 minutes.

Washing prints made on fiber-base papers is a different problem; chemicals are absorbed by the paper base, and to remove them completely by washing alone is difficult. Under favorable conditions,

prints are washed well enough for most purposes after 1 hour. If prints are intended as permanent records, they should be treated with a hypo eliminator and subsequent wash to remove the last traces of hypo that remain after normal washing.

Washing Apparatus. The water in any tray or tank used for washing photographic materials should change completely every 5 minutes. This rate of change should be achieved without excessive turbulence, which can damage the films or prints, and without splashing adjacent walls or floors.

A test to determine the rate of change of water in a washer can be made quite simply. Check either the incoming or overflow water by running it into a measuring vessel. The rate of flow should equal the volume of the wash tank or tray in 5 minutes. In the case of large tanks, a proportion method can be used. If the measuring vessel is one fifth the size of the wash tanks, it should fill in 1 minute.

Washing apparatus should always be kept clean by frequent wiping and rinsing. A 10 percent solution of sodium carbonate helps to remove slimy deposits from the interior surfaces of the washing apparatus.

Water Supply. A plentiful supply of pure water is desirable in processing photographic materials for permanence. Municipal water supplies are generally satisfactory for washing negatives and prints. Water may be either hard or soft, according to the amount of calcium or magnesium salts dissolved in it. The degree of hardness has little or no effect on stability, although very soft water permits gelatin to swell excessively; this factor may be troublesome in some processes.

If you use water from a well or other untreated source, it may contain sulfides or dissolved vegetable matter. The presence of sulfides can be detected by an odor of hydrogen sulfide when the water is heated. A greenish color in the water indicates dissolved vegetable matter. These impurities can be removed by suitable filtration or treatment.

Generally, it is safe to assume that water is satisfactory for photographic washing if it is clear, colorless, and does not have a sulfide odor when it is heated.

Washing with Sea Water. Sea water is very efficient in removing hypo from negatives and prints. This fact may be of value to those who do processing on board ship. Remember, however, that salt is detrimental to the stability of a silver image, particularly if residual hypo is present in the material. Therefore, if you use sea water for washing, it is imperative to remove the sea-water salts by a final wash of at least 5 minutes in fresh water.

Wash-Water Temperature. The temperature of the wash water has a definite effect on the rate of removal of hypo and silver complexes from both films and prints. Experiments have shown that a temperature of 4 C (40 F) will slow the removal of residual chemicals, while a temperature of 27 C (80 F) will speed it up. When practical considerations as well as the physical characteristics of film and paper are taken into account, the most suitable range of temperature for washing is 18 to 24 C (65 to 75 F). See the information in the section on hypo clearing agent in this article.

Washing Negatives. You can wash a small batch of sheet films or plates in a tray, but avoid excessive turbulence, because these materials tend to scratch one another if allowed to move about too rapidly. The Kodak automatic tray siphon is an attachment that provides adequate water change in a shallow tray without the turbulence that may damage the negatives.

Large batches of sheet negatives should be suspended in hangers and washed in a tank. With suitable hangers, both films and plates can be washed in this way. For good water circulation, place the inlet at one corner at the bottom of the tank. Allow the water to overflow at the top edges of the tank. A single outlet at the top would tend to make uniform currents that might leave certain areas in the tank comparatively stagnant, and so reduce the rate of complete water change. Roll films are usually washed on spiral reels or are hung by clips in deep tanks.

To conserve water and reduce the cost of washing, do not wash negatives much longer than the recommended 20 to 30 minutes. It is also wasteful to use an unnecessarily high rate of water flow or to wash negatives in a tank much bigger than that needed to accommodate the size or quantity of material being washed.

Washing Prints. Since the conventional photographic paper base is absorbent, it is difficult to wash the last traces of hypo and silver from prints. For most purposes, adequate washing is achieved in 1 hour if the water in the washer changes completely every 5 minutes. However, the time of washing and the rate of water flow are both meaningless if the prints are not separated constantly so that water can reach every part of each print throughout the washing time. A well-designed washer can do this fairly well with small prints up to 5″ × 7″; larger prints need frequent handling to keep them separated. A number of well-designed washers are available from photographic dealers. No washer, however, can perform satisfactorily if you wash too many prints in it at one time. Use two or more tanks and wash the minimum number of prints in each. To conserve water, you can arrange three washers in series, each one at a lower level than its predecessor. In this way, fresh water from the upper tank is used to feed the two lower tanks. Prints are moved at regular intervals from the lowest tank—where the bulk of hypo

		REFERENCE CHART—*KODAK* HYPO CLEARING AGENT			
Photographic Material	Rinse After Fixing (min.)	Hypo Clearing Agent (min.)	Wash in Running Water (min.)	Capacity (20 × 25 cm prints per litre)	Capacity (8″ × 10″ prints per gallon)
Films	none	1–2	5	12–15 or equivalent	50–60 or equivalent
Films	1	1–2	5	37–50 or equivalent	150–200 or equivalent
Single-Weight Prints	none	2	10	20 or equivalent	80 or equivalent
Single-Weight Prints	1	2	10	50 or equivalent	200 or equivalent
Double-Weight Prints	none	3	20	20 or equivalent	80 or equivalent
Double-Weight Prints	1	3	20	50 or equivalent	200 or equivalent

is removed—to the intermediate tank and then to the upper tank, where washing is completed by the incoming fresh water. Do not guess at the washing time; use an alarm clock to time the intervals. See the section on hypo clearing agent.

Water-Resistant Paper Base

In the manufacture of photographic paper, there is a trend towards the use of water-resistant paper base for black-and-white papers. Archivists and others who are concerned with the long-term keeping of prints will naturally ask about the keeping qualities of black-and-white prints on papers with this new base. The answer is that the material has not existed long enough to establish reliable data on the effects of long keeping. Therefore, users of water-resistant base material should check their processing procedures to be sure that residual hypo is at the desired level. It is also important to adhere strictly to the processing and washing times recommended for the paper. The advantages of using water-resistant paper base are in the short fixing, washing, and drying times.

Hypo Clearing Agent

As stated before, sea water removes hypo from photographic materials more quickly than fresh water. Investigations into this effect have shown that certain inorganic salts behave like the salt in sea water. Unlike sea water, however, they are harmless to the silver image. Kodak hypo clearing agent (or the equivalent) is a preparation of such substances. Its use reduces the washing time for both negatives and prints. At the same time, prints attain a degree of freedom from residual chemicals almost impossible to obtain by washing them with water alone. A further advantage in using Kodak hypo clearing agent is that adequate washing can be achieved with much colder water.

Films or Plates. Rinse films or plates in fresh water for 30 seconds to remove excess hypo and then immerse them in Kodak hypo clearing agent solution for 2 minutes with agitation. Wash them for 5 minutes in a tank where the water changes completely in 5 minutes. To minimize streaks, drying marks, and the formation of water droplets on film surfaces, bathe films in Kodak Photo-Flo solution (or its equivalent) for 30 seconds and then hang the films or plates up to dry.

Papers. Rinse prints for 1 minute to remove excess hypo. Treat single-weight papers for 2 minutes, with agitation, in Kodak hypo clearing agent solution (or its equivalent) and then wash them for 10 minutes. Observe the normal recommendations concerning water flow. The prints must be agitated and separated throughout the washing time.

Rinse double-weight papers for 1 minute in clean water, then immerse them in Kodak hypo clearing agent solution for 3 minutes. Wash prints for 20 minutes with normal water flow and with constant agitation.

Prints can be transferred to the hypo clearing agent solution directly from the fixer without an intermediate rinse. This practice, however, considerably reduces the capacity of the hypo clearing agent solution. For capacity of solution with and without intermediate rinsing, see the reference chart on the preceding page.

Processing Prints for Maximum Stability

It is difficult, if not impossible, to remove the last traces of processing chemicals from photographic papers by ordinary means. For the maximum possible stability, therefore, you should use a hypo eliminator after washing.

In the past, many different formulas have been used as hypo eliminators, but most of them failed to oxidize hypo to harmless sodium sulfate. As a result, intermediate compounds, such as tetrathionate, were formed; these compounds were just as harmful to the silver image as hypo itself. In recent years, an alkaline hypo eliminator has been used with much more success. This formula, called Kodak hypo eliminator HE-1, reduces hypo all the way to sodium sulfate, which is harmless to the silver image and soluble in the final washing.

Kodak hypo eliminator HE-1

Metric

Water	500 ml
Hydrogen Peroxide (3% solution)	125 ml
Ammonia Solution	100 ml
Water to make	1 litre

The ammonia solution is prepared by adding one part of concentrated ammonia (28 percent) to nine parts of water.

Archival Processing

CAUTION: Prepare the solution immediately before use and keep in an open container during use. Do not store the mixed solution in a stoppered bottle, or the gas that evolves may break the bottle.

Directions for Use. Treat the prints with Kodak hypo clearing agent or wash them for about 30 minutes at 18 to 21 C (65 to 70 F) in running water that flows rapidly enough to replace the water in the vessel (tray or tank) completely once every 5 minutes. Then immerse each print for about 6 minutes at 20 C (68 F) in the hypo eliminator HE-1 solution, and finally wash about 10 minutes before drying. At lower temperatures, the washing times must be increased.

Capacity of HE-1 Solution. Twelve 20 × 25 cm prints per litre (fifty 8″ × 10″ prints per gallon).

Protective Coating

Even when the last traces of hypo have been removed from a print by chemical means, the silver image is liable to attack by various substances in the atmosphere. Treatment with Kodak gold protective solution GP-1 (or the equivalent) makes the image less susceptible to such deterioration.

Kodak gold protective solution GP-1

	Metric
Water	750 ml
Gold Chloride (1% stock solution)	10 ml
Sodium Thiocyanate	10 g
Water to make	1 litre

A 1 percent stock solution of gold chloride may be prepared by dissolving 1 gram in 100 ml of water.

Add the gold chloride stock solution to the volume of water indicated. Dissolve the sodium thiocyanate *separately* in 125 ml of water. Then add the thiocyanate solution slowly to the gold chloride solution, while stirring rapidly.

For Use. Immerse the well-washed print (which preferably has received a hypo-elimination treatment) in the gold protective solution for 10 minutes at 20 C (68 F) or until a just-perceptible change in image tone (very slight bluish-black) takes place. Then wash for 10 minutes in running water and dry as usual.

Approximate Exhaustion Life. Seven 20 × 25 cm prints per litre (thirty 8″ × 10″ prints per gallon). For best results, the Kodak gold protective solution GP-1 should be mixed immediately before use.

Testing Procedures

If a single fixing bath is used for prints, test the solution frequently to avoid an undesirable buildup of silver compounds. The Kodak testing outfit for print stop baths and fixing baths contains a test solution for this purpose. When a certain quantity of the fixer is added to this test solution and a yellow precipitate forms immediately, the bath should be discarded. In using the two-bath method described previously, test the second bath only occasionally. As a rule, the test is negative if the method is operated carefully, but omissions and accidents sometimes occur in a busy darkroom. Therefore, the test is worthwhile if permanence is important.

Test for Silver. Since the quantity of silver compounds necessary to cause an overall yellow stain on a print or negative is extremely small, there is no simple quantitative method available for its determination. However, the stain that might be visible after a period of keeping can be simulated by the following drop test: Place a drop of Kodak residual silver test solution ST-1 (formula given below), or its equivalent, on an unexposed part of the processed negative or print and blot off the surplus solution with a piece of clean, white blotting paper. Any yellowing of the test spot, other than a barely visible cream tint, indicates the presence of silver. If the test is positive, residual silver can be removed by refixing the print or negative in fresh hypo and rewashing for the recommended time. Prints toned in a sulfide toner or selenium toner will not yield to this treatment, however, because the residual silver has been toned together with the image. The yellow stain so formed is permanent.

Kodak residual silver test solution ST-1

	Metric
Water	100 ml
Sodium Sulfide	2 g

Store in a small stoppered bottle for not more than 3 months. For use, dilute one part of stock solution with nine parts of water. The diluted solution has limited storage life and should be replaced weekly.

Kodak hypo test solution HT-2

	Metric
Water	750.0 ml
28% Acetic Acid	125.0 ml
Silver Nitrate,	
Crystals	7.5 g
Water to make	1.0 litre

To make approximately 28 percent acetic acid from glacial acetic acid, add three parts of glacial acetic acid to eight parts of water.

Store in a screw-cap or glass-stoppered brown bottle, away from strong light. Do not allow the test solution to come in contact with hands, clothing, negatives, prints, or undeveloped photographic material; it will stain them black.

A spot-test can be used to obtain an estimate of the amount of residual hypo in a print. A drop of the Kodak hypo test solution HT-2 is applied to an unexposed part of the processed print. After 2 minutes, the reaction is complete; the stain can then be compared with the calibrated patches on the Kodak hypo estimator.

Further Reading: Editors of Time-Life Books. *Caring for Photographs.* New York, NY: Time-Life Books, 1972; Shafran, Alexander. *Restoration and Photographic Copying.* Garden City, NY: Amphoto, 1967.

Arc Lamps

An arc lamp is an electric light source that produces illumination by a discharge between two electrodes, rather than by the heating of a metallic filament. There are many different types of arc lamps, but only a few have much use in photography—the carbon arc, the zirconium arc, and the xenon arc.

The *carbon arc* consists mainly of two rods of carbon connected to the supply of current. When the tips of the carbon rods are brought into contact and the current turned on, the ends of the rods are quickly heated; if they are then separated, the current continues to flow across the gap, producing a bow-shaped discharge (hence the name "arc"). There are several different types of carbon arcs, differing mainly in the amount of current used and the structure of the carbon rods. Low-intensity carbon arcs, using solid carbons or carbons with a core of softer carbon, are used mainly for light sources in photomechanical work and blueprinting. High-intensity arcs, using carbons having a core filled with certain rare-earth oxides, are used for projection.

The *zirconium arc* contains two electrodes of zirconium and zirconium oxide, in a glass enclosure pumped to a vacuum state. In operation, the arc forms between a pool of molten zirconium and the solid electrode. This arc is used mainly in special-purpose lighting devices, such as microscope illuminators, that require a very small, intense source of light.

The *xenon arc* consists of a glass tube having a tungsten electrode at each end and a filling of xenon gas at low pressure. Unlike the other types of arcs in which most of the illumination comes from the glowing electrode, the xenon arc produces all its light in the gas filling. Its current efficiency is very high, and its brightness is comparable to that of a carbon arc. Therefore, it is used in projection work, from compact 300-watt lamps for 8 mm projectors to 900-watt and larger units for theatrical projection. It can be fired in rapid succession at rates of up to 72 times per second. Such a "pulsed-xenon arc"* is used to eliminate the need for a mechanical shutter in some kinds of motion-picture projectors or to provide synchronized lighting for very high-speed cinematography. Because its spectral output is virtually the same as that of daylight, it is widely used for copy photography with color materials, or with panchromatic materials and full-color originals.

• *See also:* ARTIFICIAL LIGHT; LIGHTING.

Armat, Thomas

(1866–1919)
American inventor

With C. Francis Jenkins, Armat devised the first practical American motion-picture projector, which he demonstrated at Koster & Bial's Music Hall in New York City in 1896. He and Jenkins arranged to have the machine manufactured at Thomas Edison's factory. It was sold for some years as the Kinetoscope.

---

* Special integrating meters are required to measure pulsed-xenon arc illumination.

Art, Photography of

Artworks are commonly thought to consist of flat images (paintings, drawings, and prints) and sculptured work (both relief and freestanding). However, many other things are now valued and exhibited for their artistic qualities, which is taken to mean their embodiment of the taste and expressive style of a period, a culture, or an individual. A partial list of such items includes coins, jewelry, costumes, furniture, ceramics, and glass and silverware.

Thus, the photography of art involves much more than just the techniques of copying two-dimensional flat images. The general and specialized techniques of small-object photography are often required, as are the techniques of close-up photography and photomacrography, when extremely small pieces or details must be recorded. Large sculptures and groupings sometimes may require the same approach as that used for a group portrait. Photographs of murals may involve the techniques of architectural photography, while photographs of displays and exhibit installations certainly will involve these techniques. Photographs made to investigate individual works or to serve as records of condition or as guides for conservation and restoration often employ the methods and materials of scientific photography.

The techniques that apply to other fields of photography are discussed in those specific articles. This article deals with those approaches and methods that are of special concern when photographing art.

Purpose and Intent

Whatever techniques may be employed, the common factor in photographing art is the need for precision and technical excellence coupled with a sensitive understanding of the qualities of the work being recorded.

Fidelity to the Subject. One aspect of these needs is fidelity to the physical qualities of the artwork—primarily color, texture, proportion, and scale. The degree of fidelity required depends upon the intended use of the picture. A slide for general lecture purposes is intended essentially to provide a kind of first-level familiarization. It must record content and color clearly and reasonably accurately; it must be of sufficient technical quality to overcome the vagaries of presentation—notably, projectors and screens of varying quality and a wide range of stray light conditions. However, a slide need not, and indeed cannot, be of the extreme quality and fidelity required to produce a facsimile of the work —a nearly identical duplicate such as is required for

Bas-reliefs such as this Hellenistic version of the Rape of Persephone composed of many levels and often intricately carved, should be lighted to show fine details clearly. In this photo, the lights should have been better positioned to eliminate the confusing double shadows. Photo by Editorial Photocolor Archives.

The Modigliani "Nude" represents an interesting problem in reproduction, because of the widely separated contrast ranges of the upper and lower areas. By adjusting exposure for the darkest areas and shortening developing time, the contrast range can be pulled together for printing on a normal grade paper. The detail (left) has been lit to bring out the texture of the painting, a different problem requiring special lighting techniques. Photos courtesy of the Solomon R. Guggenheim Museum, New York.

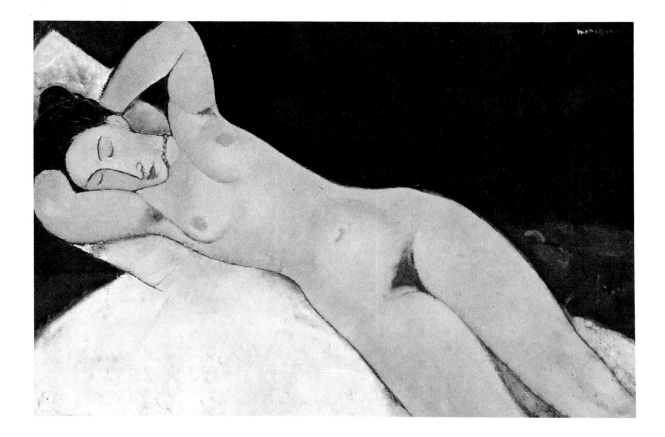

Art, Photography of

the highest quality book illustrations or for expert study. Thus, the choice of equipment, materials, and techniques is greatly affected by the desired fidelity.

Dramatization. Another major consideration in recording art is that of the photographer's approach and the resulting image. Publicity photographs of show business performers glamorize and dramatize their subjects; there is often little or no presentation of the actual human being, but rather the projection of an idealized, essentially stereotyped character. Similarly, many photographs of artworks for popular books and magazines or for superficial display are dramatized; colors are oversaturated or shifted in balance to seem "livelier"; scale is distorted to make a miniature carving look like a towering sculpture; engravings are so enlarged that the sheer graphic quality of individual lines, the "calligraphy" of the irregular deposits of ink, becomes the most important thing rather than the total image the artist created. Such distortions have a great deal to do with theatricality, but little to do with the artworks themselves.

The Straightforward Approach. To be meaningful and useful, a photograph of a work of art must be straightforward. Its purpose is to present an image in which the work speaks for itself. There is no place for manipulation or interpretation that calls attention to the photograph or the techniques used to make it; the photographer is not the artist who is to be appreciated. Unlike music, which is often intended as the starting point for highly individualized interpretation and presentation by a performer, physical works of art are self-sufficient. They must be recorded in such a way that they will be seen on their own terms.

Illustration and Display. The problem of subjective interpretation undermining straightforward presentation usually occurs only with those photographs taken for use as catalog or book illustrations or for display. When properly done, such pictures

Clarity and accuracy are essential in photographing art. Change of camera position eliminates confusing backgrounds. Adding illumination of proper color balance corrects distorted color rendition. Photo by Editorial Photocolor Archives.

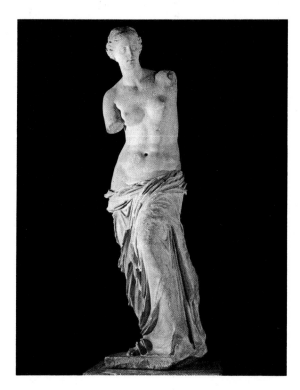

show the work from the angle and with the lighting that best reveal its beauty, grace, and strength. In the case of two-dimensional works such as paintings, this almost invariably means a head-on view lighted evenly or lighted to reveal significant texture. Three-dimensional objects may offer a variety of possible views and lighting arrangements.

Documentation. Photographs taken for purposes of documentation—for example, as file and insurance records—are not concerned with the beauty of a work, but rather with an accurate physical description. They are taken from more than one angle (front and back of a painting, for instance), with views chosen for how clearly they show size, shape, scale, condition, and identifying marks or details. Often reference devices such as a gray scale, color patches, and a centimeter-inch scale are included in the picture.

Conservation and Restoration. Photographs taken for work purposes such as conservation and restoration include overall documentation and close views that frequently concentrate on flaws and damages. Lighting and filters are carefully chosen to reveal such things as chips, cracks, dents, spots or stains, brushstrokes or tool marks, and the nature and condition of the underlying base or backing material. Pictures of this sort require extremely precise techniques because they are concerned with the minutest details of a work. Along with scientific investigation (by means of infrared, ultraviolet, or x-ray photographs), they help "fingerprint" each work for purposes of identification, authentication, dating, and attribution. For example, greatly enlarged fine line detail can aid in determining which is the earlier of two impressions pulled from the same engraving plate.

Equipment and Materials

Cameras. If the desired product is slides, a 35 mm single-lens reflex camera with through-the-lens metering is ideal. For other purposes, a larger format is desirable in order to secure images of the highest quality. A 120/220-size roll-film camera is quite suitable for installation and display records because of its maneuverability, but a small view camera may be preferred to take advantage of the adjustments that correct linear distortion, gain maximum depth of field, and make it possible to shoot past obstacles. The more controlled the shooting

In Stuart Davis' "Colonial Cubism," reds and blues are of equal tonal value, presenting special problems for black-and-white photography. Photos courtesy Walker Art Center.

situation, the larger the format can and usually should be. If the photograph is to be reproduced in color, it is valuable to shoot in a size close to that of the intended reproduction because then color quality and rendition of detail can be more accurately evaluated.

The various movements of a view or technical camera offer the greatest versatility for handling a variety of works. If most subjects are two-dimensional, other style cameras are quite suitable. However, even with flat subjects, a rising/sliding front makes it easy to center the image accurately once the camera position has been established, and a revolving back simplifies adjustments between vertical and horizontal subjects. An accessory bellows or built-in extra extension is essential for the close-ups frequently required in photographing art; rigid extension tubes and rings lack versatility.

Equally essential is a solid tripod or camera stand. Convenient lightweight supports that may be adequate for general photography are completely inadequate for this kind of work, for any vibration will degrade the image. Similarly, cameras with mirror viewing systems should permit manually locking the mirror out of the way before the shutter is released.

Shutter speeds must be tested—a simple task for a repair shop. It is not necessary to have the speeds adjusted to their marked values as long as they are

(Left) When photographed with panchromatic film, all blue and red areas merge, reproducing identically in monochrome. (Right) With yellow-orange filter, blue areas are held back and reproduce darker than red areas. This is a more normal rendition.

accurately known so that exposures can be precisely calculated. This is especially critical in color photography, and it is wise to have the speeds retested about once a year or at the first signs of variance. When the actual speeds are known, in-between adjustments can be made by a combination of *f*-stop and neutral density filter changes.

Lenses. For most work, modern standard achromatic (two-color corrected) lenses will provide excellent results. Apochromatic (three-color corrected) lenses are required only for the most critical results, and their comparatively great cost demands that there be a pressing need for them. Flat-field graphic arts apochromats deliver maximum performance with flat subjects at limited magnifications. They are such highly specialized lenses that they do not represent a good first choice for handling a variety of kinds of artworks. A slightly wide-angle lens may prove convenient for photographing large paintings in limited studio space, but with medium- and small-size works, it may bring the camera so close as to make it difficult to set up lights. For three-dimensional works, a longer-than-normal focal length is required, just as in portraiture, to avoid the foreshortened distortion caused by a too short lens-to-subject distance.

Even the best lens will deliver reduced performance if used without a shade or hood. The deepest possible hood should be used to eliminate flare and stray light, which can reduce image contrast. For a view camera, the bellows-type compendium shade provides the greatest protection and versatility.

Filters. Control of contrast and light color quality is very important in photographing art, so a wide range of filters may be called upon. Black-and-white contrast filters are used to ensure that subject colors translate into distinct, well-separated shades of gray. A No. 11 yellow-green filter should regularly be used with panchromatic film under tungsten light for proper basic translation of subject color brightnesses into equivalent gray shades. It may be that a deep red and a green will record as the same dark shade, or that a light blue and a pastel green will record as the same light tone. Filters can prevent such visual confusions, when they are chosen on the basis of the principle that a filter lightens objects of its own color and darkens those of opposite colors in the resulting black-and-white print.

Contrast Filters. Contrast filters are also valuable for eliminating marks, stains, and discolorations, or for emphasizing them, if desired for documentation. A yellow stain will disappear when photographed in black-and-white through a darker yellow filter; it will appear much stronger through a blue filter.

Filters for Color Work. For color work, conversion or light balancing filters are used to make major adjustments between light source and emulsion color balances; color compensating (CC) filters permit critical, subtle adjustments when the greatest fidelity is required.

Polarizers and Neutral Density Filters. A polarizer for the lens and for each light source is essential for controlling surface reflections and glare. Neutral density filters permit exposure adjustments without changing shutter speed or lens aperture and without shifting color balance. A series in density increase steps of one-third stop provides critical control.

Lights. Adjustability is a prime factor in selecting lighting equipment for photographing art. It must be possible to mount lights securely but to change their positions easily to accommodate works of various sizes. While electronic flash may be convenient for photographing some installations, the need to carefully adjust light placement and to balance intensity makes continuous light sources a far more practical choice.

Compared to electronic flash, continuous sources have the disadvantages of less intensity, greater bulk and heat, and, in the case of incandescent lamps, changing color balance. However, they make it possible to see exactly what the lighting effect is before any exposures are made.

Fluorescent lamps are not used because of the difficulty in precisely controlling the direction and intensity of their light, and because their output is not continuous within the range of wavelengths to which emulsions are sensitive. The relatively complex filtration required to balance fluorescent illumination with color films is not compatible with high-quality results.

Tungsten-Halogen Lamps. Tungsten-halogen lamps, so-called quartz lights, produce a great deal of light for their small size and light weight. The color temperature of the light remains virtually unchanged throughout the life of the lamp, providing consistent results without difficulty, but there is also a great deal of heat. (Some paint-removing instruments use tungsten-halogen lamps as a heat source.) Care must be taken to keep the lamps far enough from a subject to avoid physical damage or localized fading from excess heat. Accessories such as diffusers and polarizers must be kept well separated from the lamps, with plenty of ventilation, to avoid the risk of scorching or melting.

Flood and Spot Lamps. Standard tungsten photographic light sources—3200 K and 3400 K flood and spot lamps—are quite suitable when used in appropriate reflectors or in the self-contained reflector versions available in some wattages. These lamps cost less than tungsten-halogen sources, but their rated lives are significantly shorter and their output changes during use; intensity decreases and color balance shifts more and more toward the red. A good practice is to use such lamps for only about half their rated lives for color work, and then to use them only for black-and-white work. It may be valuable to record the output of such lamps when they are new as measured by a high-sensitivity color temperature meter, and to make comparison readings at frequent intervals as the lamps are used. Any significant change will quickly be apparent and may be compensated for by filter adjustments or lamp replacement.

Floodlights are useful for flat works and for general or base lighting of relief and three-dimensional works. But spotlights are required to bring out texture, provide highlights and modeling, and create

Alexander Calder's stabile "Le Petit Nez," photographed with diffused floodlight, casts a shadow that creates a distracting element in the photograph.

Bounce floodlight, created by reflecting the light from a white board, eliminates distracting shadows. Photos courtesy of the Hirshhorn Museum and Sculpture Garden, Smithsonian Institution.

specifically controlled lighting of objects. Light beams may be shaped and directed by barndoors, snoots, masks, and a variety of mirrors and other reflecting devices. Light quality and intensity can be adjusted with reflectors and diffusing materials. For critical color work, voltage-control transformers will ensure that lamps are always operating at a constant voltage for consistent color temperature output.

Films. As with camera equipment, the choice of film format is dictated by the intended use and quality requirements of the final image. The choice between color or black-and-white film is also determined by the intended use of the final image. A great deal of documentation and investigative work can be done in black-and-white; in fact, this is often the only choice because many specially sensitized emulsions are not available in color.

Black-and-White Films. Fine-grain, thin-emulsion panchromatic films are usually suitable for most black-and-white work; their relatively slow speeds are not a problem because controlled setups and long exposures are easily achieved. The major exceptions that might require fast emulsions are dimly lighted installations where it is not feasible to add illumination, and pictures of moving works such as kinetic sculptures. Specialized emulsions, including those with orthochromatic ("red blind") sensitivity or high-contrast response, may be required for copying certain kinds of prints, other photographs, and similar materials. Note that a combination of panchromatic film and a blue filter will produce results very similar to that of orthochromatic film (but the panchromatic film may not be handled under a red safelight during processing).

Color Films. Many subjects, such as engravings or metal sculptures, do not demand color rendition for effective presentation. But the bulk of presentation, display and illustrative pictures of all kinds of artworks, will be made in color, as will facsimile-quality images. The greater the need for image quality, the larger the film size must be.

It should be obvious that color film emulsions and light sources must be chosen with the intent of matching their color balances. Better results usually will be obtained from using matched lamps and emulsions than from using a conversion filter.

Virtually all color photography of art is done on positive transparency films. If color prints are required, as is increasingly the case for background and explanatory material accompanying museum displays, they may easily be made from the transparency using the excellent color reversal print materials now available. However, color prints are less suitable than transparencies for making catalog and book engraving plates, for direct study, for conservation and restoration, and for most other requirements. A serious limitation is that no color image is stable or permanent. The dyes in color images are all susceptible to color shifts and fading at various rates, depending on storage and use conditions. For this reason, color photographs are unsuitable for long-term master records. The solution is to make color separation negatives on black-and-white film that can be processed for archival permanence. New color prints can then be made at any future time without loss of quality. (*See:* COLOR SEPARATION PHOTOGRAPHY.)

Instant Print Materials. Self-processing instant print photographic materials are an important tool

(Top) When photographing sculpture out-of-doors on black-and-white film, background foliage may become a disturbing factor. (Bottom) Infrared film and a Wratten No. 25 filter will lighten the green and improve contrast. Photos of Henry Moore's "Draped Reclining Figure" courtesy of the Hirshhorn Museum and Sculpture Garden, Smithsonian Institution.

in photographing art. They are widely used for test exposures to evaluate lighting, contrast, and depth of field, especially as a preliminary to large-format color photography in which materials and processing are quite expensive. Black-and-white instant print materials are the most widely used. Color materials of this sort are less suitable because they cannot be accurately matched to the response of conventional color films, and because their results vary according to the ambient temperature at the time of use. Black-and-white instant print materials generally have much higher exposure speeds than conventional films, so it is common to use neutral density filtration to reduce the light entering the lens so that the tests can be made at the same aperture and shutter speed as for the final exposure.

Other Equipment. Accurate, tested light meters for incident- and reflected-light readings are essential. A variety of devices are required to safely hold artworks: sturdy easels of various sizes for paintings; soft boards, pins, and cloth tapes for drawings and similar works. Tables, pedestals, glass sheets, and a variety of background materials are used in photographing sculpture and other three-dimensional objects. Flats or other large baffles are used to shield the camera from light sources. A large supply of light-absorbing cloth, such as black velvet or flocked material, is essential for backgrounds, to eliminate glare in the lens from areas surrounding the subject and to prevent reflections in the subject of areas and equipment around and behind the camera. Portable black masking material and suitable support stands

When photographing works of art in color, such as Bellini's "Madonna and Child," always include in your frame a standard color bar to give accurate color reproduction. Color bar is not normally included in reproduction. Photo by Editorial Photocolor Archives.

are needed to prevent reflections in showcases or glass coverings when photographing installed works of art.

Techniques

Handling Artworks. Artworks are delicate and precious no matter what their weight and size. Extreme caution must be taken at all times to protect them from damage. This requires extra-sturdy supports and unhurried working methods.

Cleaning. Under no circumstances should the photographer attempt to clean a work to make it more presentable before photographing it. This is a job for an expert who first of all can distinguish between true dirt and the patina or other evidences of age and condition that may be considered an integral part of the work, and who knows what to use and how to use it safely if cleaning is required.

Display. Paintings and flat works should be displayed on an easel or backing board that is covered with black. Weighted cloth tapes, paper tabs, or pins can be used to secure prints and paper works in place. Cements or adhesive tapes must never be adhered to the work nor pins inserted into it (see the accompanying illustrations). Sculptures and objects should be placed at a height that permits the most convenient placement of lights, camera, and background materials.

Alignment. To be rendered without distortion, flat works must be exactly parallel to the film plane in the camera. Vertical alignment can be checked with an inclinometer, a kind of spirit level that measures the degree of tilt. It is held against a protective card over the surface of the work and the angle is noted. Then it is held against the camera back and the lens board as they are tilted to the same angle. After all is parallel, the tripod height is adjusted or the lens standard is raised to center the image. Horizontal alignment is achieved when the measured distance from the center of the lens board to each of the four corners of the work being photographed is the same. As an alternative, a small mirror can be mounted flat at the center of the subject and the camera adjusted until the lens is seen reflected in the image of the mirror on the camera's ground glass.

Lighting. Lighting is the major technique by which the qualities of a work of art are revealed. Glare from the irregular surfaces of paintings or three-dimensional objects is a lighting problem.

Glare Control. The greatest degree of glare control is achieved by using two lights equipped with polarizing screens, one on either side of the camera, and a polarizer over the camera lens. The first light is turned on with its screen in place and the lens polarizer is rotated until the maximum glare reduc-

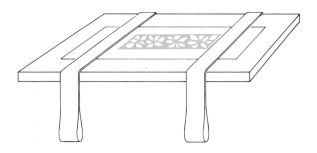

(Above) Weighted cloth tape holds paper materials flat in a horizontal position without damaging them. Tape also permits rapid changes of materials. (Below) Methods of fastening flat materials to vertical or horizontal backgrounds include: (A) stiff cardboard tab secured by a thumb tack; (B) long straight pin under a thumb tack; (C) straight pins through cloth tape. All of these overlap the border of the work and secure it by pressure. Straight pins will seldom be visible if they extend into the picture area.

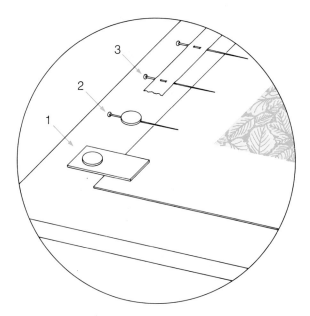

A poorly illuminated painting may show an excessive amount of surface reflection.

Surface reflection can be controlled with even illumination, a polarizing filter on the camera lens, a polarizing filter on the lights, or a combination of two or all three of these. Henri Rousseau (Le Douanier), "Artillerymen"; photos courtesy of the Solomon R. Guggenheim Museum.

Art, Photography of

tion is achieved, as seen through the camera. Then the second light is turned on and its screen is adjusted until the resulting glare has been reduced as desired; the first screen and lens polarizer are not changed during this adjustment. The complete elimination of glare may destroy all highlights on the varied form of the work, or obscure the actual texture of impasto, so the second screen may be adjusted to remove only part of the glare. If surrounding walls and equipment are reflected in the surface of the work, they must be covered with a black material.

Even Illumination. Flat works must be evenly lighted across their entire surface—an easy task with prints and paintings of up to about 3 feet in length, but more of a problem with works that may be up to 12 feet long, or more. Plenty of studio space is required, not only for camera distance, but to permit the lights to be positioned a sufficient distance from either side. If the lights are closer than 6 feet from a large work, illumination will not be evenly distributed, and hot spots near the light sources will be extremely difficult to eliminate. It is generally easier to place lights if rectangular works are turned so that the long dimension is vertical. Then multiple sources can be mounted one above another on single stands on each side. If the light direction will be evident in the final image, for example, because of strong texture lighting, shadows should fall downward or to the right because we are most accustomed to seeing things with the main light source above or at the left.

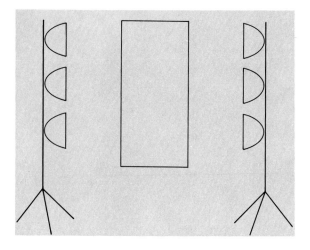

The farther the light source is from the work, the more evenly its illumination will be distributed but the less intense it will be, so banks of lights may be required. As in copy work, lights may not be placed closer than 45 degrees to the lens-subject axis without being directly reflected into the lens. With paintings, a much shallower placement is common, often with the instruments at an angle of only about 15 degrees from the surface of the painting. Texture is further revealed by adding a raking light at one side. Care must be taken that the raking light falls across the surface with equal intensity so that it does not create a hot end after the basic, even illumination has been balanced.

In photographs made for printed reproduction, a gray scale, color reference patches, and register marks should be included alongside the work *in exactly the same illumination.* They are important guides for the plate maker and printer.

Lighting Flat and Relief Artworks. Straight illustrative black-and-white copy work of line engravings and the like will need a combination of high-contrast film and flat lighting to drop out the background paper tone and capture only the ink image. But for serious documentation or facsimile illustration, panchromatic film and texture lighting must be used to retain the feeling of the entire work—the image plus the material on which it was made. The same considerations apply to works on textured paper, cloth, and wood; to collages and assemblages of actual scraps of material; to incised and relief panels and sculptures; and to similar works. The more pronounced the relief, the stronger the lighting can be from one side. Often a reflector rather than another light is used at the opposite side to reflect some illumination onto shadowed areas.

Lighting Three-Dimensional Artworks. Three-dimensional works are much more difficult to light than flat works because they must stand on some surface and be seen against some background. Both these surfaces may reveal distracting shadows, and the "horizon" line where they meet may interrupt the flow of the subject form. Shadows can be elimi-

Vertical subject orientation gives more side working space for lights, which may be mounted in banks on a single support so all move an equal distance for adjustments.

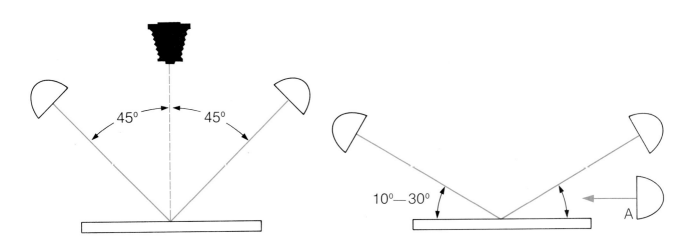

Lighting flat subjects. Lights must be at least 45° from the camera-to-subject axis to avoid direct reflection. A flatter angle and greater lamp-to-subject distance provides more even illumination. Raking light (A) brings out surface texture.

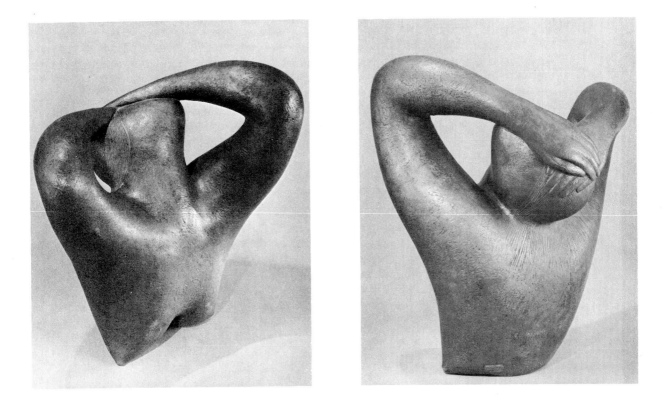

Hugo Robus' "Yearning" presents camera and lighting problems typical of sculpture. For the high camera angle chosen as most effective, the piece is placed in a floor position. Paper background is slate gray to contrast with the relatively light-toned statue. Photos above and on following page courtesy of the Solomon R. Guggenheim Museum.

nated with a ground/background of black, light-absorbing material. However, this is suitable only for light-colored objects; shadowed portions of dark objects may blend into the background. (Note that "black" papers, boards, and painted surfaces are really dark grays; they reflect too much light to become textureless and toneless in most photographs.) The more diffuse the light source, the softer the shadows it creates will be, but often a specific, intense source is required to bring out texture and form. Using a light box or placing the work a good distance from the background suspended on a sheet of glass well above the ground material are two ways to eliminate shadows. These and other arrangements can eliminate the horizon-line problem.

It is best to keep the number of lighting instruments to a minimum, for each additional light source is also an additional source of shadows. Diffuse reflectors are an excellent, trouble-free way of adding fill light to dark portions of the subject. A common technique in color photography is to use a single, intense light from above and behind to outline the subject edges and create a single, locating shadow. Front illumination is provided by a reflector picking up spill from the back light; it is soft and even and does not create problems of excessive contrast. Extremely shiny objects such as silverware can be illuminated in a surrounding translucent "tent," which diffuses the light completely. The lights are

(Above) Paper background is suspended above and behind sculpture, drawn down and forward to form a gradual slope, and weighted at front edge to hold in position. Cardboard is used to protect background while sculpture is positioned. (Below left) Lens opening for required depth of field is determined by first stopping down until variously positioned photoflood lamp sleeves all appear in acceptably sharp focus, and by then closing down two more stops for maximum definition. (Below right) Lighting is placed; main light is positioned first, then accent spotlights and fill-in floodlights are added.

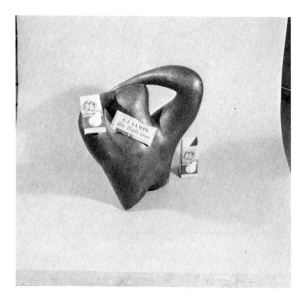

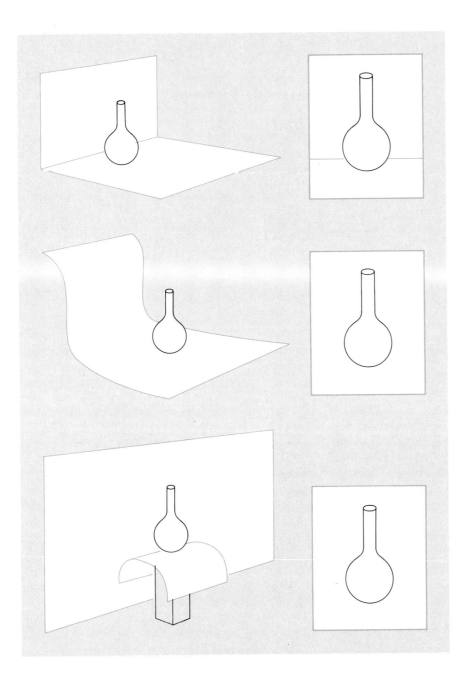

Photography of three-dimensional objects requires both ground below the object and a background. However, the line where the background and the ground below meet may be visually obtrusive. A single sheet of material may be curved to eliminate the horizon line, or the object may be placed on a stand covered with a curved material and placed in front of a background.

outside the tent, and the lens looks through a slit in the side.

Exposure. Both incident- and reflected-light meter readings are valuable in determining accurate exposures.

Incident-Light Readings. These readings (or their equivalent: reflected-light readings from an 18 percent gray card) taken at the center, corners, and intermediate positions will indicate if light intensity is even across a flat surface. They can also determine lighting ratios by measuring first the main light plus fill light intensity, then the fill light intensity only. They can also provide accurate exposure indications for subjects of normal contrast.

Reflected-Light Readings. This type of reading reveals overall contrast or brightness range when

When an object is positioned on a sheet of glass well above the ground and forward of the background, shadows fall out of camera range.

taken from the highlight and shadow areas of the subject. A spot meter is excellent for precise reflected-light readings without casting extraneous shadows. It is essential that subject contrast be measured to determine whether special processing will be required to keep it within the contrast limits of the film. Although seldom realized, this is equally as important with the areas of a painting as with a three-dimensional work. A black-and-white negative should have full dark-area detail and rich but unblocked highlights. The copy negative will look full but a bit flat as compared to normal negatives; final image contrast can be adjusted by the choice of print materials and processing.

Methods for Determining Color Exposures. Color exposures should be based on incident-light or reflected-light gray card readings. Final adjustments of color balance can be determined only by actual tests. Some modern paints contain color agents that fluoresce or otherwise emit wavelengths that will affect film emulsions differently than they do the eye. In addition, the color temperature ratings of lamps and emulsions are only nominal. For example, the "daylight" illumination produced by electronic flash units may range from 5000 K to 6800 K or higher, depending on the kind of tube, the reflector, and the

protective lens used in the unit. Similarly, the true output of various rated lamps can vary from manufacturer to manufacturer, as well as between production batches from the same manufacturer. The balance of color film emulsions is also variable, as film data sheets reveal. If the light source and the emulsion both vary in the same direction from their nominal ratings, the combined effect may significantly change the intended results.

For critical work, it is essential to make a series of light-film combination tests with each new emulsion batch or major lamp change. The test subject should be a set of Kodak color reference patches, a gray scale, and both the gray side and the white side of a Kodak neutral test card. The tests will reveal optimum exposure but, more importantly, will show whether accurate colors are reproduced along with clean, untinted whites and neutral grays. It may well be that a slight adjustment using color compensating (CC) filters is required. With color transparency film, unwanted coloration is removed by filtration of the opposite or complementary color; with color negative film, filtration of the same color as the unwanted tinge is required.

The combination of polarized illumination and a lens polarizer will result in images with saturated

136

When photographing sculpture outdoors, lighting variations as well as camera angles must be considered. Several photo sessions are desirable, to best employ changes in the sun's angle and visibility. Alberto Giacometti, "Dog"; photo courtesy of the Hirshhorn Museum and Sculpture Garden, Smithsonian Institution.

colors and some increase in contrast because light normally scattered by the surface of the work is eliminated; detail in dark areas also may be lost. In such cases, it is helpful, after the main exposure, to give the film an additional "flash" exposure to an out-of-focus white card. This will lessen overall contrast and may make dark detail more visible. The flash exposure should be about 1/50 of the first, normal exposure.

Whenever filtration, or extra extension for close-ups, is used, increased exposure is required to compensate for the reduced intensity of the image reaching the film. Correction for reciprocity is also a frequent necessity, especially with color films or with black-and-white exposures that are longer than 10 seconds.

• *See also:* CLOSE-UP PHOTOGRAPHY; COLOR SEPARATION PHOTOGRAPHY; COPYING; LIGHTING; PHOTOMACROGRAPHY.

Further Reading: Barsness, John C. *Photographing Crafts.* New York, NY: American Crafts Council, 1974; Lewis, John and Edwin Smith. *The Graphic Reproduction and Photography of Works of Art.* Salem, NH: Faber and Faber, 1969; Mates, Robert E. *Photographing Art.* Garden City, NY: Amphoto, 1966.

Artificial Light

Artificial light is illumination from man-made sources, rather than the natural light of the sun, moon, and stars. (Note that in another sense the "natural," meaning existing or available, light in a scene may come from artificial sources.) Artificial light sources may produce illumination continuously or momentarily (intermittently). Almost all sources rely on electric power, but some (for example, candles, magnesium ribbon or powder, and phosphorus) may rely on physical/chemical action.

The most common continuous-emission artificial-light sources are:

1. Tungsten filament bulbs—household, photoflood, or photo bulbs.
2. Continuous-discharge gas lamps—fluorescent or mercury- or sodium-vapor lamps.
3. Tungsten-halogen bulbs—so-called "quartz" bulbs.
4. Arc lights—continuous-discharge electric spark lights

Intermittent/momentary sources are:

1. Conventional flash bulbs, cubes, and strips—filament or foil-filled.
2. Electronic flash tubes—instant-discharge gas tubes.

There are two basic approaches to using artificial light. The first is to supplement, reinforce, or correct the natural light in a scene (for example, to unobtrusively raise the overall brightness level or lighten dark areas). The second is to create the entire pattern of light or shade in the scene. In either case, artificial light has the advantage that it may provide complete control of the quality, color, intensity, and direction of subject illumination. However, it has the

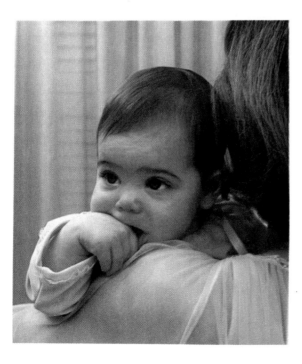

(Top) Artificial light is made to seem more natural when it is reflected (bounced) off white walls or ceiling. (Bottom) While direct artificial light may appear harsh, bounced light gives a softer, more diffused, and more evenly balanced effect.

disadvantage of requiring additional equipment and set-up time.

• *See also:* ARC LAMPS; ELECTRONIC FLASH; FLASH PHOTOGRAPHY; INCANDESCENT LAMPS; LIGHTING.

ASA, ASAP Speeds

ASA, ASAP speeds are systems for rating the speed, or sensitivity to light, of photographic emulsions according to methods approved by the American National Standards Institute (ANSI), formerly called the American Standards Association.

The prefix "ASA" designates an American National Standard film speed; "ASAP" designates an American National Standard paper speed. When practical experience or testing shows that under certain conditions an emulsion may be more accurately rated at another speed, the new rating is an *exposure index* and should be designated "EI," not "ASA." Similarly, ratings arrived at by other national standard methods should be properly designated. ASA speeds are numerically equal to BSI (British Standards Institute) Arithmetic Speeds and to JSA (Japan Standards Association) speeds; they are approximately equal to the Russian GOST speeds, and are related to but not equal to the German DIN (Deutsche Industrie Norm) speeds.

The numbers in the scale of American National Standard Speeds (see the accompanying table) are arithmetic; a number that is twice as much as another represents twice as much sensitivity to light. However, in order to have the speeds separated by convenient intervals, it takes three steps on the scale for a numerical doubling to occur. It is easy to determine the adjacent steps to any given speed, if required. The next higher speed is 0.25× more than the given speed; the next lower speed is 0.8 of the given speed. For example, the next speed above 400 is: 400 + (400 × 0.25) = 400 + 100 = 500. The next lower speed is: 400 × 0.8 = 320. The numbers are rounded off as necessary to maintain the sequence of doubling at every third step.

A useful rule-of-thumb is that the ASA speed of a film is inversely proportional to the exposure time required at *f*/16 for an average subject in bright frontal sunlight. So, an ASA 100 film requires an exposure of 1/100 sec. at *f*/16 with such a subject, while an ASA 400 film requires 1/400 sec. at *f*/16 with the same subject. This correlation makes it possible to make a rough test of a film of unknown speed. Expose it to such a subject at *f*/16 and a variety of shutter speeds. The shutter speed used for the most satisfactory exposure indicates the approximate ASA speed: 1/50 sec. would indicate ASA 50.

• *See also:* ANSI; BSI SPEEDS; DIN SPEEDS; GOST SPEEDS; SENSITOMETRY, SPEED SYSTEMS.

American Standard Speeds
3200
2500
2000
1600
1250
1000
800
650 *
500
400
320
250
200
160
125
100
80
64 *
50
40
32
25
20
16
12
10
8
6
5
4

*The actual ANSI values are 63 and 630; manufacturing practice is to label films as shown in the table.

Aspheric

Aspheric, taken literally, means *not spherical*. In lenses, the term is applied to surfaces that have been ground to nonspherical shapes. Such shapes are almost always paraboloid because this shape can be designed to correct spherical aberration. Of the five Seidel Aberrations, only spherical aberration is caused by the spherical shape of the lenses. Therefore, only it can be affected by the use of aspheric surfaces. However, spherical aberration can be corrected in other ways, and since grinding aspheric surfaces is a difficult and expensive process, most designers prefer to avoid their use.

Aspheric lenses are used mainly in condenser systems of projectors. Since condenser lenses are not required to form sharp images, simple molded and fire-polished lenses can be used.

• *See also:* LENSES; OPTICS.

Astrophotography

The photography of astronomical objects is called astrophotography. You can start taking astrophotographs with no knowledge of astronomy and with a minimum of equipment. All you need is a good camera that can make time exposures, a cable release, a rigid tripod, and some fast film.

Since many of your pictures will be time exposures, one of the most important requirements for astrophotography is a steady camera. Therefore, place your camera on a rigid tripod before taking pictures. Also use a cable release. This will help you get sharp pictures by keeping camera vibration to a minimum when you open and close the shutter.

Photographing Star Trails

Stars are good subjects for your first astronomical picture-taking experience because they are so

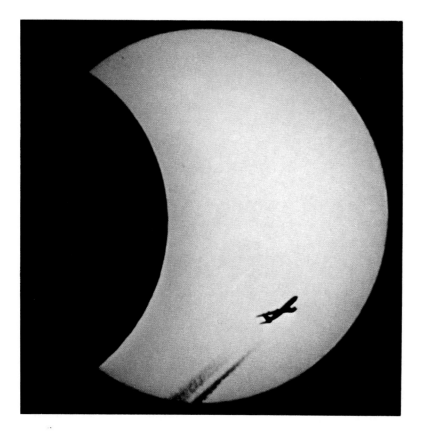

This photograph of a jet plane crossing a partially eclipsed sun is a rare catch. Photo by Mike Sankey and Wayne McGill, taken with an 8-inch Celestron; courtesy of Celestron, Inc.

These star trails over Kitt Peak National Observatory in Arizona were photographed on Kodachrome-X film with a 35 mm focal length lens at f/3.5. The star trails were exposed for six hours; the interiors of the buildings were exposed by turning the lights on for four seconds; and the exterior of the observatory was illuminated with several flashes from an electronic flash unit used near the building. Photo by Richard H. Cromwell.

easy to photograph. Stars do not remain stationary in the sky. They appear to rise and set because of the rotation of the earth. When you take time exposures of stars, you will discover that stars create interesting effects, called "star trails," on your film.

Procedure. Load your camera with a fast film such as Kodak Tri-X pan film. Open the camera lens to its maximum opening and set the focus at infinity. With your camera on a tripod, aim it toward a group of stars and open the shutter for a 4-minute exposure. At the end of the exposure, close the shutter, reduce the lens opening by 1 stop, and wait for 1 minute. Then make another 4-minute exposure on the same frame or piece of film, if possible. Continue this procedure, making a series of exposures ending at f/16.

After your film has been processed, you will find that the stars have been recorded as a series of streaks, or star trails. From these star trails you can determine the best exposure. If the trails are needle-sharp, you know that your lens is in sharp focus at the infinity setting. If the trails are straight and not jagged, you know that your camera support is sufficiently rigid.

You can use longer exposures and get the best pictures on dark, moonless nights away from the bright lights of cities. Moonlight and city lights produce a general background light in the night sky. This skylight limits the maximum exposure time

that you can use without overexposing the background areas of your pictures.

Be sure to keep your camera lens free of dew from the night air. A lens cap is helpful in keeping dew off the lens between exposures. If you don't have a lens cap, you can make one from cardboard. When dew gets on the lens, wipe the lens surface with a clean, soft, lintless cloth or lens tissue, such as Kodak lens cleaning paper. However, don't clean the lens while you're making an exposure.

Polaris. You can obtain interesting circular star trails by photographing the sky area around the North Star. The North Star, called "Polaris" by astronomers, is located near the earth's celestial pole point. The earth rotates around the celestial pole point at the rate of 15 degrees per hour, or 1 degree every 4 minutes. This causes the stars to appear to rotate around Polaris. Polaris is the star at the end of the handle of the Little Dipper constellation, called Ursa Minor.

If you make a time exposure of 5 minutes or more of the area of the sky that includes the star Polaris, your photograph will show circular star trails made by the stars revolving around Polaris. Since Polaris is about 1 degree away from the true celestial pole-point, your photograph will show that Polaris has also made a short trail.

Constellations. For other fascinating picture-taking possibilities, try some pictures of constella-

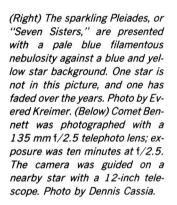

(Right) The sparkling Pleiades, or "Seven Sisters," are presented with a pale blue filamentous nebulosity against a blue and yellow star background. One star is not in this picture, and one has faded over the years. Photo by Evered Kreimer. (Below) Comet Bennett was photographed with a 135 mm f/2.5 telephoto lens; exposure was ten minutes at f/2.5. The camera was guided on a nearby star with a 12-inch telescope. Photo by Dennis Cassia.

tions such as the Big Dipper, Orion, or Cassiopeia. Experiment with exposure times of 5, 10, or 15 minutes, with the lens wide open. You can add interest and dimension to your astronomical photographs by including silhouettes of objects such as trees, your home, a church, or a landscape in the foreground of your pictures.

Films. You can take beautiful pictures of celestial objects in color or black-and-white. Since your eyes have low sensitivity to color when they become adapted to the dark, you may not realize that the stars have different colors. You can capture the colors of stars with color film. Set your camera lens wide open and expose for 10 to 30 minutes or more. The longer the exposure, the longer the star trails will be on your film.

Photographing Comets

When a bright comet is due to appear in the sky, it is an event that makes the headlines. Some comets

Astrophotography

METEOR SHOWERS AND WHEN THEY OCCUR

Name of Meteor Showers	Occurrence
Quadrantids	January 1–4
Lyrids	April 19–23
Eta Aquarids	May 1–6
Delta Aquarids	July 26–31
Perseids	August 9–15
Orionids	October 18–23
Leonids	November 14–18
Geminids	December 10–13

appear regularly, having a cycle of several years; others appear only once. You may be able to photograph them while they are visible for a period of a few days or weeks.

To photograph comets, use a fast film, open the camera lens all the way, and expose the film for 10 to 30 minutes. With a stationary camera, you will get a blurred image of the comet because of the rotation of the earth. For sharper pictures, follow the comet by using a guided camera. (See the section on astrophotography with a guided camera in this article.)

Meteor Pictures

Photographing meteors is a challenge and takes a great deal of patience. Although they appear much more often than comets, the position of meteors in the sky is unpredictable; they appear in all parts of the sky. You can take pictures of meteors in the same way as you photograph star trails.

Meteors vary greatly in brightness and frequently in color. These small bits of matter enter our atmosphere at about 25 miles per second, and they are only 50 to 70 miles above the earth's surface.

On a clear, dark night away from city lights, you may see about 5 to 10 meteors an hour. They occur more frequently after midnight and are more common in the second half of the year. Dark, moonless nights are best for observing and photographing meteors.

There are certain periods of the year when meteor showers occur. The showers may last for several hours or a few days, but each meteor will be visible for only a few moments. If you find out when meteor showers are due and where to look in the sky, you may have a chance to photograph them. When a spectacular meteor shower is expected, your local newspaper may publish the date in advance. The table above indicates the times of the year when meteors are most likely to appear.

Aurorae

The Northern Lights (or the Southern Lights) vary greatly in form, intensity, color, and height. They are excellent subjects for color or black-and-white pictures. To photograph an auroral display, set your camera lens at its widest opening, and use a fast film such as Kodak Tri-X pan film for black-and-white prints or Kodak high speed Ektachrome film (daylight) for color slides.

If you use high speed Ektachrome film in 135 and 120 sizes, you can request special processing by Kodak, which increases the film speed 2 times. To obtain the special processing, buy the Kodak special processing envelope, ESP-1, from your photo dealer. Complete instructions come with the envelope. Other processing laboratories may also process the film to the increased speed.

Since an auroral display has such a wide range of intensity and brightness, exposure times can vary from 1 second to 2 minutes. In order to increase your chances of getting a good picture, take pictures at several different exposure times.

Man-Made Satellites

The appearance of satellites is very predictable, since they orbit the earth every 90 minutes or so. For information on the position of man-made satellites and their orbits, write to the Independent Tracking Coordination Program.

You won't get any detail in photographs of satellites when you use a telephoto lens or a telescope because satellites are too small and far away. Pictures of satellites will be better if you use a normal-focal-length lens on your camera because they will include more of the satellite's path. This will make it easier for you to aim your camera toward the passing satellite. In addition, you can use longer exposures, since it takes longer for the satellite to move across the camera's field of view. Finally, a normal-focal-length lens minimizes the effects of camera vibration. Longer focal-length lenses are more difficult to hand-hold, so the effects of camera vibration are increased.

To take pictures, load your camera with a fast film and set the lens wide open. When the satellite comes into view, point your camera toward the satellite's path (it will be too dark to use your viewfinder). Open the shutter on B (Bulb) or T (Time), and wait until the satellite passes out of your camera's field of view. Then close the shutter. You can make your picture even more impressive if you plan the timing so that you take the picture as the satellite passes through or passes near a prominent constellation.

Photographing the Moon

Since the moon is our closest celestial neighbor, it presents exceptional opportunities for astrophotography. Because the moon is a sunlit subject, the full moon requires the same exposure as a sunlit subject here on earth. The gibbous moon (between half and full) requires two times as much exposure as a full moon (1 stop more); the half moon requires four times as much exposure as a full moon (2 stops more); and a crescent moon (less than half) requires ten times as much exposure as a full moon (3½ stops more).

Although the moon appears large to your eye, it is a very small subject to photograph. For example, with a 50 mm camera lens, the image of the full moon will be less than .5 mm (1/50 inch) on your film, hardly more than a speck. But you can take excellent pictures that will show some surface detail if you use a lens of at least 300 mm (12 inches) focal length and make a photographic enlargement to gain additional magnification. (*See:* ECLIPSE PHOTOGRAPHY.)

You can determine in advance the approximate diameter of the moon's image that you'll get on your film by dividing the focal length of your camera lens by 110. Use the same units—inches or millimeters—for both the image diameter on the film and the focal length of the camera lens.

$$\frac{\text{Focal Length}}{110} = \frac{\text{Moon Image Diameter}}{\text{on Film}}$$

(Below left) A total lunar eclipse not quite in the center of earth's shadow. Photo by S. Schultz, Jr. (Below right) A crescent moon, the moon two days old. Photo by J. K. Rouse.

Astrophotography

Sky Charts and Astronomical Tables

Sky charts, such as those published in *Sky and Telescope* magazine (Sky Publishing Corporation) each month and in many local newspapers each week, indicate the positions of celestial objects and the times that they are visible. When you use a sky chart, imagine that the chart is pasted on the ceiling so that the compass directions agree with your location. The stars on the chart will then appear in their correct positions.

A "Rotating Star and Planet Finder" is a helpful guide for locating celestial objects. When the dial is set for the month, day, and hour, the dial indicator shows all of the constellations overhead. It is distributed by Edmund Scientific Company.

Graphic Time Table of the Heavens is a chart published annually by the Maryland Academy of Sciences. It includes the rising and setting times of celestial objects, and other pertinent astronomical information.

Astrophotography with a Guided Camera

So far we have been talking about stationary cameras. You can improve your astrophotographs by using your camera on an equatorial mount in order to follow astronomical subjects. This compensates for the rotation of the earth and keeps the images stationary on your film during the long exposures that may be necessary for good pictures of faint objects. An equatorial mount provides a heavy, firm support and orients your camera for convenient tracking of celestial objects. You can purchase an equatorial mount, without motorized drive, from scientific supply firms. (See supplier references under the head "Telescope Mounting and Drive System" in this article.)

How to Use an Equatorial Mount. Set the polar axis parallel to the earth's axis by pointing it at the celestial pole point near the North Star. When you do this, the angle between the polar axis and the horizontal will be equal to the latitude of your loca-

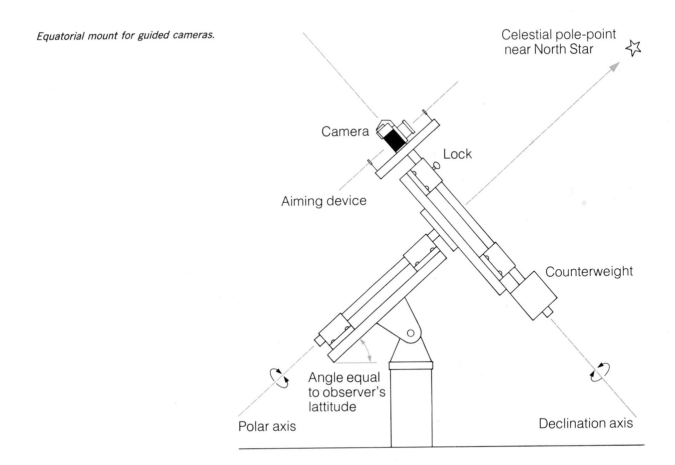

Equatorial mount for guided cameras.

Celestial pole-point near North Star

Camera

Lock

Aiming device

Counterweight

Angle equal to observer's lattitude

Polar axis

Declination axis

tion. You can measure this angle with a protractor and a level. Once you have properly aligned the polar axis, you won't have to change it unless you move the telescope to another latitude.

Next, mount the camera at the end of the declination axis as shown in the illustration on the preceding page. Point the camera toward the object you want to photograph and lock the declination axis. This permits you to rotate only the polar axis in order to follow an astronomical subject accurately. An aiming device aligned parallel to your camera lens axis will help you center your camera on the subject. You can use a simple aiming device made from two screw eyes available from hardware stores, but a small telescope or binoculars attached near the camera will be more accurate.

If you guide your camera carefully, stars will appear as points of light with no appreciable diameter. The brighter stars, however, will produce larger images because of light spreading in the film. You cannot magnify star images with long-focal-length lenses because stars are much too far away from us. However, the moon, sun, and comets do have definite image diameters. When you photograph these subjects, you can obtain larger images by using a telephoto or long-focal-length lens on your camera.

A spectroheliogram made in hydrogen's red light shows great surface and prominent detail. This enlarged section shows a single tongue of flame bursting out to 100,000 miles or more. Such a flame would encompass many earths. Note the material falling back to the surface. DANGER: Never look at the sun through any optical device without adequate protection, as you may permanently damage your eyes. Photo by Walter Semerau.

Photographing the Sun. Do not attempt to photograph the sun without suitable protective camera filters over the lens—you could damage your camera and film (see the exposure recommendation table). DANGER: Never look at the sun through any optical device without adequate protection because the sun can burn your eyes and permanently damage them without your being aware of it at the time.

To look at the sun safely, you must look through protective filters for visual use. Medical authorities indicate that a neutral density filter of metallic silver, such as developed black-and-white photographic film of at least 6.0 density, will provide adequate protection. Such a filter is for *visual use only;* it is not suitable for photographic use. Place the filter *in front of your eyes before facing the sun.* You can make such a filter from two thicknesses of black-and-white film, such as Kodak Verichrome pan film, which has been completely exposed and developed to maximum density. Expose the film by unrolling it in daylight. **Do not use color film as a viewing filter** because the dyes used in color film will not block the harmful rays of the sun.

A solar eclipse taken at the moment of totality, July 1963. Very interesting eclipse photographs can be taken with ordinary cameras, standard focal length lenses, and the proper eye protection provisions. Photo by Paul H. Preo.

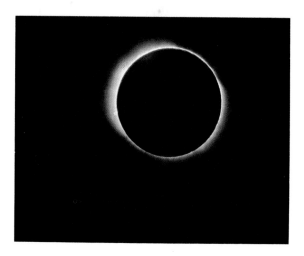

Jupiter's red spot and shadow of the moon Io, which is nearly as large as our moon, as photographed from Pioneer 10. Jupiter is the largest of our planets; the red spot could swallow several earths. Photo courtesy of NASA.

Polarizing filters and neutral density filters used for photography transmit infrared energy that is harmful to your eyes. **Do not use either of these types of filters to observe the sun.**

Astrophotography with a Telescope

To photograph astronomical subjects in greater detail, you will need a telescope. There are two major classes of telescopes: refracting and reflecting. These two types are nearly alike with respect to their use in astrophotography. The refracting telescope forms an image of an object by transmitting the light rays through a lens system similar to camera or binocular lenses. The reflecting telescope collects the light rays with an accurately curved mirror that forms the image. With both telescopes, the primary image is magnified by an eyepiece. Reflecting telescopes are less expensive and are generally better at focusing different colors in the same plane. This feature is important in obtaining sharp images.

Astronomers use the term "objective lens," or "objective," when they refer to the telescope's main or primary lens that collects the light from the sub-ject. The "objective" may be either the objective (front) lens of a refractor telescope, or the mirror of a reflector telescope. When we discuss telescope lenses in more detail, we will use these terms.

Telescope Mounting and Drive System. An equatorial mounting with a motorized drive system will allow you to use the long exposures that are necessary for astrophotography of many interesting objects far out in space, such as the planets, nebulae, galaxies, and star clusters. Equatorial mounts with clock drives are available from scientific firms, such as Edmund Scientific Company and A. Jaegers.

Operating a motorized mount is similar to operating a simple equatorial camera mount. Turn the telescope about the declination axis to the desired position, and lock the declination axis into place. The telescope and declination axis will rotate about the polar axis (either with a drive system or manually) in order to keep the desired object in view and stationary on your film. You can take good pictures of the brighter objects without using a drive system, but a drive system is almost a necessity for photographing faint objects requiring long exposures.

The full moon as seen through an astronomical telescope. It was photographed with a 10-inch aperture f/9 reflector scope, 0.8-inch image at prime focus. Photo by Henry E. Paul.

When you use a drive system, set it to rotate the polar axis one revolution per day. Professional astronomers rotate the polar axis of their telescopes once every sidereal day (23 hours, 56 minutes, and 4 seconds of clock time), which is the true rotational period of the earth. However, even their guiding mechanisms are not perfect. Refraction by the earth's atmosphere changes the apparent position of celestial objects; therefore, slight guiding corrections are required. An ordinary 24-hour clock drive is good enough for most astrophotography; you can correct for the slight guiding discrepancy manually, if necessary.

To observe the tracking accuracy of your drive system, you can view the object relative to the cross hairs of a reticle used with an illuminated eyepiece on your telescope, or you can use a guide telescope aligned with the main scope. In addition, a small finder telescope is often necessary to help you locate celestial objects because the field of view of the high-power main scope is extremely small.

Telescope and Camera. The four basic telescope-camera systems are:

1. eyepiece-camera lens
2. eyepiece projection
3. prime focus
4. negative-lens projection

The system you use depends primarily on your equipment and on the desired image size.

Eyepiece-Camera Lens System. This is probably the most convenient for those who are new to astrophotography because you don't need a special camera or a camera with a removable lens. You can take astrophotographs with an ordinary camera positioned close to the eyepiece of your telescope. However, this system does not transmit as much light as the other systems because the light has to pass through more lenses and some of it is absorbed.

There are several kinds of optical instruments that you can use for the telescope part of your eyepiece-camera system. These include binoculars and spotting scopes as well as astronomical telescopes with eyepieces. To take pictures with your camera and telescope, you'll need a simple mounting device to attach the two units. The mounting device should provide both precise alignment of your camera lens with your telescope eyepiece and a rigid, vibration-free support for your camera. Although the mount should furnish a lighttight guard between the two units, this guard is not absolutely necessary. A black, lint-free cloth will do. You can purchase mounting devices from optical firms such as Optica b/c Company and Edmund Scientific Company.

With the other three telescope-camera systems, you do not use your camera lens. Therefore, you'll need a camera with a removable lens and a shutter that's built into the camera body. The camera body you use should have some provision for focusing on a substitute film plane (see section on focusing). Cameras that do not fulfill these requirements must be altered.

An excellent camera for astrophotography with a telescope is the single-lens reflex camera with a removable lens. You can use this type of camera with all four telescope-camera systems by using the camera with or without its lens, depending on the system you employ. When you look through the viewfinder of a single-lens reflex camera, you are looking through the lens system. This enables you to position the image and focus your telescope-camera system conveniently and accurately.

You can purchase specially built astrocameras from telescope manufacturers, such as Unitron Instrument Co., Criterion Manufacturing Co., and Celestron Pacific.

Eyepiece-Projection System. With this system, you attach your camera, with its lens removed, to the telescope eyepiece. The eyepiece projects the image directly onto the camera film plane. Since you don't use the camera lens, there are fewer lenses for the light to pass through. As a result, less light is absorbed and there are fewer lens aberrations to affect the image.

Also, with the eyepiece-projection system you can increase magnification by moving the film plane farther from the eyepiece. However, as you do this, the image-forming light is spread over a larger area

The dim North American nebula high in Cygnus presents its true continent form in this 30-minute exposure with a 10-inch focus f/2.0 camera lens. Photo by Henry E. Paul.

and therefore becomes fainter. So there are practical limits.

To focus the image on the film plane, it is necessary to move the eyepiece outward slightly from the setting for visual use. See the section on focusing procedures.

Prime-Focus System. In this system, the objective of the telescope focuses the image directly on the camera film plane, thus eliminating extra lenses. Consequently, the main advantage of this system is that it transmits the most light while keeping lens aberrations to a minimum.

Negative-Lens Projection System. This system is similar to the prime-focus method in that the image is projected directly onto the film plane. In negative-lens projection, a negative achromatic lens, usually referred to as a Barlow lens, is placed inside the focus of the objective. This produces more image magnification without greatly increasing the length of the telescope. This principle is used in telephoto lenses.

Focusing Procedure and Camera Alignment. The way in which you check for alignment and sharp focus of your telescope and camera will depend on the type of camera you use.

With a single-lens reflex camera and a suitable mount, line up your camera so that it is centered on the optical axis of your telescope. If you use the camera lens, place it close to the eyepiece of the

telescope. Next, put a piece of tracing paper or tissue paper over the front of the main tube of your telescope, and illuminate it evenly with a 100-watt light bulb in a reflector about .6 metre (2 feet) away. Set the camera lens at its smallest opening. Then move the camera back and forth slightly to obtain the most uniform illumination in your viewfinder. If the camera lens is either too close to or too far from the eyepiece of the telescope, the corners of the viewfinder will be dark.

For focusing, take the paper off the end of the telescope and point the telescope toward a bright astronomical subject, such as the moon or a bright star, NOT THE SUN! If you use the camera lens, open the lens to its maximum opening and set the lens for infinity. Then adjust the focus with your telescope (or binoculars). When the image looks sharp on the ground glass of your viewfinder, it will be sharp on your film.

With a nonreflex camera, use the same mounting setup and alignment procedure. To line up and focus this type of camera, you will need a piece of ground glass to fit the film plane of your camera. Ground glass is available through your photo dealer or from Edmund Scientific Company. You can use a piece of wax paper or matte acetate (thin plastic sheeting that has a matte surface) as a substitute, but be careful not to bend or buckle it; the wax paper or matte acetate must be flat in the film plane.

A superb photo showing the famous "diamond ring" effect occurring as the last rays leave or the first rays emerge from behind the moon. Fractions of a second are important when photographing such events. Photo by Mark Bowers.

Astrophotography

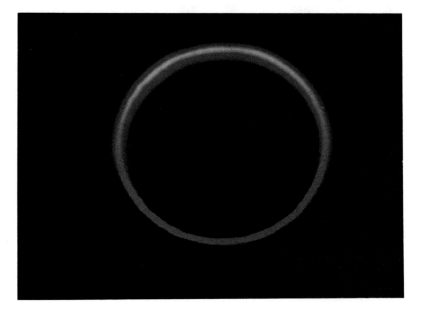

A rare solar event, an annular eclipse—the moon is nearer to the sun, and since it is close to the horizon, air refraction causes the flattening or oblateness. Photo courtesy of Ralph Dakin.

Before loading this type of camera with film, open the camera back and place the ground glass over the film plane of the camera, with the ground surface toward the lens. Make sure that the glass is resting on the film-plane frame or rails; then fasten it in place with tape.

Open the camera shutter on T (Time) or B (Bulb). If you use the B setting, use a locking-type cable release to keep the shutter open. Then with the camera lens wide open and set on infinity, adjust the focus with your telescope and observe the image on the ground glass with a magnifier, such as the Kodak achromatic magnifier, 5×. When the image appears in sharp focus on the ground glass, it will be sharp on your film. After focusing, lock all adjustments and remove the ground glass. Then load your camera with film. Be careful not to disturb the focus.

Lens Speed. The lens speed of a telescope-camera system indicates its light-transmission capability. This is expressed by *f*-number or objective diameter, depending on the particular subject you are photographing.

In astrophotography, there are two general types of subjects—extended objects and point-source objects. Extended objects are large enough or close enough to use so that they can be magnified. For example, the moon, sun, planets, and large nebulae are extended objects. Point-source objects, such

as stars, cannot be magnified because they are too far away.

When you photograph extended objects, as in conventional photography, the light reaching the film in your telescope-camera system compared to another telescope-camera system is inversely proportional to the ratio of their *f*-numbers squared. For example, an *f*/4 telescope-camera system transmits 4 times as much light as an *f*/8 system. $f/8^2 \div f/4^2 = 4$ times. A picture taken at *f*/4 requires an exposure time ¼ as long as a picture taken at *f*/8.

However, when you take pictures of point-source objects (stars), the image intensity that reaches your film depends upon the diameter of the telescope or binocular objective, *not the f-number*. In this situation, the lens speed of telescope objectives is directly proportional to the ratio of the squares of their diameters. A 77 mm (3-inch) objective transmits 2.25 times as much light as a 51 mm (2-inch) objective; $3^2 \div 2^2 = 9 \div 4 = 2.25$ times. Your exposure time will be 1/2.25 as long with the 77 mm (3-inch) objective.

The *f*-Number of Your Telescope-Camera System. The *f*-number of your system is determined by your telescope (or binoculars). When you take pictures through a telescope and you use your camera lens, set the camera lens at its widest opening.

Eyepiece-camera lens

$$\text{f-number} = \frac{F \times F_c}{D \times F_e}$$

or

$$\frac{\text{Telescope power} \times F_c}{D}$$

Eyepiece projection

$$\text{f-number} = \frac{F \times L}{D \times A}$$

Prime focus

$$\text{f-number} = \frac{F}{D}$$

Negative-lens projection

$$\text{f-number} = \frac{F \times C}{D \times B}$$

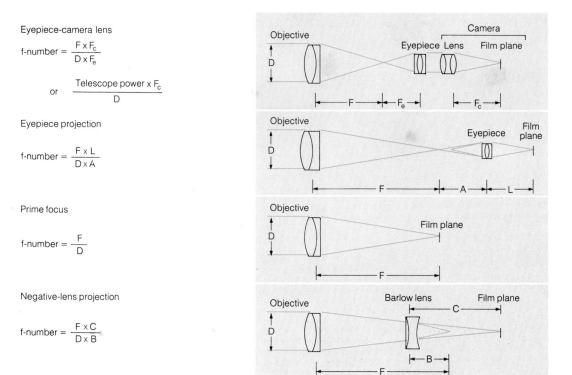

Telescope-camera systems.

F = *focal length of telescope objective*
F_e = *focal length of eyepiece*
F_c = *focal length of camera lens*
D = *diameter of telescope objective*
L = *distance of eyepiece from film (eyepiece projection only)*
A = *distance of eyepiece from normal focus of telescope objective (eyepiece-projection system only)*

C = *distance of Barlow lens from film*
B = *distance of Barlow lens from normal focus of telescope objective*
Telescope power = power printed on the telescope eyepiece, on the binoculars, or given in the instruction manual for the equipment. NOTE: Use the same units for all dimensions.

The formulas and diagrams in the accompanying figures will help you determine the effective *f*-number of each of the telescope-camera systems. With the eyepiece-camera lens system, you can use the formula that includes telescope power if you don't know the focal length of your telescope objective or eyepiece but you do know the power of your telescope, spotting scope, or binoculars.

Film Selection

Film speed is an important consideration in astrophotography; the faster the film, the shorter your exposure time can be. Shorter exposures minimize the effects of guiding errors and atmospheric shimmer, and this produces sharper astrophotographs.

The film speed is listed on the instruction sheet that comes with the film.

Speeds of films for pictorial photography are based on average exposure times used in taking conventional pictures. If your calculated exposure time is much longer than 1/10 sec., you should regard your exposure estimate as the basis for trial only. So make a series of test exposures at ¼, ½, 1, 2, 4, and 16 times the calculated exposure.

Film graininess is also an important factor to consider in selecting a film for astrophotography. Graininess is the "salt-and-pepper" appearance, or sandlike pattern, that is sometimes evident in enlarged photographs. As a general rule, slow-speed films have the finest grain. When you want to make a photographic enlargement of your astrophotograph, it is best to use the finest-grain film you can. However, the film you select should have not only fine grain but also adequate speed for your picture-taking situation.

Filters

You can take excellent astrophotographs without using filters, but sometimes filters may be helpful for purposes such as reducing the effect of background light. Moonlight scattered by the earth's atmosphere produces a predominantly blue background light in the sky. If your exposure time is very long, this light causes overexposure in the sky areas of your picture. You can use filters to reduce the effect of background light. With panchromatic black-and-white film, use a No. 8 yellow filter or a No. 15 deep-yellow filter over the camera lens. This will permit you to use longer exposure times without overexposing the background areas of your picture. Since filters decrease the intensity of the light reaching your film, increase your exposure time by multiplying by the filter factor listed on the instruction sheet that comes with the film or the filter.

The Apparent Brightness of Astronomical Subjects

The Greek astronomer Hipparchus devised a system of classifying stars according to degree of brightness, which is still in use today. He designated the 20 brightest stars as *first* magnitude; the next 50, in order of brightness, as *second* magnitude; and so on. Stars that are barely visible to the normal, unaided eye are *sixth*-magnitude stars. Objects such

This photograph of the Lagoon nebula was taken with a 14-inch Celestron—cold camera. Photo by James Matteson and courtesy of Celestron.

as the sun and moon, which are brighter than first-magnitude stars, receive a Hipparchus classification that runs from less than $+1$ into the minus numbers. For example, the brightness of the sun is -26.7.

This brightness relationship is useful because it can help you determine exposure time. Each magnitude classification difference of 1 indicates a brightness difference of 2.5. For a given astrophotographic setup, this means that fourth-magnitude stars will require 2.5 times the exposure time of third-magnitude stars, and so on. Textbooks on astronomy in your public library contain tables of relative magnitudes for various celestial objects. You can estimate magnitude classification to a high degree of accuracy by comparing the celestial object of interest with objects of known magnitude.

Estimating Exposure

General exposure recommendations are given in the accompanying table. Since there are so many variables in taking astrophotographs, such as equipment, speed of the film, and atmospheric conditions, the table gives exposure ranges to serve as a basis for your own pictures.

You may find exposure data with astrophotographs in books and magazines. You can relate this data to your own astrophotography setup. For example, assume that the exposure for a photograph of the moon is given as 1/125 sec. at $f/8$ with Kodak Panatomic-X film (ASA 32). If your telescope-camera system has an effective f-number of $f/32$ and you are using Kodak Plus-X pan film (ASA 125), what should your exposure time be?

GENERAL EXPOSURE RECOMMENDATIONS FOR AMATEUR ASTROPHOTOGRAPHY

Subject	Instrument	Mount	Objective	f-number	Films & Plates	Exposure
Star Trails and Comets	Camera with time exposure	Rigid support	Any lens	Wide open	Fast, b & w and color	Up to 30 min. or more
Meteors	Camera with time exposure	Rigid support	Good lens	$f/6.3$ or wider	Fast, b & w and color	10 to 30 min.
Aurorae	Camera with time exposure and fast lens	Rigid support	Fast lens	$f/4.5$ or wider	Fast, b & w and color	1 sec. to 2 min.
Man-Made Satellites	Camera with time exposure and fast lens	Rigid support	Fast lens	$f/4.5$ or wider	Fast, b & w and color	Hold shutter open for pass duration
Moon	Camera, or camera with telescope	Rigid, or equatorial with or without drive	2.6 cm diameter or larger	About $f/11$	Medium speed, b & w and color	1/125 sec. to 10 sec.
Stars and Comets	Camera, or camera with telescope	Equatorial with guiding sights	2.6 cm diameter or larger	$f/6.3$ or wider	Fast, b & w and color	10 min. to 1 hr.
Star Clusters, Nebulae, and Galaxies	Camera, or camera with telescope	Equatorial with sights and drive	2.6 cm diameter or larger	About $f/6.3$	Fast, b & w and color	10 min. to 1 hr.
Planets	Camera with telescope	Equatorial preferably with drive	2.6 cm diameter or larger; for detail, 15.6 cm and up	Use f-number determined by your system	Fast, b & w and color	1/2 to 15 sec.
Sun (Never look at the sun through any optical device without adequate protection.)	Camera, or camera with telescope	Rigid, or equatorial with or without drive	Neutral density filters 4–6 over 2.6 cm or larger main objective	$f/11$–$f/32$	Slow, b & w and color	1/30 to 1/1000 sec. with neutral density filters 4–5 over main optical objective (not the eyepiece)

Since the moon is an extended object, the normal f-number relationship is valid. Therefore, to determine the exposure compensation for the smaller f-number of your system, use the following formula.

$$\frac{(\text{your system } f\text{-number})^2}{(\text{example } f\text{-number})^2} = \frac{\text{exposure}}{\text{compensation}}$$

In this instance $32^2 \div 8^2 = 16$; therefore, your system requires 16 times as much exposure. However, your film is 4 times as fast as the film used in the example, so it requires ¼ of the exposure. Combine both factors by multiplying ¼ × 16. The answer, 4, indicates that you need a total of 4 times as much exposure as was used in the example. To determine your exposure time, multiply the exposure time used in the example by 4. Since 4 × 1/125 second = 1/30 (approximately), the exposure time for your setup is 1/30 second.

In photographing a point-source object (star), the size, or diameter, of your telescope or binocular objective, not the f-number, determines the intensity of the light that reaches your film. Consequently, exposure data for photographs of point-source objects should include objective diameter rather than f-number. To compute the exposure compensation for differences in objective diameter, use the following formula.

$$\frac{(\text{example objective dia.})^2}{(\text{your system objective dia.})^2} = \frac{\text{exposure}}{\text{compensation}}$$

Then multiply the exposure time used in the example by the exposure compensation. Also compensate for differences in film speed, if any.

Low Temperature Astrophotography

A most challenging segment of amateur astronomy is the photography of deep sky objects, an area usually left to the professionals. Considerable ingenuity, patience, and practice are needed with modest equipment, but striking photographs make up for the time spent. One fascinating method that goes beyond the usual techniques is that of taking pictures while the film is at temperatures far below freezing. This method has given some truly amazing results—only modest exposure times are needed to obtain photographs of faint nebulae and galaxies—rivaling those taken by tedious prolonged exposure

Nebula are glowing areas of highly rarefied gas or dust in space. The Orion nebula, only about a thousand light years away in our galaxy, was photographed by James Matteson with a 14-inch Celestron—cold camera. Photo courtesy of Celestron.

or by much lower aperture ratio instruments. All work has been done with a 312.5 mm (12½-inch) f/7 reflector, quite a modest size by professional standards. Much could be accomplished with the average amateur's 150 mm or 200 mm (6- or 8-inch) f/8 reflector using this low temperature technique.

Background Information. Very long exposures are necessary to get good density on deep sky photographs with commonly available films because of their poor sensitivity to the low intensity light from these distant objects. Indeed, it may not be possible to record very faint light at all in a reasonable exposure time. To reduce exposure time, one can select a "hot" film by testing different code dates under long exposure conditions in the darkroom or use special spectroscopic-type films. Other methods would be treating the film chemically, baking, and flashing the film with light before exposure. But these give varying degrees of fog, which may be objectionable. Gains are most often quite modest. It has been known for a long time that low temperatures will decrease the sensitivity of an emulsion to light of high intensity, yet increase it to very low intensities. While this reversal of the reciprocity failure effect at low temperatures is just what is needed to permit shorter exposure times, only in very recent years has any serious effort been made to put this effect to use in astronomy.

Some Problems. Cooling the film below the dew point of the air will cause moisture to condense on the surface. Of course when the film is below freezing, frost will form. Keeping frost off the film surface, then, is the most difficult problem to contend with. One method of doing this is to place the film in a chamber having a front window facing the objective, the film back resting on a cooling plate at the rear. Dry air can then be used to "flush out" the chamber before it is sealed. Making air absolutely dry is difficult, and, because of a refrigerator action, frost soon forms on the outside of the window, necessitating a heater. The air in the chamber conducts much heat to the film. A far better method is to evacuate the air from the chamber with a vacuum pump. Any pump pulling down to about 0.1 mm of mercury will suffice for this purpose. Not only is the moisture removed, but good insulation results as well.

Constructing a Vacuum Chamber. Only a few construction hints and a schematic drawing are given here, as anyone building a similar unit will probably want to try other ideas or improvements. As shown in the accompanying drawing, the chamber is constructed of heavy sheet metal (heavy enough so that air pressure will not bend it) and soldered. The window is bonded to the chamber with silicone rubber, and the gasket around the top of chamber, on which the cold box frame rests, is also silicone rubber. The film holder sits on a lucite rest for insulation, which must be strong enough to support the atmospheric pressure on it coming from the area of the cold box. Because the cold box has atmospheric pressure on it, it must be strong enough not to bend and cause the film holder, which is in contact with it, to go out of focus. The cold box is bonded with silicone rubber in a lucite frame for insulation.

The cold box can be cooled by filling it with dry ice chips, or more conveniently, by allowing liquid CO_2 from a bottle to escape through a small orifice and into the box (the liquid turns to snow instantly) yielding about *minus* 43 C (109 F). An accurate way to control temperature would be to use a thermoelectric device for cooling. It is essential that there be no leaks, for even though the pump can maintain the vacuum, moisture in the air coming through the leak will form frost on the film.

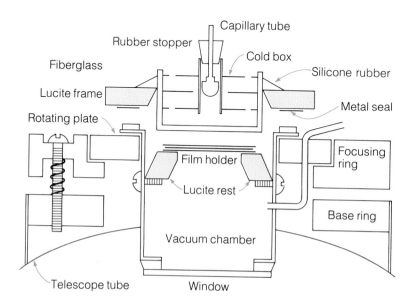

Capillary tube

Rubber stopper

Cold box

Fiberglass

Silicone rubber

Lucite frame

Metal seal

Rotating plate

Focusing ring

Film holder

Lucite rest

Base ring

Vacuum chamber

Telescope tube

Window

A schematic drawing of a vacuum chamber with a guiding head unit. Expanded carbon dioxide gas serves as a coolant. Original line drawing by Evered Kreimer.

Operating a Vacuum Chamber. The vacuum chamber is mounted and used in the form of a guiding head. It consists of a base ring that fastens to the telescope tube at the Newtonian focus. On the base ring, a focusing ring is mounted with three spring-loaded screws. A plate, which can rotate 360 degrees, supports a guiding microscope and goes in the focusing ring. The vacuum chamber is then mounted in the center of the rotating plate. A different method of mounting the vacuum chamber would be used in installations where a separate telescope is used for guiding.

To operate the vacuum chamber, center the object to be taken, find a guide star with the microscope, place the film holder on the rest, and put the cold box in place. After the vacuum pump has run a couple of minutes, you can admit the dry ice or expand the CO_2 and begin the exposure. When taking a series of pictures, the cold box must be allowed to warm up a bit so that moisture can be wiped off the platen before starting.

Black-and-White Results. Some types of emulsions will show much larger speed gains than others, and each type will have an optimum exposure temperature. As temperature control seems difficult in the simple camera using dry ice, a film that shows the fastest speed at the fixed temperature of dry ice must be used. In most cases, this film is Tri-X pan film in 120 rolls. If a cooled and an uncooled picture are taken of the same object, and both are exposed for the same sky fog density, the cooled one will show bright areas as being noticeably less "burned in." Carrying this a step further, a cooled picture can be given two or three times the "normal" exposure time and can then be developed in a low-contrast developer, such as diluted Kodak developer D-76. The resulting negative can be printed on No. 5 paper with little or no dodging and will show detail in the bright areas. Cooling makes the exposure necessary for this technique practical. Overexposure and underdevelopment also improve the "signal to noise ratio."

As a true galaxy, the whirlpool of stars in Andromeda, visible to the eye, is a photographically striking object. Photo by Alan McClure.

A solar eclipse is a major scientific event. The phases of the eclipse range from partial eclipse, through the "diamond ring" effect, to totality. This photograph presents totality with its full coronal beauty, as recorded with a 3½-inch Questar telescope. Photo by Boysinger and Peterson (from Denver Museum of Natural History Expedition) at Lake Rudolph, Kenya. Photo courtesy of Questar Corp.

Color Results. Experimenting has been done with just Kodak high speed Ektachrome film (daylight), and speed gains with cooling seem to run about three to six times. However, speed gains aside, many code dates will show a more important substantial improvement in color balance. Other code dates show little, the color balance being quite good even on a long, uncooled exposure. These variations result because the three emulsion layers react differently to cooling. By testing a particular code date in the darkroom beforehand, the exact color balance with cooling can be determined by comparison with a standard. Pictures taken on this code date can then be viewed through the proper color-correction filter. Actually, the color variations between different emulsions are relatively small when they are cooled. The eye is able to adapt and ignore these differences quite easily, unless you are trying to identically match two pictures.

Exposure time on cooled high speed Ektachrome film (daylight) with the *f*/7 reflector system is about 60 to 90 minutes to get down into the sky fog for very faint objects. As color film does not seem to have the contrast of black-and-white film, these faint objects will not show up well on the bright background. To improve the contrast and overall appearance, the original is copied onto reversal color film, such as Ektachrome, with an exposure to darken the sky background and bring it closer to what might be termed "normal." Although contrast is improved, faint reds and blues will tend to be lost in the copying process unless a light magenta filter such as a Kodak Wratten CC10M or CC20M is used. Sometimes the original will have a greenish cast to the unexposed base, and more dense magenta CC filtering will be needed to keep the green color from getting out of hand on the copy. Other CC filters can be added if it is desired to exaggerate slightly in the blue or red direction. With careful copying, the resulting picture can be almost spectacular, and yet as genuinely true as color film can reproduce astronomical objects.

• *See also:* ECLIPSE PHOTOGRAPHY; MOON, PHOTOGRAPHY OF; SUN, PHOTOGRAPHY OF.

Further Reading: Cortright, Edgar M., ed. *Exploring Space with a Camera.* WA, DC: Scientific and Technical Information Division, Office of Technology, Utilization, NASA, 1968; Keene, George. *Star-Gazing with Telescope and Camera.* Garden City, NY: Amphoto, 1967; Paul, Henry E. *Outer Space Photography,* 4th ed. Garden City, NY: Amphoto, 1976; —— *Telescopes for Skygazing.* Garden City, NY: Amphoto, 1976.

Atmospheric Haze

Atmospheric haze is a suspension of water vapor, smoke, dust, and other solid particles in the air, which scatters visible (especially blue-violet) and ultraviolet energy wavelengths. Its effects are most visible in the print or slide images of distant objects; they are lighter and less contrasty in both black-and-white and color pictures, and color pictures will also be less saturated and bluer. Under some conditions, haze effects may be reduced or eliminated by using filters. Atmospheric fog—ground-level mist (suspended water particles rather than vapor)—often combined with smoke and dust—cannot be penetrated by filtration. Success depends on the luminance of the subject itself.

• *See also:* AERIAL PERSPECTIVE; FILTERS.

Astrophotography

(Left) Black-and-white film picks up ultraviolet light scattered by atmospheric haze. (Right) No. 25A red filter absorbs UV light, reducing effect of haze.

Audiovisual Planning

The degree of success achieved by a slide or filmstrip presentation, or a motion picture, is directly proportional to the thoroughness of the planning that precedes the actual production. An inadequately planned presentation invariably costs more than a comparable production that has been well prepared.

The planning of a presentation or motion picture is facilitated by the use of equipment such as planning boards, planning cards, slide-sequence illuminators, and Kodak Ektagraphic write-on slides (for slide shows). These items are used regularly by planning departments at Kodak and other industrial organizations, and by many professional producers of slides and motion pictures. They are relatively simple to make from readily available materials. Obviously, the materials and dimensions given here are not fixed; they can be modified to suit individual requirements.

Planning Boards and Planning Cards

Planning boards and cards are valuable for:

1. Generating, collecting, and organizing ideas and visuals
2. Planning and producing lessons, slide sets, filmstrips, and informational motion pictures
3. Pretesting programs before production begins
4. Communicating assignments to writers, photographers, and artists
5. Coordinating production steps
6. Creating integrated visuals and narration
7. Preventing wasted effort
8. Visualizing productions in rough form
9. Preparing scripts or presentation outlines
10. Providing for checking the daily status of a project
11. Storyboarding

Planning Board. This is a very helpful device at the various stages of organizing a presentation; it is sometimes called a "storyboard" later in the planning process. For a lengthy presentation, several boards may be needed; a modest production usually requires only one.

Plain white 76 × 127 mm (3″ × 5″) or 102 × 152 mm (4″ × 6″) index cards are commonly used in the initial planning stage. On each card, write one idea or point you want to include to achieve the slide or filmstrip objective. Put the first card on the board; write another idea on another card and put it on the board; repeat the process until no more pertinent thoughts come to mind. If more than one person is involved at this step in planning, the brainstorming or random-thinking technique is adopted. Every idea that occurs to anyone—no matter how unlikely it may seem at the time—should be written on a card and placed on the board. Often, even a seemingly impracticable suggestion can spark an excellent idea.

It is possible to lay the cards on a table or floor, rather than to use the planning board. The advantages of the board are that the cards are held quite firmly and not easily dispersed, and the whole board can be carried to another room (for more work or for submission for approval) without disturbing the sequence of ideas.

When sufficient thoughts have been recorded and placed on the board, an editing process takes place: cards bearing similar or overlapping points are grouped; ideas that are impractical for filming, or that are inconsistent with the objective, are set to one side but not discarded—there may be reason to refer to them later. If new possibilities occur during this editing, they are written on cards and added to the board. Finally, the cards are arranged to represent the continuity of the ideas in the completed

A planning board will help organize a presentation. This board is for 102 × 152 mm (4″ × 6″) planning cards.

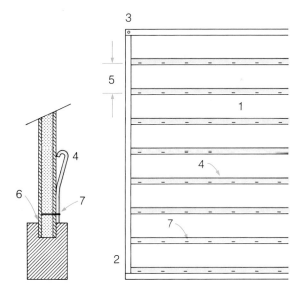

Planning board construction.
1 Panel: 6 mm (¼-inch) fir plywood, 1.22 × 0.81 m (48" × 31 ⅞").
2 Frame: 25 × 19 mm (1" × ¾") pine, rabbeted 6 × 6 mm (¼" × ¼") to fit panel.
3 Provision for hanging: 8 mm (⁵⁄₁₆-inch) diameter holes, slightly beveled at both ends, to fit over 6 mm (¼-inch) diameter metal pegs or rods; or use screw eyes in top of frame.
4 Card retainers: 1.19 mm (47-inch) plastic strips to hold cards in place. Mount strips beaded side toward panel.
5 Retainer spacing: 102 mm (4 inches), center to center for 102 × 152 mm (4" × 6") cards.
6 Rabbet detail.
7 Retainer staple: 6 mm (¼-inch) gun-type.

film. When the planner is satisfied with the result, it is presented to the proper authority for approval. It might also be a good idea to photograph the board at this time for future reference, in the event the composition is changed.

Planning Board Construction. The board is quite simple to make. Essentially, it consists of a piece of 6 mm (¼-inch) plywood set in a frame made of 25 × 19 mm (1" × ¾") pine. Special plastic strips are stapled on one or both sides. A board can be painted to give it a finished appearance. Holes can be drilled through the top for hanging, or the board can stand on a display rack or easel. These boards hold 56 cards. Ready-made planning boards and printed cards (holds 40), 76 × 127 mm (3" × 5")

are available from Medro Educational Products.

Planning Card Use and Design. With approval of the plan as represented by the ideas on the planning board, the next step is to visualize in detail the points written on the previously mentioned plain white cards. At this stage, some users consider that they are through with the *planning board* and are turning to a *storyboard*. Instead of plain white cards, specially prepared 76 × 127 mm (3" × 5") or 102 × 152 mm (4" × 6") cards are now employed.

These cards can easily be composed, and then duplicated in quantity on almost any office copier. If a very large number is needed, it would probably be simpler to have them produced by a local printer.

The layout for printing is shown in the accompanying illustration. Any common type size, including typewriter, can be used for the legends. The rectangular area on the card should occupy the upper lefthand corner and it should have the same proportions as a 35 mm transparency. (For a square or vertical image, an appropriate portion of the rectangle should be used.)

The rectangle on the card provides a frame for a rough sketch of the anticipated shot. Fine artistry is rarely needed; stick figures and general outlines of subjects can serve. Before sketching each shot, visit the location where it is to be made, if at all possible; without on-the-spot viewing, you may easily visualize a shot that later proves impossible because of space limitations, immovable objects, or other restrictions. Photographs, shot on scouting locations, can also be attached to the frame on the card.

Job. Show the number (or the title) of the production—for identification, filing, and bookkeeping. If a series of films, slide sets, or filmstrips is being planned, the sequential job-number should be entered on each card.

Illustration. Indicate presentation sequence of the slide or movie scene. Slide pairs for use in dissolve presentations might be marked 1A, 1B; 2A, 2B; and so forth. (The letters identify the slide trays.) The illustration numbers should be marked in pencil, then changed to ink or other permanent mark after the final sequence has been determined. Changes during planning can be accommodated by renumbering, deleting cards, or using subscripts (for additions).

Production Notes. This space is for information that will be needed by the photographer and artist

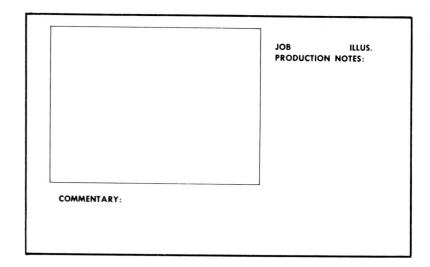

The planning cards should have space for all pertinent information—job number, illustration number, production notes, commentary, and a sketch of the anticipated shot.

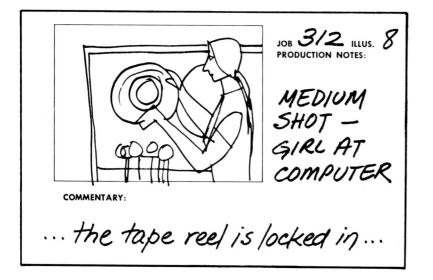

The complete planning cards are very helpful for organizing a presentation. In this way, there is a record of slide or filmstrip ideas.

—such as background color, lettering style, camera angle, and progressive-disclosure details.

Commentary. Information recorded here may be only a word, phrase, or single sentence. It can be expanded later, if desired, even to include the final narration.

If a job is for release to an outside producer, copies of the completed cards should be made on an office copier or similar equipment. For large-group evaluation of the proposed presentation, a slide set or filmstrip of the visuals on the cards can be made.

Slide-Sequence Illuminators

Slide-sequence illuminators are practically indispensable for:

1. Comparing different slide sets
2. Arranging slides in sequence before loading tray(s)
3. Editing slide sets
4. Comparing slide sets with planning boards and scripts
5. Creating narration
6. Viewing filmstrips and uncut slide film

A slide-sequence illuminator is used for viewing, organizing, and comparing slides.

7. Marking slide mounts
8. Inspecting slides
9. Organizing slide talks from existing slides

Building a Slide-Sequence Illuminator. The materials needed are:

1. 19 mm (¾-inch) plywood for illuminator box
2. Gloss-white paint for box interior
3. 1.2 m (48-inch), 40-watt, cool-white deluxe fluorescent lamps with fixtures (set of three for average use; set of four where room light is 60 footcandles or higher at the face of the illuminator; set of six with illuminator twice this size). Note that because of the spectral characteristics of the fluorescent lamps, the illuminator should not be used for copying transparencies or for making critical evaluation of color.*
4. Viewing panel of 3 mm (⅛-inch) plastic or flashed opal glass—height, 422 mm

(16⅝ inches); length, as required. Rigid white translucent plastic, such as Plexiglas No. W-2447 available from Rohm and Haas Company, is recommended. IMPORTANT: If Plexiglas is used, size the panel to allow for 3 mm (⅛ inch) of possible expansion at each end. Make any screw holes in the plastic somewhat oversize and use flat washers on the screws.

5. Panel hinges or clips; rubber feet; lamp-support brackets or cleats; toggle switch. If a toggle switch with an extra-long sleeve or a bushing is needed, it is available from Arrow-Hart Inc., Part No. 21615BD or 21615BE. Alternatively, the area around the mounting hole can be routed out for a 12 mm (¹⁵⁄₃₂-inch) bushing; or an enlarged mounting hole with a metal mounting plate can be used.

6. 9 mm (⅜-inch) quarter-round, 6 × 9 mm (¼″ × ⅜″) shoe molding, or 19 × 6 × 9 mm (¾″ × ¼″ × ⅜″) counter edging (or cap) for slide-support strips. (The 9 mm quarter-round was used on the illuminator shown in the illustration that appears on the following page.)

---

*Special fluorescent lamps are available that are photographically balanced to be the equivalent of daylight. The use of such lamps permits a better judgment of slide color and permits photographing slides on daylight film without filter corrections.

Explanatory Notes. The slide-support strips should be cemented in place if a glass viewing panel is used. They can be glued, cemented, or screwed to a plastic panel.

As described, the illuminator accommodates up to 144 slides in 51 × 51 mm (2″ × 2″) mounts. If the illuminator is to be used with the Kodak 110 plastic slide mount (30 × 30 mm), then the space between slide supports should be reduced by 19 mm (¾-inch); about 333 of the plastic slide

mounts will be accommodated. The dimensions can be altered to suit the individual needs.

For adequate ventilation, place the illuminator at least 13 mm (½-inch) away from the wall. Alternatively, drill additional vent holes in the top of the illuminator box (or near the top in the ends of the box).

For critical evaluation of facial expression, mount alignment, sharpness, and other details in the slides, use a high-quality magnifier, such as the Kodak achromatic magnifier, 5×, or the Edmund Scientific magnifier, 9–12×.

If it is desired to hold strips of film for viewing, Kodak color film clips can be attached to the end panels of the illuminator. Similarly, clips attached to the top of the illuminator, near the front edge, can be used to hold sheet film for viewing.

Ready-made illuminators are available from Matrix Systems Ltd.

Kodak Ektagraphic **Write-On Slides**

When an instructor is previewing a slide set, he may see the opportunity to insert a slide or two that will tie the subject directly to something that the class has studied or has experienced. On occasions such as this, some of the special values of the Kodak Ektagraphic write-on slides become apparent.

Each slide consists of a 51 × 51 mm (2″ × 2″) mount containing a square of Kodak Estar film base with a matte surface on one side. The writing area measures 38 × 38 mm (1½″ × 1½″).

You can add your own drawings, diagrams, comments, or last-minute notices to a slide presentation by using write-on slides and almost any kind of pencil or fiber-tip pen. For a neat, professional look, try easy-to-use transfer letters.

You can create projected flash cards or progres-

Construction diagram of a slide-sequence illuminator. (For metric equivalents see the accompanying table.)

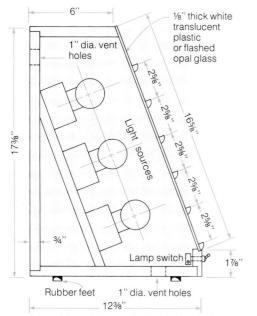

Support lamp fixtures with cleats or brackets attached to inside of end panels.

METRIC EQUIVALENTS OF LINEAR DIMENSIONS

Inches	⅛	¼	⅜	¾	1	1½ × 1½	1¾	1⅞
Millimeters	3	6	9	19	25	38 × 38	44	48

Inches	2⅛	2⅝	2 × 2	4½	6	12⅜	16⅝	17⅜
Millimeters	54	67	51 × 51	114	152	314	422	441

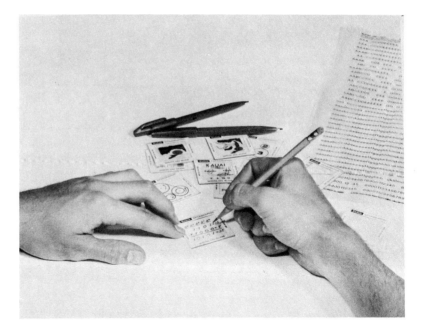

Write-on slides are useful for adding drawings, diagrams, comments, or last-minute notices to a slide presentation, without the need to prepare extra artwork that must then be photographed.

sive-disclosure sets. Students can make slides easily to present reports, describe experiments, or develop other presentations of their own.

Write-on slides can be used as temporary slides in the planning and previewing of slide sets and synchronizing sound and music while the finished artwork and photographs are being completed. These preview slides can be shown to persons or groups that must approve the program.

Kodak Ektagraphic write-on slides are available only through dealers in Kodak audiovisual products. Note that these slides are not recommended for use in automatic-focusing projectors.

• *See also:* PROJECTION, AUDIOVISUAL; PROJECTION CABINETS; PROJECTION SCREENS; SLIDE PRESENTATION; SLIDES AND FILMSTRIPS.

Further Reading: Brown, James S. *Audio-Visual Instruction: Technology, Media, and Methods,* 5th ed. New York, NY: McGraw-Hill Book Co., 1977; Bullard, John R. and Calvin E. Mether. *Audiovisual Fundamentals: Basic Equipment Operation and Simple Materials Production.* Dubuque, IA: William C. Brown Co., 1974; Erickson, Carlton W. and David H. Curl. *Fundamentals of Teaching with Audiovisual Technology,* 2nd ed. New York, NY: Macmillan Publishing Co., 1972; Kemp, J. E. *Planning and Producing Audio-Visual Materials,* 3rd ed. New York, NY: T. Y. Crowell, 1975; Langford, M. J. *Visual Aids and Photography in Education.* New York, NY: Hastings House, 1973; Ring, Arthur. *Planning and Producing Slides and Filmstrips.* Belmont, CA: Fearson Publications, 1974.

Automatic Exposure Systems

Many modern cameras are made with internal metering, but this alone is not considered automatic exposure adjustment, even where a system of matching the meter needle to a reference is used.

For a system to be considered automatic, it must actually perform the setting of either the lens diaphragm, the shutter speed, or both, without any action by the photographer. A system should be considered *automatic* only if it sets *both* lens aperture and shutter speed without manual movement of a control by the operator. All other systems should be considered *semi-automatic.* Both kinds of systems require a preliminary setting of the film speed in use.

Semi-automatic systems fall into two classes, depending upon whether the automatic control operates the lens diaphragm or the shutter speed. The operator has to set one value; the automatic control sets the other.

Systems in which the operator chooses a suitable aperture setting are commonly called "aperture-preferred" systems. The camera's exposure control sets the proper shutter speed for that aperture according to the brightness of the subject. In a semi-automatic "shutter-preferred" system, the operator decides on an appropriate shutter speed, after which the camera sets the lens aperture.

Fully automatic systems, which operate both the lens-aperture and shutter-speed setting automatically, still require the operator to set the film speed when loading the camera. In some cases, however, the film-speed setting is made by a notch or other key on the film magazine and requires no attention by the photographer at all.

The most common example of the fully automatic system is in the Kodak Trimlite Instamatic® camera. Insertion of a film magazine sets the system for the speed of the film in use; the "electric-eye" system then operates both lens aperture and shutter speed according to a fixed program. In the brightest light, the shutter speed remains at its maximum setting, while the lens is set at its smallest aperture. As the light diminishes, the shutter speed remains at maximum, while the lens aperture opens as required for correct exposure. When the light becomes so dim as to require the maximum aperture of the lens, the control switches over to the shutter and produces appropriately slower speeds, extending in some cases to time exposures of several seconds.

Many automatic systems provide a method of switching the automatic controls off when the photographer prefers to decide upon his own exposure. It is also necessary to disengage the automatic exposure controls to make pictures with flash. In the case of the Kodak Trimlite Instamatic cameras, this is accomplished automatically. Inserting a flashcube disconnects the electric-eye control and connects the lens-aperture control to the focusing device. Thus, the lens aperture is set according to the flash-to-subject distance, as in ordinary work using the flash guide-number system.

• *See also:* EXPOSURE METERS AND CALCULATORS.

Available-Light Photography

Available-light photography, also called ambient-light or existing-light photography, comprises the making of pictures with whatever light happens to be available, and without the addition of any light source by the photographer. Thus, available light is not only natural light, it is also whatever artificial light may exist in the scene, either indoors or outdoors, and conversely, any daylight that may enter an interior scene.

Available light includes the light from table and floor lamps, ceiling fixtures, fluorescent lamps, spotlights, neon signs, windows, skylights, candles, fireplaces, and any other light source that provides the available light. In other words, available light is the type of light found in homes, schools, museums, churches, restaurants, stage shows, and auditoriums. Outdoor scenes at twilight or after dark are considered to be available-light situations. Available light is characterized by lower light levels than you would encounter in daylight outdoors.

Advantages of Available-Light Picture-Taking

Your available-light pictures look realistic because you haven't altered the illumination in the scene. Even a skillfully lighted flash or photolamp picture may look artificial and contrived when compared with a good available-light picture.

White card held near girl's face reflected light into shadows. White walls and curtains also reflected light.

Available-light picture-taking gives you a bonus, too. It lets you take pictures that you couldn't take with other lighting techniques. For example, flash may not be appropriate during a wedding ceremony in a church or during a stage show. Not only would flash disturb the proceedings, but it usually can't carry far enough to light your subject. Fortunately, these scenes are often well lighted and you can photograph them with available light.

Available-light picture-taking is inexpensive and convenient. Without accessory lighting equipment to think about, you can concentrate on getting the best pictures of your subjects, and you have greater freedom of movement. Speaking of subjects, people will really appreciate your available-light approach to picture-taking because they won't be disturbed by flashes from flashbulbs or by bright photolamps. In fact, they may not even notice you're taking pictures, which will give you an added bonus in relaxed, candid expressions.

Equipment and Film

The availability of high-speed films and cameras with fast lenses eliminates the need for a tripod for most scenes and gives you the capability of making candid pictures in available light. Today, the saying

Large subjects photographed from a distance cannot be illuminated by flash, but with existing light, exposure is not affected by camera-to-subject distance. Kodak high speed Ektachrome film (daylight), 6 sec. (with tripod) at f/5.6. Photo by Herb Taylor.

Available-Light Photography

This photograph was taken using only the light given off by the lamps in the room. Kodak high speed Ektachrome film (tungsten), push-processed to EI 400, 1/30 sec. at f/2.

"If you can see it, you can photograph it" is nearly a reality.

Camera Requirements. If you have an adjustable camera or an automatic camera that has a sensitive exposure meter, either one with an $f/2.8$ or faster lens, you're all set for taking many available-light pictures with a hand-held camera. If your camera lens isn't that fast, you can still explore the world of available-light picture-taking, but sometimes you'll need a tripod so that you can make time exposures. If your camera doesn't have an exposure meter, a separate meter that is sensitive to low light levels will be a big help in determining the correct exposure.

Films for Available-Light Picture-Taking. For greatest versatility in most available-light situations, use a high-speed film, such as Kodak high speed Ektachrome films for color slides, or Kodak Tri-X pan film for black-and-white prints. A special processing service offered by Kodak is available at photo dealers. Kodak will push-process your high speed Ektachrome film in the 135 and 120 sizes to 2 times its normal speed.

Each color film is designed for use with a specific type of light. To obtain the most pleasing color rendition in your pictures, expose the film under the lighting conditions recommended by the manufacturer. For example, some high speed Ektachrome films are balanced for daylight illumination. When you expose these films by tungsten lighting (without a light balancing filter), the pictures will look "warm," or yellow-red. Some Ektachrome films are designed for 3200 K tungsten illumination. These films produce pleasing results under most existing tungsten light (regular light bulbs or tungsten floodlights). For taking pictures under fluorescent illumination, daylight film is best, although your results still may appear greenish. Outdoors at night you can use either type of film.

Some important points to remember are:

Take pictures by available light for natural expressions and realism.

Use a camera with a fast lens, $f/2.8$ or faster, and a high-speed film for hand-held pictures.

If your camera has a slower lens, use a tripod to make time exposures.

For color pictures, use daylight color film with daylight or fluorescent illumination; use tungsten film for tungsten illumination. For color pictures outdoors at night you can use either type of film.

Available-Light Photography

Daylight as Available Light Indoors

You can take very pleasing pictures with daylight coming through the windows of your home, and you don't have to concern yourself with the weather. The lighting on overcast days is excellent for informal portraits indoors. It has a soft, diffuse quality that is flattering for pictures of people. It is even better when there is snow on the ground, since this acts as a reflector.

Existing daylight coming through the windows is usually brighter than the artificial light in the home. Take advantage of the light from all the windows in the room by opening the drapes or curtains. This increases the light level in the room, making it easier to get enough exposure, and makes the lighting more even and less contrasty.

On sunny days, the areas in the room that are *not* in direct sunlight are usually best for picture-taking. The lighting is less contrasty and is similar to the diffuse lighting on overcast days. But you can also get some good pictures when your subject is in direct sunlight near a window. Have the subject turn his or her face toward the window, or select a camera angle that includes a minimum of shadow area. The bright sunlight lets you use higher shutter speeds and smaller lens openings or a slower-speed film than you can use for most other available-light pictures.

A subject in front of a bright window may photograph as a silhouette. You can avoid this silhouette effect by shooting from a position beside the window or by exposing for the shadow side of the subject. If there are no other windows in the room to help lighten the shadows, try to stand so that the window is behind you.

(Left) Bright sunlight from a window directly behind the subject may result in a semi-silhouette. Avoid this by making a close-up meter reading of the subject's face. (Right) Change the camera angle or turn the subject toward a window to illuminate the face and eliminate silhouette effect. Kodak high speed Ektachrome film (daylight), rated at EI 400, 1/60 sec. at f/4.

SUGGESTED EXPOSURES					
	Picture Subject	ASA 50–64	ASA125–200	ASA200–400	ASA1000–1250
At Home	Home interiors at night —Areas with bright light; Areas with average light	1/15 sec. *f*/2 1/4 sec. *f*/2.8	1/30 sec. *f*/2 1/15 sec. *f*/2	1/30 sec. *f*/2.8 1/30 sec. *f*/2	1/60 sec. *f*/4 1/30 sec. *f*/4
At Home	Candlelighted close-ups	1/4 sec. *f*/2	1/4 sec. *f*/2.8	1/15 sec. *f*/2	1/30 sec. *f*/2.8
Outdoors at Night	Indoor and outdoor Christmas lighting at night, Christmas trees	1 sec. *f*/4	1 sec. *f*/5.6	1/15 sec. *f*/2	1/30 sec. *f*/2.8
Outdoors at Night	Brightly lighted downtown street scenes (Wet streets add interesting reflections.)	1/30 sec. *f*/2	1/30 sec. *f*/2.8	1/60 sec. *f*/2.8	1/125 sec. *f*/4
Outdoors at Night	Brightly lighted nightclub or theater districts—Las Vegas or Times Square	1/30 sec. *f*/2.8	1/30 sec. *f*/4	1/60 sec. *f*/4	1/125 sec. *f*/5.6
Outdoors at Night	Neon signs and other lighted signs	1/30 sec. *f*/4	1/60 sec. *f*/4	1/125 sec. *f*/4	1/125 sec. *f*/8
Outdoors at Night	Store windows	1/30 sec. *f*/2.8	1/30 sec. *f*/4	1/60 sec. *f*/4	1/60 sec. *f*/8
Outdoors at Night	Floodlighted buildings, fountains, monuments	1 sec. *f*/4	1/2 sec. *f*/4	1/15 sec. *f*/2	1/30 sec. *f*/2.8
Outdoors at Night	Skyline—Distant view of lighted buildings at night	4 sec. *f*/2.8	1 sec. *f*/2	1 sec. *f*/2.8	1 sec. *f*/5.6
Outdoors at Night	Skyline—10 minutes after sunset	1/30 sec. *f*/4	1/60 sec. *f*/4	1/60 sec. *f*/5.6	1/125 sec. *f*/8
Outdoors at Night	Fairs, amusement parks	1/15 sec. *f*/2	1/30 sec. *f*/2	1/30 sec. *f*/2.8	1/60 sec. *f*/4
Outdoors at Night	Fireworks—Displays on the ground	1/30 sec. *f*/2.8	1/30 sec. *f*/4	1/60 sec. *f*/4	1/60 sec. *f*/8
Outdoors at Night	Fireworks—Aerial displays (Keep shutter open on "BULB" or "TIME" for several bursts.)	*f*/8	*f*/11	*f*/16	*f*/32
Outdoors at Night	Lightning (Keep shutter open on "BULB" or "TIME" for one or two streaks of lightning.)	*f*/5.6	*f*/8	*f*/11	*f*/22
Outdoors at Night	Burning buildings, campfires, bonfires	1/30 sec. *f*/2.8	1/30 sec. *f*/4	1/60 sec. *f*/4	1/125 sec. *f*/5.6
Outdoors at Night	Night football, baseball, racetracks†	1/30 sec. *f*/2.8	1/60 sec. *f*/2.8	1/125 sec. *f*/2.8	1/250 sec. *f*/4

SUGGESTED EXPOSURES (cont'd.)				
Picture Subject	ASA 50–64	ASA125–200	ASA200–400	ASA1000–1250
Niagara Falls— White lights Light-colored lights Dark-colored lights	15 sec. f/5.6 30 sec. f/5.6 30 sec. f/4	8 sec. f/5.6 15 sec. f/5.6 30 sec. f/5.6	4 sec. f/5.6 8 sec. f/5.6 15 sec. f/5.6	4 sec. f/11 4 sec. f/8 4 sec. f/5.6
Moonlighted— **Landscapes** **Snow Scenes**	30 sec. f/2 15 sec. f/2	15 sec. f/2 8 sec. f/2	8 sec. f/2 4 sec. f/2	4 sec. f/2.8 4 sec. f/4
Basketball, Hockey, Bowling	1/30 sec. f/2	1/60 sec. f/2	1/125 sec. f/2	1/125 sec. f/4
Boxing, Wrestling	1/60 sec. f/2	1/125 sec. f/2	1/250 sec. f/2	1/250 sec. f/4
Stage shows—Average **Bright**	1/30 sec. f/2 1/60 sec. f/2.8	1/30 sec. f/2.8 1/60 sec. f/4	1/60 sec. f/2.8 1/125 sec. f/4	1/60 sec. f/5.6 1/250 sec. f/5.6
Circuses—Floodlighted **acts** **Spotlighted acts** **(carbon-arc)**	1/30 sec. f/2 1/60 sec. f/2.8	1/30 sec. f/2.8 1/125 sec. f/2.8	1/60 sec. f/2.8 1/250 sec. f/2.8	1/125 sec. f/4 1/250 sec. f/5.6
Ice shows—Floodlighted **acts** **Spotlighted acts** **(carbon-arc)**	1/30 sec. f/2.8 1/60 sec. f/2.8	1/60 sec. f/2.8 1/125 sec. f/2.8	1/125 sec. f/2.8 1/250 sec. f/2.8	1/250 sec. f/4 1/250 sec. f/5.6
Interiors with bright **fluorescent light**	1/30 sec. f/2.8	1/30 sec. f/4	1/60 sec. f/4	1/125 sec. f/5.6
School—Stage and **auditorium**	—	1/15 sec. f/2	1/30 sec. f/2	1/30 sec. f/4
Swimming pool— **Tungsten light indoors** **(above water)**	1/15 sec. f/2	1/30 sec. f/2	1/60 sec. f/2	1/60 sec. f/4
Church interiors— **Tungsten light**	1 sec. f/5.6	1/15 sec. f/2	1/30 sec. f/2	1/30 sec. f/4
Stained-glass windows, **daytime—from inside**	Use 3 stops more exposure than for the outdoor lighting conditions.			
Glassware in windows, **daytime—from inside**	Use 1 stop more exposure than for the outdoor lighting conditions.			

Indoors in Public Places (side label spanning lower rows)

For color pictures, use tungsten film for the most natural color rendition. You can also use daylight color film, but your pictures will look yellow-red.

For color pictures of these scenes, use daylight film. You can also use tungsten film with a No. 85B filter over your camera lens. When you use this filter, give 1 stop more exposure than that recommended for daylight film in the table.

For color pictures of these scenes, you can use either daylight or tungsten film. Daylight film will produce colors with a warmer, more yellowish look. Tungsten film produces colors with a colder, more bluish appearance.

†When the lighting is provided by mercury-vapor lamps, you'll get better results by using daylight film. Your pictures will still appear greenish.

Use a tripod or other firm support for shutter speeds slower than 1/30 sec.

The span of this bridge with the city skyline was photographed at dusk. All illumination except skylight came from the lights on the bridge and the buildings. With large subjects, where flash is impossible, long exposure times must be used. Note the particularly effective use of a star filter to point up the individual lights and create an illusion of greater brightness.

Your reflected-light exposure meter or automatic camera can be misled by a bright window included in the scene. Either make a close-up meter reading of the subject or select a camera angle that doesn't include the window in the picture.

You can reduce contrast by using a reflector, such as a piece of white cloth, white cardboard, or crumpled aluminum foil, to fill in the shadows. Place the reflector on the shadow side of your subject so that the reflector is facing the window that provides most of the light. Make sure the reflector is far enough away so that it is not included in the picture. Strictly speaking, this is not pure available light, but you can forgive yourself for stretching the truth a little when it helps you improve the basic lighting.

On clear days, when you are taking pictures in an area of the room that is not in direct sunlight, but where the blue sky is providing most of the light, you can use a skylight filter (No. 1A) to reduce the blue tint in your color slides. This filter does not require any increase in exposure.

Artificial Lighting

Artificial lighting at home is usually contrasty because it includes brightly lighted areas around lamps and comparatively darker areas in the other parts of the room. Turning on *all the lights* in the room reduces the contrast of the lighting and raises the light level so that you may have enough light to hand-hold your camera and obtain proper exposure. (See the exposure table.) House lamps with translucent shades are best for most available-light pictures. Pole lamps or gooseneck lamps, which give more directional light, are handy to use when you want direct light on your subject or want a spotlight effect in the scene.

Most household lamps have tungsten light bulbs. Use a color film designed for tungsten light to get pleasing color rendition in your pictures. In rooms illuminated by some fluorescent light, use daylight color film without a filter. For accurate color renditions, correction filters can be used.

Since black-and-white film doesn't record the color of the light in the scene, you can use it with any kind of lighting.

It is difficult to judge visually the differences in the amount of light from one scene to another in the home. Use an exposure meter or an automatic camera to determine exposure. A lighted lamp included in the scene may mislead your reflected-light meter, so take a close-up reading of the principal subject, excluding the lamp.

Outdoor Scenes at Night

Outdoor night scenes usually include large areas of darkness broken by spots of light from signs, streetlights, and buildings. Pictures of such scenes are easy to take because you can get good results over a fairly wide range of exposures. Short exposures emphasize the bright areas by preserving the detail while the shadows go dark. Long exposures show more detail in the shadows and reduce detail in the brightest areas. The large dark areas in many night scenes make it difficult to use an exposure meter from the camera position. You can either make a close-up meter reading of the important areas in your picture or use the exposure recommended in the exposure table in this article. When you are photographing evenly illuminated subjects, such as floodlighted buildings, statues, and store windows, try to get close enough to take an exposure-meter reading. When you go outdoors for night pictures, take along a small flashlight. This will help you make your camera settings in the dark.

For outdoor picture-taking at night, you can choose either daylight film or tungsten film. This is a matter of personal taste. Pictures taken on tungsten film may look more natural, while pictures taken on daylight film will have a "warmer," more yellow-red appearance. Both types of film produce pleasing results.

An excellent time to take pictures of street scenes, floodlighted buildings, city skylines, and other outdoor night subjects is at twilight, just be-

Night scenes photographed on tungsten film look more natural; those on daylight film appear warmer, yellower. Kodak high speed Ektachrome film, long exposure times (note blurred car lights).

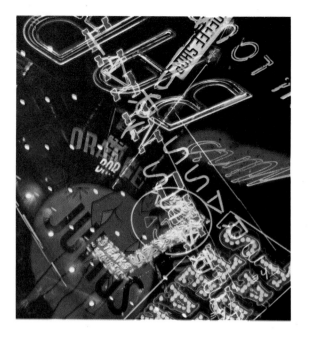

A montage can be created by making several exposures on the same frame of film. Kodak high speed Ektachrome film (tungsten) at ASA 320; exposure 1/125 sec. between f/4 and f/5.6.

on the *same frame of film.* By placing the signs in different locations on the film, you can create an unusual montage. Make a mental note of the placement of the sign for each exposure so that you will create a pleasing design. Check the instruction manual for your camera to see whether you can try this fascinating technique.

Store windows often have elaborate and colorful displays with dramatic lighting effects. Take a close-up meter reading through the window glass and try to select a camera angle that minimizes distracting reflections from the window.

Outdoor Christmas Lights. Around Christmas, many neighborhoods, downtown streets, and shopping centers are ablaze with color. Buildings with outdoor Christmas lights make good subjects for color pictures. If there is snow on the ground, you can get pictorial effects by including the reflections of the colored lights on the snow. On very cold nights, keep your camera tucked inside your coat until you're ready to take pictures. Cold weather may make some shutters sluggish.

Floodlighted Buildings, Fountains, and Statues. Many buildings, fountains, and statues look rather ordinary in the daytime, but at night they are often

fore complete darkness. Your pictures will show a rich color in the sky instead of just black. Usually the lights are turned on at dusk, before the sky becomes completely dark. While there is still some light in the sky (about 10 minutes after sunset), you can make pictures at 1/60 sec. at f/4 on some Kodak high speed Ektachrome films. Since the lighting conditions are so variable at this time of day, you may want to bracket your exposure.

Street Scenes. Signs in theater, nightclub, or shopping districts make brightly colored subjects for your pictures. The best time to take pictures in business districts is on shopping nights, because more buildings are lighted. An excellent time to take these pictures is during or just after a rain. The lights will produce a myriad of colorful reflections on the wet pavement, adding interest to otherwise black, empty areas of your pictures. For a colorful abstraction, move in close to a rain puddle so that the reflections become the main subject for your picture.

If your camera permits double exposures, you can make several exposures of different neon signs

Special department-store displays make delightful photographs. Select camera angle carefully to avoid reflections of light on the glass.

Available-Light Photography

beautifully lighted. Try framing this type of subject with an object in the foreground, such as a tree branch. You can make interesting comparison pictures by shooting the same buildings or fountains during the day and at night.

Outdoor Sporting Events at Night. Sporting events at night are usually well lighted and provide excellent subjects for available-light pictures. Outdoor sporting events may be illuminated with tungsten light, but many modern sports stadiums have installed mercury-vapor lamps, which look slightly blue-green when compared to tungsten lamps. With mercury-vapor lighting, you will get better pictures on daylight film, although they will probably look blue-green because the lights are deficient in red.

When possible, use a very high-speed film so that you can use shutter speeds high enough to stop some action. See the exposure table in this article. Don't worry if you can't stop the action completely. Motion that is somewhat blurred gives pictures a look of action. Stopping action is discussed in greater detail under the heading "Indoor Sports" in this article.

Fairs and Amusement Parks. Fairs and amusement parks become a wonderland of colored lights at night. The gay and imaginative outdoor lighting that you will find in these places is superb for availa-

This silhouetted statue adds interest to spectacular fireworks. Kodak Ektachrome-X film at f/8; shutter on "Bulb" or "Time."

ble-light pictures. You can take hand-held pictures of lighted buildings, the midway, and the many colorful signs. Since lighting is such an important part of modern living, world's fairs and similar expositions display the latest lighting innovations. It is truly a world of color for your camera.

Fireworks. Fireworks displays are easy and fun to photograph. You'll get the best pictures of aerial displays if you put your camera on a tripod and capture several bursts in the same picture by making a time exposure. Focus your camera on infinity and aim it in the direction of the display. Exposure is not critical. A larger lens opening will make the lines in the burst thicker and lighter; a smaller lens opening will make the lines thinner and darker. Set the lens opening on your camera according to the exposure table, and with the shutter set on "Bulb" or "Time," keep the shutter open for several bursts.

If you don't have a tripod for making time exposures, you can get successful results by hand-holding your camera and using an exposure of 1/30 sec. at f/2 on Kodak Ektachrome 64 film. Take your pic-

Sports pictures taken outdoors at night during almost motionless moments do not require that fast a shutter speed.

(Left) This peanut-vendor's stall on Crete appears as an island of light in the darkness. Kodachrome II film, 1 sec. at f/2. (Right) The circus offers a wealth of activities to photograph, and lighting presents few problems. Kodak high speed Ektachrome film, Type B, rated at EI 400, 1/125 sec. at f/5.6. Photos by Herb Taylor.

tures when the fireworks bursts are at their fullest.

You can add interest and a feeling of depth to your fireworks pictures by including lighted buildings, a city skyline, lights reflected in water, or silhouettes of objects in the foreground. If you have a telephoto lens for your camera, use it to take "close-up" pictures of fireworks displays.

Since fireworks displays on the ground last several seconds or longer and don't move across the scene, you can use shorter exposure times. For ground displays, you don't need a tripod; you can take pictures by hand-holding your camera and using a shutter speed of 1/30 sec.

Lightning. Taking pictures of lightning is similar to photographing fireworks, except that you don't know exactly when or where it will strike. To capture the lightning in your pictures, put your camera on a tripod and hold the shutter open for one or more flashes. Since you and your tripod would be a likely target for lightning, be very careful to avoid open spaces outdoors. Take your pictures from inside a building through an open window or from some other location (not under a tree) that offers protection.

Since you don't know exactly when or where the lightning will streak across the sky, use a normal or wide-angle lens on your camera. This will increase your chances of having your camera aimed in the right direction, because these lenses include more of the sky than a telephoto lens does. You may have to hold the shutter open for quite some time, so it is best to take pictures of lightning away from city lights and car lights. If there are no bright lights around, you can hold the shutter open for a minute or two when necessary, until the lightning streaks across the sky. If a car goes by, cover your camera lens temporarily with an object such as a hat so that the car lights don't spoil your picture.

Indoor Opportunities for Available-Light Pictures

Museums and Galleries. Museums, art galleries, and other public buildings can provide many subjects for available-light pictures. Some museums offer a great variety of unusual sights, from giant models of prehistoric animals to priceless gems in exquisite settings. The lighting is often arranged to enhance the items on display. Take advantage of this artful lighting when you take pictures.

The elaborate dioramas in many museums make especially good subjects for available-light pictures

Available-Light Photography

Dioramas usually have painted backgrounds, so use a large lens opening to throw the background slightly out of focus and make the diorama look realistic.

Museums and art galleries sometimes have "daylight" fluorescent lights or skylight windows that let in daylight illumination, so use daylight film for best results under these lighting conditions.

When taking pictures of objects in glass display cases, be aware of the reflections on the glass. To prevent the reflections from being recorded in your pictures, you will have to hold your camera right against the glass or use a polarizing filter.

Some museums and galleries don't allow picture-taking, although these restrictions aren't too common. Others do not permit the use of tripods or flash units, but do permit you to hand-hold your camera for taking pictures by available light. It's a good idea to check with the museum personnel before taking

pictures. You may even want to telephone the museum ahead of time.

Circuses and Ice Shows. Photographing these colorful spectaculars by available light is natural because they are well lighted and the subjects are usually too far away for you to use flash. The brilliant costumes and lighting give outstanding results with color film. You may want to get a printed program for the show before you take your seat; it will help you plan your picture-taking.

The lighting at circuses and ice shows is provided by two general kinds of light: carbon-arc spotlights and general tungsten lighting. You can use either daylight or tungsten film—it is a matter of personal preference. Daylight film gives the best color rendition for acts lighted by carbon-arc spotlights; pictures of these scenes made on tungsten film will look somewhat bluish. Since the general, overall lighting that illuminates the arena or ice is usually tungsten, tungsten film gives the most natural color rendition; daylight film will give yellow-red results. When colored filters are used over the lights, both types of film will give equally good results. Since you will probably want to use one type of color film, use Kodak high speed Ektachrome films for color slides or Kodacolor films for color prints.

Churches. Many important family events, such as weddings and baptisms, take place in church. Flash is often inappropriate for picture-taking on such occasions. However, you can record these meaningful events without causing any disturbance when you take pictures by available light. For example, you can get very good pictures of a wedding ceremony from the balcony, where you can be unobtrusive about your picture-taking and can steady your camera on the balcony railing. Take long shots that include much of the church interior and then use a telephoto lens for close-up views.

Sun filtered through stained-glass windows makes a lovely pattern. Kodak high speed Ektachrome film (daylight), 1/60 sec. at f/4.

During your travels, you may visit churches rich with historical significance, or tour creations of modern architecture filled with the promise of the future. Churches make interesting and colorful subject matter for available-light pictures.

The illumination in churches may be primarily tungsten or daylight, depending on how much light the windows let in and the time of day. Choose the appropriate type of color film for the predominant lighting. After you have taken an overall view of the church interior, move in close for pictures showing the detail of the structure, such as intricate carvings and statues.

Stained-Glass Windows. Stained-glass windows also make unusual and extremely colorful picture subjects. Photograph them from inside the church with daylight shining through the glass. Move in close to the window to make your meter reading so that the meter reads only the light coming through the window. If you don't have a meter, try an exposure with the lens opening three stops larger than you would use for the outdoor lighting conditions. For example, if the sun is shining on the window, an "average" exposure for a film with a speed of ASA 64 is 1/125 sec. at $f/4$. On a clear day when the sun isn't striking the window, try 1/30 sec. at $f/2.8$. It is a good idea to bracket your exposure.

School Events. Many events that take place in school, such as plays, parties, graduation ceremonies, and indoor sports events, make good subject matter for your pictures. In the daytime, there is usually plenty of light for indoor picture-taking if the school has large windows. At night, the light will be dimmer, but the overhead lighting is usually sufficient for taking pictures. It is best to use an exposure meter.

Stage lighting in auditoriums is usually provided by tungsten lights. In classrooms, gymnasiums, and swimming pools, the overhead lighting may be tungsten or fluorescent. In the daytime, daylight is usually combined with the artificial overhead lighting.

Indoor Sports. High school and college sporting events are fun to photograph, particularly if a friend or relative is a member of the team. Professional sporting events also offer color and action for you to photograph by available light.

You may want to find out in advance whether the gymnasium lighting is tungsten or fluorescent and take along the appropriate film. To determine the exposure, take a close-up exposure-meter reading of the gym floor area before the action begins.

Several techniques can help you stop action in your pictures. Use the highest shutter speed that the lighting conditions will allow. You can use higher shutter speeds with a high-speed film, such as Kodak Tri-X pan or Royal-X pan film, or high speed Ektachrome films with special Kodak processing.

Most sports activities include moments when the action is temporarily halted or slowed—the "peak" of action. For example, when basketball players are at the highest point of a jump, there is little motion during the split second of suspended action. Snapping the picture at the peak of action "freezes" the motion in your picture.

The direction of motion has a large effect on stopping action. It is easier to stop the action if the subject is moving toward you or away from you. You must use higher shutter speeds to stop the motion of subjects going by at a right angle to your camera than you would need for other directions of motion.

Another way to help stop the action is to "pan" your camera with the moving subject. Move your camera smoothly to keep the subject centered in your viewfinder as you take the picture. Your subject will be sharp and the background blurred. This enhances the feeling of motion in a still picture. Panning works best with a subject moving at a steady speed, such as an ice skater.

Subject distance is also an important factor in stopping action. The farther away you are from your subject, the easier it is to stop the action.

Stage Shows. Musicals and plays provide beautiful settings for pictures. Available-light pictures of stage productions are easy to take because you can use one basic camera setting for most of the show. For example, with Kodak high speed Ektachrome 160 film, the camera setting for a brightly lit professional stage show is 1/60 sec. at f/4. Tungsten film will produce the most pleasing color rendition with stage lighting. Focus on a point in the center of the stage about 3 metres (about 10 feet) behind the footlights and you are ready to take pictures. You should have enough depth of field for most stages so that refocusing usually isn't necessary.

If there's a lot of action on the stage, you can time your picture-taking to catch brief instants when the actors are relatively motionless. For example,

In certain situations, such as religious ceremonies, where flash is not only distracting but also difficult because of camera-to-subject distance, available light is the only solution. In this wedding scene, illuminated only by the interior lights without the addition of flash, warmth is actually added by the light technique used.

most dance sequences include moments when the dancers pause as they finish a spin or change direction. Slight subject blur, caused by moving arms or legs, for example, can add a feeling of movement to the picture so that it does not look static.

When you use the basic exposure setting given in the table in this article, your pictures will become lighter or darker as the stage lighting changes, reflecting the mood of the different scenes. When spotlights emphasize one stage area and the rest of the stage is dark, your pictures will capture the same effect. When all of the stage is dimly lighted, open up your lens one stop from the basic exposure. If the lighting is *very* dim, open the lens two stops from the basic exposure.

Don't worry if the lower part of your picture

Available-Light Photography

Illumination by firelight is lovely but not very bright. Push-process developing increases film speed, allowing for hand-held pictures of dimly lighted subjects. Kodak high speed Ektachrome film (tungsten), ASA 320, 1/30 sec. at f/2.

includes the heads of a few members of the audience; they will give the picture dimension and help frame the stage. For an unobstructed vantage point, try to get seats in the front row of the balcony. You may want to use a telephoto lens to get close-ups of the actors.

Remember that the people around you want to enjoy the performance, too. Be unobtrusive about your picture-taking so that you don't spoil your neighbors' enjoyment. Some professional theaters prohibit picture-taking during the performance because they feel it detracts from the show.

One of the best times to photograph a stage presentation is during the dress rehearsal. You will be able to get close to the cast and choose the best viewpoints for your pictures without disturbing an audience.

Shooting tips include:

Take a pocket flashlight along so that you can see to make your camera settings under dim lighting conditions.

Outdoors in cold weather, put your camera under your coat between exposures to keep the shutter working properly.

A good time to take outdoor night pictures is at twilight, before the sky goes completely dark.

For pictures of aerial fireworks displays, put your camera on a firm support and hold the shutter open for several bursts.

To help stop the action in sports photography, use a very high-speed film and the highest shutter speed that the lighting conditions permit. Then snap the picture at the peak of the action. Panning with the subject also helps stop subject motion in pictures.

Exposure for Available-Light Pictures

Available light varies considerably in intensity. Since your eyes adapt easily to changes in illumina-

tion, the actual light level in a certain situation may be misleading. To get correct exposure, use an automatic camera, an exposure meter, or the exposure table in this article.

Usually the objective in available-light photography is to reproduce the scene so that it appears as realistic as possible. Incorrect exposure can drastically alter the way the scene appears in your picture.

Because of the low level of most available light, underexposure is more common than overexposure. However, you can sometimes overexpose very dimly lighted scenes without realizing it. You will usually want pictures of scenes such as those found in dark restaurants or outdoors at night to look dark when the original scene looked dark to you. But when you use color-slide film and expose these scenes normally according to an exposure meter, you may give too much exposure. The meter indicates exposures that will make the scenes look average in brightness. As a result, the slides look lighter than the original scenes. The slides may be quite acceptable, but they are not accurate reproductions of the scenes. An example of this effect is a time exposure of a scene lighted by moonlight that looks as though it were taken in the daytime. You will get this effect most often when you photograph dimly lighted scenes that have no lights in them. Lights serve as points of reference as to how light or dark the scene actually appeared.

To make natural-looking color slides of dark scenes, try ½ to 1 stop *less* exposure than the meter indicates. This exposure effect does not apply to negative films because the lightness or the darkness of a print is controlled primarily during the printing process.

• *See also:* EXPOSURE METERS AND CALCULATORS; EXPOSURE TECHNIQUES.

Further Reading: Adams, Ansel. *Natural-Light Photography.* Boston, MA: Little, Brown and Company, 1952; Amphoto Editorial Board. *Night Photography Simplified,* rev. ed. Garden City, NY: Amphoto, 1974; Editors of Time-Life Books. *Light and Film.* New York, NY: Time-Life Books, 1970; Nurnberg, Walter. *Lighting for Photography,* 6th ed. Garden City, NY: Amphoto, 1968; Petzold, Paul. *Light on People.* Garden City, NY: Amphoto, 1971; Wooley, A. E. *Photographic Lighting,* 2nd ed. Garden City, NY: Amphoto, 1971.

When photographing lightning, shoot from inside a building or some other sheltered area. Position your camera on a tripod and hold the shutter open for one or more flashes of lightning.

Baby and Child Photography

Pictures of babies are easy to take because babies are so expressive—and they ignore cameras. A noisy toy can evoke enough expressions in just a few minutes to fill an album with pictures. Even the baby's daily attempts at learning to get along in the world provide an endless variety of picture opportunities. Keep a loaded camera in a convenient place around your home so you will be ready to catch impromptu activities. If you wait to take these pictures, you will miss photographing important stages in your baby's development. You can't go back and get these pictures later. You have to take them as things happen —and many things happen only once.

In their first few months, babies grow rapidly; take pictures at least once a week. From six months until the first birthday, plan to take pictures every second or third week. This may sound like a lot of picture-taking, but babies change so much in their first year that it's worth planning a picture-taking schedule to make sure you will get all the pictures you want.

It may help to have the baby's mother nearby to attract the attention of and to position the baby. This picture was taken with a 35 mm single-lens reflex camera fitted with an 85 mm lens. Photo by Don Maggio.

Make a Picture Story

Start taking pictures of the baby right in the hospital; they will provide a good comparison with later ones.

The light in some hospital nurseries is bright enough to permit picture-taking without flash if you have an automatic or adjustable camera with an $f/1.9$ or $f/2.8$ lens. Use Kodak Ektachrome film for color slides or Kodak Tri-X pan film for black-and-white prints, or equivalent films. Be careful not to include any bright outside windows in your picture. The light from the window will mislead the meter of an automatic camera and cause anything in front of the window to appear as a silhouette.

The First Few Weeks. No photographic record of infancy should ignore the many "firsts" in the new life of family-plus-baby: mom or dad fixing formula; grandfather and grandmother holding the baby; and the first bath. Since the first bath is quite an experience for everyone involved, you will want several pictures to tell the story.

From Three to Six Months. Babies become capable of really doing things at this age. Although perhaps not ready to sit unaided in a high chair or baby seat, they manage admirably when propped up by a couple of pillows.

Give a baby a small stuffed toy, a rattle, or a soft blanket, and he or she will supply interesting picture possibilities. Whenever you have control over the location of the picture subject, choose a plain, uncluttered background. If the baby loses interest in the toy before you have finished taking pictures, have someone make noise with a toy, a coin in a tin can, or vocally.

From Six Months Onward—The Age of Discovery. Events such as the first encounter with a pet, or an inanimate object like a lollipop, demand more than one picture. A series of pictures will capture the whole story, and improves the possibility that one of your pictures will turn out to be something extra special. In professional photography of babies, it is essential to shoot several pictures to ensure getting the desired result.

A baby's first attempts at feeding him- or herself are never-to-be repeated moments. For those pictures of the food going everywhere but in the mouth, shoot everything that the baby tries to do during the first few weeks.

Photographing Children

The First Haircut. One of the biggest events of a child's first year is that first trip to the barber.

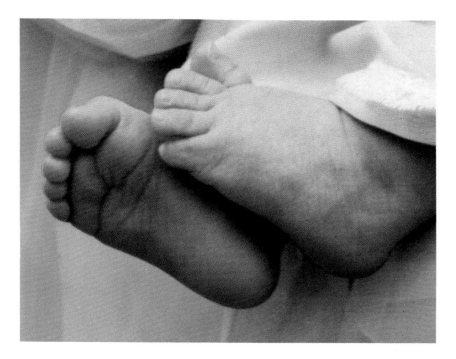

Close-ups such as this can provide interesting variations of the subject. Try to find new angles for your picture-taking. Photo by Don Maggio.

Baby and Child Photography

Party pictures record important events and produce memorable expressions. The guest of honor is the center of attention, so move in and take plenty of close-ups.

There may be enough daylight coming through the window to shoot without flash if you use Kodak Ektachrome 200 film, or its equivalent. If you do use flash, avoid reflections by shooting at an angle to mirrors and by making sure that your image doesn't show in the mirror.

Birthdays. The big event that ends a baby's first year is the first birthday. While the child is all dressed up for this special occasion, take at least one picture as a record of growth. For a fascinating series, stand the baby near something big, such as a door frame, a fireplace, or a stairway, and take the picture. Then every year on the child's birthday, take a picture in the same location.

Of course, birthday parties are always special occasions for children of any age, and they deserve good picture coverage. Make a complete picture story of the party. Start by taking pictures when the first guest arrives at the door, and keep on shooting until the last guest has departed. The birthday boy

or girl is the center of attention, so move in and shoot some close-ups of him or her. You will treasure the expression and detail of these close-up shots.

Ages Three to Ten. The stages of growing-up pass swiftly. Only in pictures will a family still find the toddler, the kindergarten scholar, the Space Cadet, the Red Cross nurse, the summer camper, and the intense teenager. Taking memorable pictures of growing children is as easy as taking pictures of babies. The biggest difference is that the older children move around faster.

In the long run, the pictures of children that mean the most are those which show them engaged in the business of being themselves. The biggest key to natural-looking pictures of children is to keep them doing something or to catch them doing something. When children are engaged in an interesting activity, they forget about the camera, and you can capture a natural expression.

Many of a child's activities take place outdoors. The everyday events may not seem special at the time, but photographs will provide delightful memories in later years.

Taking Pictures of Children Around the House. The everyday things—children taking a bath, playing in the snow, building castles in the sandbox, or taking a dip in a wading pool—provide pictures of events that may not seem special at the time, but will be very special in a few years.

More often than not, children in the house are playing on the floor. One of the most important points to remember is to take the picture from their level. At the same time, move in close to them. Ask them to go right on with their activities while you shoot.

Outdoors. At the beach, the sand and waves provide plenty of entertainment to keep children busy. Children love playgrounds, too. They can climb, swing, and hang to their hearts' content. Shoot through the bars of a jungle gym and use them to frame the picture. Try a low angle to emphasize how high the bars and children go.

Catch the action of subjects, such as a child on a fast-moving swing, by snapping the shutter when the action reaches its peak. With simple cameras, shoot the action head on. Any movement at right angles to the camera is hard to stop when you can't

186

adjust your shutter speed. With an adjustable camera, use a shutter speed of 1/200 or 1/250 sec. or higher to stop action. Actually, some blurring of the hands or feet shows that the subject was moving rapidly, and may not be objectionable.

Informal Portraits. You can make informal portraits by using two methods to get your young subjects to hold still: props and an assistant.

Props can be very helpful in getting a natural expression. A prop may divert the child's attention from the camera, or it may just give the child something natural to do with his or her hands. Any object that captivates or absorbs a child's interest will help show that special delight or absorption. A few of the most common and successful props for little children are toys, musical instruments, small animals, articles of clothing, books, food, and all kinds of ticking, moving, or flexible gadgets. Sometimes a piece of sticky tape on a young child's finger will create interest for a few minutes. Try to keep your prop out of sight until you are all set up and ready to take the picture. Then ask someone to hand it to the child. The initial expression often becomes the best picture.

An assistant can be a great help in posing a child for an informal portrait. An assistant can get the child into position and arrange his or her clothing while you are composing the picture in the viewfinder. When you are ready to take the picture, the assistant can talk with the child or hold up a prop to help get a natural expression.

Older children, while easier to direct, are a great deal less easy to divert. Approach them with a camera and there's no disguising what you have in mind. Props, though, are still beneficial—not so much to draw the subject's attention from the camera as to give the subject something to pose with.

Placing an animal in the hands of an older child may evoke a response, and chances are, that response will be the best ingredient of your picture.

Movies of Babies and Children

Babies and children are perfect subjects for movies that will be among your most prized possessions.

From the day a new baby comes home until the day you attend his or her wedding reception, you'll want to document the important events and everyday fun times in that growing life. Color movies keep yesterday alive because the children in these movies never grow up.

There are two basic approaches to filming babies and children; you'll want to use both of them. One approach is to film movie stories of interesting and important events. The other approach is always to keep your movie camera loaded and in a convenient place around the house for unexpected happenings. Then you can capture those moments when your baby or child is indulging in the many candid activities that are always worth two or three scenes.

After the scenes are processed, you can edit them into an interesting movie. By filming both complete movie stories and isolated bits of spontaneous childhood activities, you'll accumulate an interesting and valuable chronicle of those important but soon-gone childhood activities.

Ideas for Baby Movies. You'll find many opportunities during your baby's first years to record interesting storytelling events. Since babies can't move about as fast as older children, you will have to create much of your own action. Here are just a few ideas for some interesting movie stories.

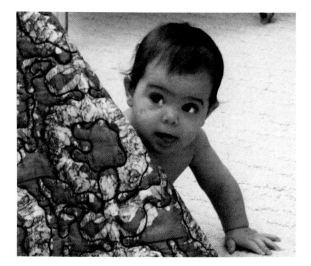

Some of the best times to take movies of a baby are when he or she is busy exploring. For accurate perspective photograph from the baby's own level. Photos by Don Maggio.

Baby and Child Photography

The Newborn Comes Home. The following scenes are just the beginning of the many important events that will take place with the arrival of a new baby.

> Close-up scene of birth announcement.
> Scenes of baby's room with crib, dressing table, toys, and other paraphernalia.
> Long shot of hospital entrance, preferably with hospital name included in scene.
> Sequence of mother and baby leaving hospital and entering car.
> Scene of mother bringing baby into house.
> Mixture of medium shots and close-ups of mother and baby sitting on sofa.
> Scenes of relatives and friends looking at baby.
> Sequence of mother putting sleeper on baby.
> Sequence of mother placing baby in crib.

Baby in High Chair. Feeding time is an event in a baby's life that you won't want to miss capturing on film.

> Close-up of mother preparing baby's bottle.
> Medium shot of mother setting warming dish on high chair.
> Mother putting food in dish to warm.
> Dad getting baby from crib.
> Dad placing baby in high chair.
> Close-up of mother putting bib on baby.
> Sequence of mother feeding baby.
> Close-up of baby's face covered with food.
> Close-up of mother wiping baby's face.
> Close-up of mother's approving face.
> Baby drinking from bottle.
> Dad picking up baby from high chair.

Baby's First Steps. Only movies of a baby's first steps can capture the excitement and importance of such an accomplishment.

> Baby standing in crib.
> Dad picking up baby and standing him or her on floor.
> Sequence of dad holding baby while guiding the first few steps.

The most interesting time to take movies of children is when they are engaged in their own activities.

> Close-up of dad's hands holding baby's hand.
> Medium shot of dad releasing grip as baby toddles onward.
> Baby walking.
> Sequence of baby stumbling, getting up— with a little assist from dad, if necessary —and walking again.
> Medium shot of baby walking into mother's outstretched arms.
> Mother carrying baby back to crib.

These are only a few of the movie story possibilities for the baby's first year or two. In most of these stories, one of the parents is providing most of the action or is helping the baby to provide the action. To add a feeling of action to your movies of a baby, it's a good idea to change filming distance and camera angle frequently and to take lots of close-ups. You'll also want to keep a camera handy at all times for impromptu action when the baby learns to sit up, roll over, crawl, and demonstrate the other baby

skills he or she picks up. And, scenes of the baby rocking in a chair or playing with the crib swing or toys are all good movie subjects. At these times, you may want to film only two or three scenes—whatever is needed to record the interesting action.

Children are Active Subjects. When babies grow into children, they are even more fun to film. Growing children move around faster, providing plenty of action for your color movies.

Many of your best opportunities will occur when the children are busy with any of a limitless number of normal childhood activities. After a while, the children will get used to your movie-making and won't freeze or go into a clown routine when you point the camera at them. Try to film children from a low angle. Remember, they're small and are often sitting on the floor or ground. They will look more natural when filmed from their own level. Try to take some pictures from their point of view. Editing will let you insert a shot of whatever the child looks at outside the frame: a tall adult, the Christmas tree, or a romping pet, for instance.

Filming Action. Most of your children's movie-worthy activities will take place right around home. In the backyard, they will be romping in the inflatable pool, playing football, or sliding on their sleds. Indoors, they will be drawing pictures, setting up a doll house, or laying out a track for the slot-car set.

(Above) Children will be more natural if they are unaware that you are filming them. (Right) You can provide a child with something to do that will make an interesting movie.

Baby and Child Photography

Outdoors, light will be no problem. Indoors, you may want to add light in some situations. A movie light mounted on the camera and pointed at the subject gives a harsh light that may be distracting and will cause squinting every time the child glances your way. Also, it creates sharp shadows that will move distractingly every time you pan the camera to follow the action. It is better to aim one or two movie lights at a white ceiling so that a softer overall light is reflected or bounced over the entire area. The visual results are more natural and more pleasing to look at, and action can move throughout the lighted area without those following shadows. (Note: Avoid bouncing light off a colored ceiling or walls; skin tones and white objects in the scene will be recorded with tinges of that color.)

Watch out for sudden bursts of fast action—your child may dart out of the shot or have you rapidly panning to keep up with him or her. When physical activity starts to build, zoom back to a wider view so your subject can move without being lost on the film.

It is always easier to film children when they are concentrating on what they are doing, and not on you. Don't interrupt or give directions; they may cause a loss of naturalness in the subject and a loss of interest in the projects. Move around to find the filming position that best shows the child without interfering with what he or she is doing. This helps you get candid, lifelike movies. It also makes the movie-making experience pleasant for the youngster, which is important when you want to take movies again later.

There are special times in a child's world that are worthy of a whole movie story. There are birthday parties when friends come over, Halloween when the children are busy making a jack-o'-lantern and dressing up in their costumes, Easter and the big egg hunt, and Christmas with all the gift-opening and new toys. Trips to the park, zoo, and beach are also great for movies of children.

You can even create interesting diversions for your children. Giving an artistically inclined child a

To show what seems like an endless stream of children climbing out of a barrel, set the camera on a tripod or some other firm support and film each child coming out. To avoid later cutting and splicing, stop the camera after each child emerges and wait until the next child has entered the barrel and is ready to come out.

When traveling, photograph children in each country you visit. This is an excellent way to record various national characteristics of dress, hairstyle, games, and other ethnic attributes. This group of young boys was photographed in Mexico City. Photo by Herb Taylor.

set of finger paints can lead to a movie-making session. Setting up a basketball hoop on the garage will provoke instant action for a movie story.

Keep your mind open to the possibilities at all times and film the action when it happens. It is enjoyable and easy to do—and well worth it as your children grow older.

Teenagers—New Topics to Film. You don't have to make a great transformation in your moviemaking when children turn into teenagers. The activities just change, that's all. Now there are school trips, sports, hobbies, picnics, parties, and many other new experiences.

An important point to remember when photographing teenagers is to be as inconspicuous as possible. Many teenagers are naturally self-conscious in front of a movie camera. However, if they have become accustomed to having movies made of them during their earlier years, this should not be much of a problem. In any event, it's best to film them while they are involved in some activity so that they aren't overly conscious of your movie-making.

The formula remains the same for movies of all your children, regardless of age: Film the important times and the fun times.

• *See also:* CHILDREN, PHOTOGRAPHING.

Further Reading: Editors of Time-Life Books. *Photographing Children.* New York, NY: Time-Life Books, 1971; Fearnley, Bernard. *Child Photography.* Garden City, NY: Amphoto, 1972; Szasz, Suzanne. *Child Photography Simplified.* Garden City, NY: Amphoto, 1976.

To make the best movie stories be aware of the action possibilities and be ready to film instantly.

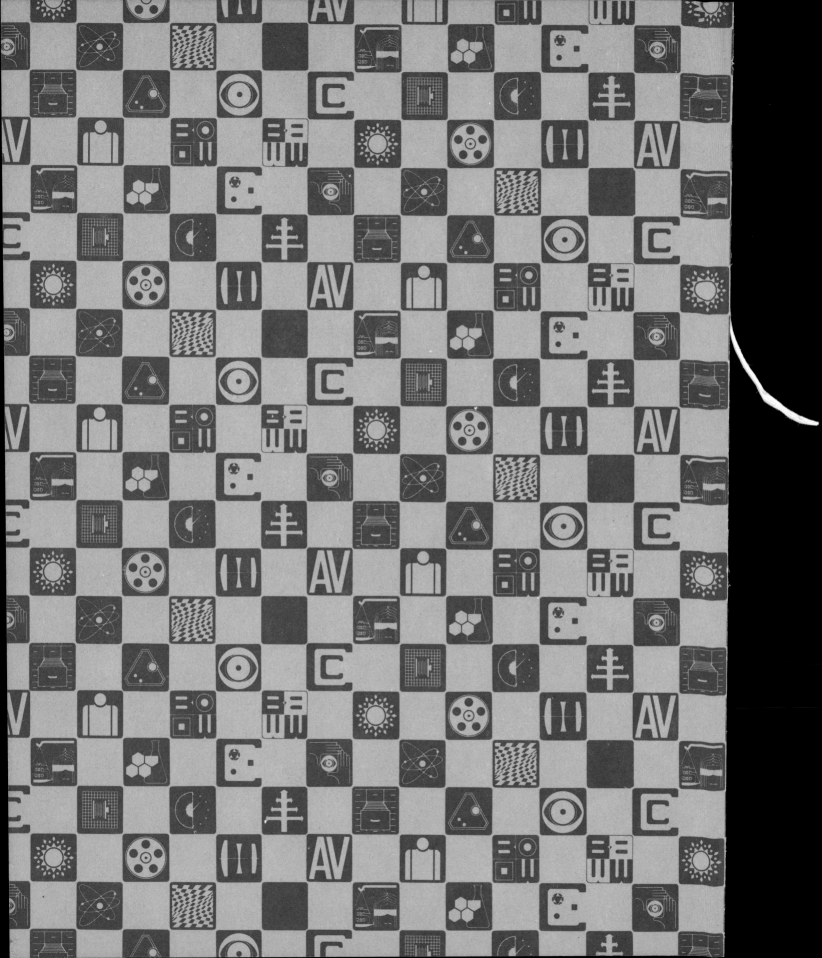